Development in Zambia: A Reader

Edited by Ben Turok

Zed Press, 57 Caledonian Road, London N1 9DN

Development in Zambia: A Reader was first published by
Zed Press, 57 Caledonian Road, London N1 9DN at the
request of the University of Zambia, in November 1979.

ISBN 0 905762 08 8

Copy-edited by Lorne Larson
Designed by Mayblin/Shaw
Typeset by Lyn Caldwell and Kathy Munro
Proofread by Penelope Fryxell, Noelle Goldman and
    Sarah Onions
Printed in U.S.A.

First reprint, June 1981

Acknowledgements

The author would like to acknowledge the help of
Mary Turok, Robert Klepper and Ilse Mwanza in
the preparation of the book for publication. Life
would have been much more difficult without their
assistance.

This book has been prepared for the students of
the University of Zambia who are desperately short
of reference material as a result of Zambia's
economic crisis. It is also a small gesture to them
in appreciation of the friendly environment they
have created for me and my visiting colleagues.
No teacher could ask for more cooperation and
greater motivation than these students have
shown.

Contents

Ben Turok
Introduction

The production of a book on Zambia today is a hazardous undertaking. Zambia is today one of the world's best known trouble spots, the cockpit of many conflicting forces in Southern, East and Central Africa, and the confluence of many differing interests and ideologies. How could one hope to capture the spirit of this ferment in one hastily assembled volume, and even if one succeeded, how long would it remain valid?

Zambia gained its Independence in the comparatively calm waters of the 1960s when peaceful and orderly transition was much valued by coloniser and decolonised alike. As a result, its institutions, ideology and approach to development all have the stamp of that epoch upon it. Yet this same Zambia has become caught up in a vortex of Frontline statism whose principal concerns are far from peaceful and orderly transition, but the pursuit of the successful outcome of a power struggle for the liberation of the South. The terms of social change are now vastly different from those of Zambia's past and the partners in the alliance are different to those found in the early years of the African Independence struggle.

Decolonization is not what it was: it is based on the use of force, the advocacy of advanced theories of socialism and the establishment of regimes of a new type not previously experienced in Africa. Even peaceful and moderate Tanzania has undergone a transition in outlook and must now be considered as a state in arms, with the capacities of popular mobilization. All this has had its effect on Zambia. Hoping to make progress with its development plans in peace and order, it is surrounded by turmoil. Since it is landlocked on all sides (having eight frontiers to contend with) its transport routes remain a perpetual worry. Hoping to establish some kind of rhythm in its exports and imports, the sources of supply are bedevilled by frequent incidents while some markets remain out of reach when most needed. Trying to assess the full magnitude of its own problems and deficiencies, the harassment of Rhodesian bombs and incursions makes calm reflection impossible. Zambia is subjected to all the vicissitudes of a war situation while it is not itself at war.

In every direction, behind every issue, lurk the unresolved problems of the whole region so that local affairs of state are intertwined with the fate of the sub-continent. It would be a mistake to regard this as a purely military affair as though normality will return when the shooting stops. With the creation of new regimes around Zambia new relationships must emerge requiring a re-orientation at the political and the economic levels.

Even now, as development goals and objectives come under discussion there is an awareness that some neighbouring states have chosen a different ideological orientation to that of Zambia and that they are trying different development options. Cross-national comparisons are made increasingly frequently, at least at the University of Zambia, legitimated by the seemingly close camaraderie that is manifested between the Presidents of the Frontline states. It cannot be long before greater cross-fertilisation takes place since necessity must here be the mother of innovation. No matter what contrary tendencies might be present within Zambia itself, this country cannot but take cognizance of the transitions taking place in Tanzania, Mozambique, Angola and now Zimbabwe, for all these countries hold the lifeline for Zambia to the sea. It is argued that the South is a necessary source of supply and route out in emergencies, but Zambia's destiny is linked far more with its immediate neighbours in the long run. The point is, however, that Zambia's surrounds makes the study of this country more difficult and tentative.

Another source of difficulty is the fact that Zambia is in the midst of a deep economic crisis, a phenomenon now common in the underdeveloped world. But, since Zambia stood so tall in its successes in the early years of Independence, its taste of the depths of depression is all the more bitter now. All the copper in its subsoil cannot bail it out as long as world prices remain at the margin of profitability. With all the other economic problems, it remains for the present a country under severe stress seemingly unable to shake off the straightjacket of underdevelopment and distorted growth that was its inheritance from colonial times, reinforced by some wrong policies adopted after Independence. How to escape from this trap is Zambia's present preoccupation and the essays in this book show how differing approaches are adopted on a wide range of topics. In the essays the explicit or implicit needs of development constitute the main theme throughout.

Some of the essays are based on first hand research while others are theoretical and analytical. Others again seek to provide an overview of a major sector of Zambia's social formation throwing up the main issues under discussion. An area that has not been covered is the international context and this is a major weakness. The necessary material has simply not been available to the editor on this occasion. As a consequence the book has a somewhat parochial feel, reflecting the preoccupations of Zambians about their own internal problems, within their own milieu. Thus the essays of Kashoki and Tembo seem somewhat remote from the harsh realities of multinational corporations, world markets, or even Frontlinism and economic crisis. They seem to be musing aloud about the direction Zambia's intellectual life might be taking, seemingly unconcerned by the more critical factors disturbing the country's equilibrium. Yet, the issues raised about the stirrings of Zambian consciousness in reaction to 'cultural imperialism' from Western universities are of paramount importance. There can be no liberation of the society as a whole without challenging the assumptions of Western orthodoxies which still remain so pronounced in Zambia.

This book had as one of its principal objectives the creation of a vehicle for Zambians to write about Zambia, and the bulk of the contributions are of this kind. Additionally, almost every essay is written by a current member of staff at the University of Zambia, thereby hopefully providing a sense of immediacy in the issues discussed.

The book was also conceived as a supportive teaching text for interdisciplinary courses in the Social Sciences and the contributions have been selected with this objective in view. The intention is that a variety of methodological concerns should be brought out in the teaching situation, including the research procedures adopted in the more empirical studies. Finally, it will probably be apparent that the work has been compiled under great pressure to meet a very short deadline. This is because the drying up of Zambia's foreign exchange has brought about a dearth of books for UNZA's students and this book is a small contribution towards filling this gap, however inadequately. Even then, without the support of the Vice-Chancellor Dr Jacob Mwanza it might not have happened at all.

Ben Turok
Lusaka
April 1979

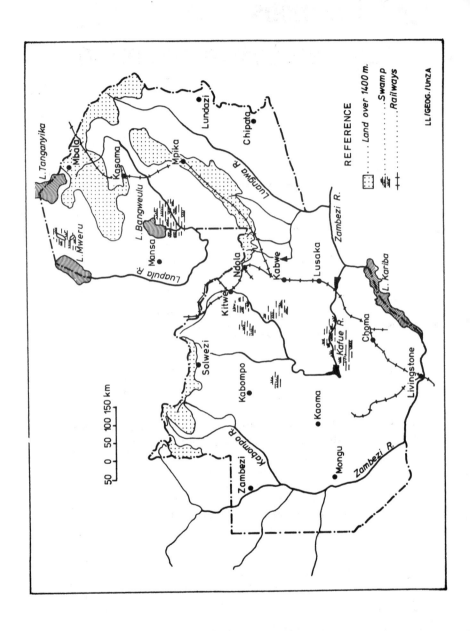

REFERENCE

.... Land over 1400 m.
␛␛␛␛ Swamp
┼─┼─┼ Railways

LL/GEOG. /UnZA

50 0 50 100 150 km

L. Tanganyika
L. Mweru
Mbala
Kasama
L. Bangweulu
Luapula R.
Mansa
Mpika
Lundazi
Chipata
Luangwa R.
Ndola
Kabwe
Kitwe
Lusaka
Zambezi R.
L. Kariba
Choma
Livingstone
Kafue R.
Solwezi
Kabompo
Kaoma
Mongu
Zambezi R.
Kabompo R.
Zambezi

x

1. H. J. Simons
Zambia's Urban Situation

A great many Zambians show a strong liking for urban living. Party and
Government leaders sing the praises of country life and call on townsmen
not productively employed to go back to the land. Yet, despite such appeals
and attempts to improve conditions for villagers, they continue to vote with
their feet for the towns. Population figures tell the story.

Table 1
Population (in thousands)

	Rural	Urban	Total
1963 census	2,843	667	3,510
1974 estimate	3,039	1,656	4,965
Increase in number	196	989	1,185
Total increase (%)	7	148	34
Average annual increase (%)	1.2	6.8	3.0

Table 1 shows that the urban population grew twenty-one times faster than
the rural, and four times faster than the national population between 1963
and 1974. Townsmen do not produce more children than villagers. The
growth rate differences are therefore the result of a big and ongoing movement of villagers to the towns. Population movements of this kind are taking
place throughout the world. Urbanisation is a global process; to reverse the
process, or even to stop it, needs a major national effort to bring about far-
reaching changes in way of life, attitudes, ambitions and values.

The Spread of Urbanism
Africa was a late starter in the urbanising process and remains the least
urbanised of all the great land masses. Four out of five people live off the
land in most African countries, and only one in ten of the continent's
population live in towns of more than 20,000 inhabitants. Zambia's urban
proportion of 35 per cent is well above the continental average.

Yet Africa has the highest urban growth rate as measured by the increase
in the population of cities with more than 100,000 inhabitants. United

1

Nations' estimates show that the per cent increase between 1900 and 1950 was 629 in Africa, 444 in Asia and 254 in the world at large. The 'population explosion' is accompanied by an even greater 'urban explosion'. If growth rates and the rural exodus continue on the present scale, the world's population will nearly double in the next twenty five years and more than half the total will have been urbanised by the year 2000. Table II gives Homer Hoyt's projections.[1]

Table 2

	1960	1975	2000	1960	1975	2000
	(Millions)			*(Per cent)*		
Urban	1,003	1,615	3,416	33.9	42.2	54.5
Rural	1,959	2,213	2,851	66.1	57.8	45.5
Total	2,962	3,828	6,267	100.0	100.0	100.0

Zambia's population growth and movements are in line with world trends. Half the population will be living in towns by 1990 at the present rate of urbanisation. The social pressures responsible for the migration vary but the cumulative effect points consistently towards the city. The Party and Government have decided to go against the stream by mobilising people and resources behind a national programme of rural reconstruction, yet the aim of balanced growth remains a dream.

Country and Town
For comparison, 'urban' is taken to mean a fairly close settlement of at least 20,000 people who do not grow their own food but live by working in industry, commerce, domestic service and other kinds of non-farming activities. The bigger the settlement, the more it develops a high level of specialisation and division of labour, two important features of urban society. But size alone is not the chief quality of urbanism. A small community attached to a mine in a rural area is urban, whereas some thousands of farmers living closely together form a rural settlement. It is the mode of production that distinguishes urban from rural. Townsmen look to farmers for foodstuffs and industrial raw materials. An urban settlement cannot exist unless it draws a surplus from cultivators who produce more than they use for themselves.

Before colonialism people lived under independent chiefs and kings; farmers, fishermen, cattle-owners and hunters produced a surplus over their family needs. They traded part of the surplus for hoes, spears, salt, bark-cloth and other goods. Another part went in tribute to the rulers for the up-keep of the royal palace and government officials. The tribute was freely given out of respect for the king, in recognition of his position as supreme owner of the land, and in return for his protection and help in times of hunger.

Colonial capitalism upset the traditional economy by imposing private ownership, wage labour and commodity production for a market. In classical economic theory, capitalism works best when numerous producers compete freely on a market regulated by a price system that none controls. Adam Smith (1723-90), who formulated these principles at an early stage of industrial capitalism, wove them into a concept of balanced growth that became a commonplace of conventional thinking. A progressive farming community, he observed, needs the services of many kinds of craftsmen who tend to settle in the same neighbourhood, thus forming a small town. It grows in proportion to the improvement of agriculture and the surrounding countryside. In the nature of things, therefore, agriculture comes first, manufacturing afterwards and foreign trade last of all. The town depends on farmers for food and raw materials, and pays them by sending back a part of its manufactured product. Though both town and country gain in equal measure from the exchange, the towns are more dependent. They draw their subsistence from the rural surplus and can increase only as it increases. The improvement of rural areas, therefore,'must, necessarily, be prior to the increase of the town, which furnishes only the means of convenience and luxury.'[2]

Smith's historical sketch had already been falsified by 1776, when his book first appeared. There is a parallel between his conception of 'natural' urban growth and Zambia's policy of decentralisation, village re-grouping and rural industries. Both contemplate a concentration of people and resources in growth points throughout the countryside. Zambia's acute imbalance between scattered villages and big urban-industrial complexes is closer, however, to the realities of industrialising societies in nineteenth-century Europe than to Smith's idyllic model.

Industrial Capitalism

Two great changes in Western Europe upset the 'natural' balance of rural and urban growth. One was the revolution in farming methods and land ownership during the 1700s. At an earlier period, villagers grew crops and grazed livestock on common lands, very much like the practice in most parts of Zambia under customary land tenure systems. The new style of rotation farming went hand in hand with large capital investments in agriculture. Big landowners and landlords took possession of the common lands under Acts of Parliament, put up rents, and forced thousands of villagers and small farmers to leave their homes in search of work. The invention of weaving and spinning machines speeded up the output of cloth by small farming families and rural craftsmen. The new machines enabled this cottage industry to double output, but the steam engine — first used in 1776 — led to the rise of factories. Unable to compete with factory-made cloth, the cottager lost his source of livelihood and often moved with his family to the new manufacturing towns that arose near coalfields or along canals and railroads. The age of industrial capitalism began with the introduction of power-driven machinery in coal mines, copper mines, iron foundries, cotton mills, breweries and factories.

Towns came into being long before the use of power-driven machinery. But industrialisation speeded up urban growth in all countries, partly because people migrated from rural areas to seek work in factories and mines, and partly because of an increase in population that followed improvements in health services and food supplies. Large sums of capital and many workers were needed to build the mines and factories, produce machinery and raw materials, and operate the machines of the new industrial plants. The capital came from domestic agriculture, industry and commerce, foreign trade, trafficking in slaves, and wealth taken by force from colonies in America, Asia and Africa. Many of the workers were landless farmers whose common lands had been enclosed and craftsmen whose products could not compete with cheaper factory-made goods.

Land seizures and the breaking down of village communities threw masses of people on the industrial labour market. They had neither land nor tools, and could live only by selling their labour power to owners of mines and factories, whose profits came from the surplus value that the workers produced in return for their wages. Karl Marx observed that the basis of capital accumulation was the process which drove the cultivator off the land, stripped him of all means of livelihood other than his capacity to work, and turned him into a wage earner.[3] In contrast to Adam Smith's theory of balanced growth, Marx noted that industrial capitalism gave rise to great cities, concentrated wealth and the ownership of the means of production in a small class, neglected agriculture, increased the urban population far more than the rural, and placed the countryside under the rule of towns. Goods made in factories took the place of goods made in villages. The destruction of rural cottage industries went hand in hand with the separation of manufacturing from agriculture, and made possible the growth of a single internal market such as capitalism required.

Colonial Capitalism

The growth of Europe's home markets could not keep pace with the growth of industry. More goods were produced than could be sold at a profit within the industrial countries themselves. Western capitalism needed new markets and new sources of raw materials—copper, tin, gold, oil, rubber, cotton, phosphates, sugar and tropical foodstuffs. Capitalist countries turned to the colonies for markets, raw materials, and outlets for capital investment at high rates of profit. Imperialism, wrote J. A. Hobson in 1902, 'is the endeavour of the great controllers of industry to broaden the channel for the flow of their surplus wealth by seeking foreign markets and foreign investments to take off the goods and capital they cannot sell or use at home'.[4]

Explorers, traders, missionaries, chartered companies (such as the British South African Company), administrators and soldiers poured into Asia, Africa and South America and opened the way to colonial rule. The big powers carved up and annexed all of East and Central Africa between 1884 and 1895. This act of expropriation marked the beginning of capital accumulation in Zambia. Colonial capitalism operated under the same laws as industrial capitalism, and also accumulated capital out of surplus value produced by wage earners. But it had special features, arising from foreign rule, white settlement, race discrimination, industrial colour bars and the underdevelopment of African agriculture, industry and trade. The colonial government, as the agent of imperial authority, had a monopoly of power and used it to make the colony safe and profitable for expatriate farmers, mineowners, businessmen, and above all the big industrial and financial houses in Europe. The colony was managed as a business enterprise in the interests of overseas capitalists and their local representatives.

Another big difference resulted from the time factor and order of events. When power-driven machinery came into general use, factory owners in Europe had at hand large numbers of landless people uprooted from the countryside by earlier changes. This was not the position in Zambia and other African countries whose inhabitants were largely self-sufficient landed proprietors. There was no ready-made army of unemployed persons looking for employment. One of the first aims of the British South Africa Company was to create such an army, to turn villagers into wage-workers, to separate men from their wives, families, fields, cattle, rivers and hunting grounds. The measures adopted to bring about these changes initiated a process that gave rise to the present condition of rural displacement and urban overgrowth.

The small trickle of work-seekers who left their villages at the beginning of the century — mostly to find jobs in Southern Rhodesia and South Africa — soon grew into a large and steady stream. By 1920 about 50,000 Zambians were working outside their country, a larger number than those employed for wages within; and ten years later about 113,000 had entered the labour market, 78,000 of them within Zambia.[5] Towns were built by men from the villages, and many settled down to become urban residents. People moved from rural areas to urban, from one town to another, on such a scale that in 1969 one out of three Zambians lived outside the district of their birth.

Work Seekers

Why did men leave their villages for the town? There is no single answer: living conditions, colonial policies and the attitudes of people varied from place to place and from time to time. Allowing for these differences, we can list a number of country-wide factors. Tax collectors, labour recruiters, traders and missionaries gave the movement a big push in the Eastern, Northern and Luapula Provinces, and a smaller one in North-Western and Western Provinces. Villagers in the railway belt could combine wage-earning with the sale of surplus foodstuffs; others, in distant areas, depended more on wages earned in towns. In one way or the other, Zambians were drawn into the market system.

Capitalism needed a growing market, and created one by killing the demand for the products of village craftsmen. Nowadays we talk of 'import substitution' but the colonial capitalists reversed that process, and replaced Zambian goods with imports. Cotton cloth took the place of bark cloth;

iron pots drove out earthenware pots; factory-made hoes, axes and knives replaced the tools made by the village blacksmith. Shop goods without an exact equivalent in the traditional economy — such as tea, sugar, paraffin, candles, clothes — had an appealing use-value, and became necessities in many villages. Mission stations encouraged people to wear imported clothing, attend church and school, buy books and pay church dues. The money for these goods and services came for the most part from wages.

The alienation by sale or leasehold of about three million hectares of land to expatriate farmers also had important long range effects. One was the overcrowding that took place among villagers living close to the commercial farmers. The pressure was eased by a transfer and resettlement of people in reserves that were marked out in 1928-29, but many reserves in turn became overpopulated and eroded. Land scarcities may have been a cause of labour migration, but there is no clear evidence of actual landlessness. In contrast to Marx's model of a proletarian — the worker who is free in the double sense of having no property and also no ties binding him to a lord or master — Zambians were landowners. Those who set out to work in towns retained a base in their home areas with a view to returning sooner or later.

Another even more important effect was the hold that the white settler farmers had over the agricultural market. The colonial government expected them to feed the urban population and encouraged them with subsidies, high prices and free technical assistance. Their dominant position continued long after Independence in the production of tobacco, dairy products, pigs and sugar, and they supplied a large share of poultry, maize, beef, fruit and vegetables.[6] In contrast, the colonial government failed to adopt measures for the improvement of farming standards in village settlements.

Rural underdevelopment was a two-pronged strategy: it gave white farmers a near-monopoly of the agricultural market, and it narrowed the range of choices open to villagers who needed money. E. A. G. Robinson, the economist on the 1932 Merle Davis Commission, recorded both sides of the process. He concluded that villagers often grew maize more cheaply than expatriate farmers and increased their output where they had an assured market at reasonable prices. The mines, one of the main sources of demand, bought on a large scale and required a good quality. 'For these reasons they have hitherto obtained their supplies in the main from the European growers and from outside the Territory. There has thus emerged the present paradoxical system whereby European farmers grow Native crops for Native consumption.'[7]

In buying maize grown on settler-owned farms rather than maize grown on village lands the mines discouraged the improvement of village agriculture and encouraged villagers to sell their labour instead of their produce. The link between these choices appeared clearly in 1910, when the administrator of the North-West region stopped the Kaonde from selling maize to mines in Katanga. 'It would seem to be a better policy,' he wrote, 'to encourage the energies of the Bakahondi in the direction of mining rather than agriculture.'[8]

Traders were not interested in promoting a balanced trade between village producers and urban manufacturers, and made little effort to help villagers to sell their produce. Those traders who accepted grain in payment usually stored it for selling back to the growers at higher prices when household supplies ran out. As Robinson observed, 'It has in effect served as a security until someone shall go to the mines to earn the money to make the final payment.'[9]

He gave a simple explanation of labour migration. 'Having nothing else to sell, the Native has sold himself. The need to find the money to pay his taxes, his mission or education dues, and to buy the products of the store, has led him to seek work in the towns, on the farms, at the mines, both in Northern Rhodesia and the surrounding countries.'[10] He had 'nothing else to sell' — no surplus for the market — because capitalism wanted his labour and not his produce.

Tax Collectors

Villagers who were only slightly exposed or responsive to the agents of social change could carry on with their traditional occupations. Apart from seasonal food shortages and occasional droughts or floods, they were able to satisfy their needs for food, clothing and shelter from their own resources. It was not possible, however, for the great majority to remain wholly outside the capitalist economy. The demands of the tax collector forced them to enter the market.

Colonial taxation took the place of tribute given to chiefs and demonstrated the power of the new rulers. Company officials, backed by police or army units, moved from village to village, registering families and collecting taxes in 'tours' that brought them face to face with people, many of whom had never before set eyes on a white man. The tax was an important source of revenue for the payment of salaries and other costs of government. African taxation yielded £148,000 in 1931-32, more than was paid in income tax by expatriates, and formed one-sixth of government revenues from all sources. The obligation to pay tax — or suffer a criminal penalty — compelled villagers to sell their produce or their labour.

From 1905 onwards taxes had to be paid in cash, except in areas far from the centres of employment where men could earn a tax receipt by working for a month at the local boma or in road-making and construction. The annual rate was 7s. 6d. in the North-West, 8s. in Western Province, 10s. in the North-East and 12s. 6d. in the railway belt. But an expatriate paid no tax whatsoever on an earned income of less than £96 a month if he had a wife and two children. These were the rates in 1930, when unskilled wages averaged 15s a month in towns and for surface work on the mines, while underground miners were paid 1s. a day. Men could therefore find the tax money by working for a month provided that they spent nothing on themselves or their families. That being an impossible condition, they usually spent several months in wage employment before returning home, the average period of service of miners ranging from six to twelve months in the early 1930s. The

tax may then have been only a small part of the villager's cash needs, but it
remained a compulsory factor that made wage labour unavoidable for many
thousands of men. It was also deeply resented, as appeared in 1935 when
Copperbelt miners, reacting to reports of a tax increase, went on strike for
the first time and lost six of their comrades who were shot dead by the
police.

Taxes and shop debts in underdeveloped rural communities were sufficient
reasons for the growth of the wage-earning class, from 120,000 in 1931, to
300,000 in 1951 and 400,000 in 1971.[11] A circular, self-perpetuating process
set in. Underdevelopment in an established market economy left villagers with
no alternative to wage employment. Their absence from the village accentuated the state of underdevelopment, which gave rise to a corresponding increase
in the outward flow of villagers. Women followed their menfolk to the towns,
and rural depopulation became noticeable in one out of three districts. The
cumulative effect of the capitalist economy was to make wage labour a
habit, a way of life, an institution that needed no reason or justification other
than its existence.

Living Standards
The pressures that made wage labour appear both desirable and unavoidable
also conditioned workers into putting up with low standards of housing, food
and wages. An abundant supply of 'cheap' labour was a widely advertised
colonial asset, and the colonialists took steps to exploit it fully. They argued
that though wage-earning was necessary for economic growth, blacks should
circulate between village and town until old age or sickness forced them to
retire for good to the rural community. Workers' wives and families were not
wanted in the towns. They were expected to remain at their rural home and
support themselves from their fields and the contributions made by their
menfolk out of wages.

A wage is the price of labour power and that share of the worker's product
which goes back to him for the purchase of things needed to keep himself and
his dependants in a state of good health. In a competitive capitalist society
with a free labour market and a large landless working class, wage rates vary
with changes in the supply and demand for labour. At all times, however,
wages must cover the cost of maintaining the worker and his family. A
colonial economy that rested on the use of forced or recruited migrant
workers had a different wage structure, in which wage rates were related to
the assumed basic needs of a single man, a villager who had no schooling and
was content to eat *nshima*, wear a blanket, and sleep on an earthen floor. For
so long as officials, traders and recruiters induced villagers to enter the labour
market in sufficient numbers, wages could be kept stable at a level well below
the subsistence needs of a family unit. Real earnings — adjusted to price
changes — of Copperbelt miners rose from £21 to £25 annually in the period
1937-49. An urban family could not manage on such a low income. An
investigation made in 1943 showed that an average family required £6.11s.7d.
a month for a reasonable living standard, but earnings ranged from £2.5s.10d.

in secondary industries to £4.14s.7d. in mining. Malnutrition diseases were common and tuberculosis was making headway.[12]

Housing conditions in the segregated ghettos were bad. 'Single' urban Zambians lived in bachelor quarters in barracks, compounds or locations. Others who had their families with them were expected to build their own houses. They could not afford to build or pay an economic rent for a decent dwelling, nor would the government, or employers generally, subsidise one for a man supposed to be a temporary and family-less worker. For these reasons the 'shanty town' and 'squatters camp' emerged in the early days of urban growth. Urban workers erected pole and dagga shelters and sun-baked brick houses, drew water from nearby streams, wells and an occasional stand-pipe, and for sanitation used pit latrines and the surrounding bush. Local authorities, which applied stringent British-type building regulations in ex-patriate residential areas, turned a blind eye to conditions in compounds and locations.

Ndola's municipal location, said to be typical of such settlements in the early 1930s, had a population of 4000 living in 1700 mud huts spaced twelve feet apart. Huts infested with mice and vermin were torn down and replaced with new structures. Fifty communal latrine pits behind grass screens served the needs of the inhabitants and were gradually filled to overflowing. Though inspected daily 'they are so horrific that, in spite of the risk of arrest, the surrounding land is fouled with night soil'. About one-third of the residents were married and lived in separate quarters. An estimated 150 men lived with women other than their wives for periods of weeks or years. 'These temporary wives are turned over to others or abandoned. Little notice is taken by the management unless inter-family friction should develop.'[13]

Of 94,000 people living in compounds and locations in 1944, 50 per cent were men, 23 per cent women, and 27 per cent children. 'On average in the urban local authority areas 8.1 persons squeezed into each housing unit and 7.3 persons into each room — from which it may be inferred that only 10.3 per cent of the housing units were made up of more than a single room.'[14] The offical version of a familyless, transient, migrant worker had become a fiction. It was an excuse for starvation wages and slums. Eight per cent of the men were unemployed, forming a labour reserve that could be drawn upon when labour demand rose or to replace sick, disabled and outgoing workers. Their presence showed that the supply of work-seekers had out-stripped the demand and that employed men faced competition from new or returning migrants. Without trade unions or other means of collective bargaining, the industrial workers of the 1940s were unable to cope with the competition and put effective pressure on employers to increase wages to a level at which they could support the families that emerged as women settled in the towns.

Women go to Town
The history of labour migration reveals a tendency for men to pioneer the movement to urban settlements. In consequence, the urban areas have a

surplus of men and the rural areas a surplus of women. This imbalance is tolerable if the men go back to their villages after a fairly short period of absence in wage employment and keep in touch with their families while away at work. The women are tied down by responsibilities for their families and household property, and also by a strong disapproval in rural communities of urban life for women. Resistance to the outflow of women slackens as wage-earning becomes a regular and preferred source of livelihood. A growing proportion of men settle in towns permanently or for long periods and cut down the number of their visits to home villages. Abandoned wives and unmarried girls look for husbands outside the village community and follow the men, often on their own account and in defiance of local sentiment. Some wives join their husbands in town, while some men marry women whom they meet in town. A growing number of men migrate with their wives to the employment centres. In such various ways, the urban female population tends to grow faster than the urban male population under conditions of permanent urbanisation, until the sexes are more balanced in both town and country.

Few white settler governments recognised the inevitable or responded to it by building urban homes for women and their families. The Belgian Congo was a singular exception. Its 'stabilised labour' policy demonstrated the advantages of a permanent industrialised African working class settled in urban townships with family housing and basic services. The regime's authoritarian nature, the government's large holdings in major enterprises, the absence of an elected legislature, the refusal to entrench white artisans behind colour bars enabled the mining companies to adopt the kind of labour organisation that suited their purpose. Stabilisation was introduced in the first place to protect rural communities from the effects of excessive migration but employers were the ultimate beneficiaries. They saved on recruiting costs and could draw on successive generations of urbanised workers committed to wage earning and increasingly efficient. Employed on a wide range of skilled jobs, often at wages only slightly more than unskilled rates, the African labour force of Katanga showed itself 'capable of undertaking technical operations of considerable complexity, far surpassing those so far entrusted to it in the copper-mines of Northern Rhodesia'.[15]

Northern Rhodesian officials also wanted stabilisation at an early stage in copper mining, but the slump in copper prices and the revolt of African miners in 1935 precipitated a sharp swing towards the familiar migratory labour system. The industry's long-term prospects were in doubt; and white settlers objected to the growth of an urbanised African population which would press for political rights and admission to skilled trades. Short-sighted, racially-biased administrators yielded to these fears. They urged employers to recruit and repatriate villagers in an endless circulatory chain, ostensibly to preserve customary ways of life — as though rural stability could be bought at the price of urban instability! The official reason was a myth in the absence of effective programmes of rural development, but it encouraged housing authorities to ignore the needs of urban workers who had their wives with them.

Employers had no incentive to revive the redundant, expensive recruiting system as they could hire for indefinite periods all the men they needed from among the many workseekers who travelled at their own expense to labour centres. Unable to control the exodus, the government sought to ensure the men's return by keeping women as hostages in the villages with the aid of traditional leaders, the chiefs and headmen who represented male-dominated societies. Women were prohibited under Native Authority rules from moving to towns unless accompanied by their husbands or in possession of an official permit. The rules, though ineffectively applied and of doubtful validity, strengthened the prevailing notion that it was improper for women to join their husbands or seek work on their own account in urban areas.

A substantial number of women defied the man-made convention. They found their way to the towns and by their presence there compelled the government and mining companies to adopt a more realistic approach. Balanced stabilisation, as the new policy was called, 'meant that though some family units should legitimately live in the urban system the bulk should be prevented from doing so'. From the early 1950s onwards the government 'ceased to impede the influx of women into urban systems'.[16] But decades of hostility to female urbanisation inflicted a lasting injury on women's economic prospects. Their sex was held to disqualify them from heavy manual labour, although they were, and still are, the chief source of labour in traditional farming communities. As regards lighter work in domestic service, manufacturing and the distributive trades, men, by virtue of being first-comers, established a monopoly which women have not seriously challenged because they are conditioned to the convention that their proper function is to serve the family and manage household affairs.

Townships for Zambians

Copper prices soared after the war, from an average per ton of £62 in 1941-45 to a peak of £352 in 1955. Production costs also increased, but more slowly. High outputs and profits in 1946-55 made it the most prosperous decade in the industry's history. Job opportunities, increasing in like measure, attracted yet more villagers to urban settlements, thereby aggravating the chronic housing shortage. Senior administrators at long last admitted that a permanent proletariat, properly housed, might offset increases in housing costs by improved levels of efficiency. Legislation introduced in 1948 obliged local authorities to build family houses, for which the central government provided funds. There never was enough to keep pace with demands, but the decision marked an important stage in the advance to a positive urban policy.

Political trends after the war also favoured a forward movement. Notable events included the formation of the Northern Rhodesia African Congress in 1948 (renamed the African National Congress in 1951), a parallel growth of African trade unions, mounting opposition to Federation (imposed in 1953) and government attempts to conciliate African opinion. Nationalist and trade union leaders objected strenuously to colour bars, low wages and bad housing. A successful strike of African miners in 1952 brought substantial wage increases, lifting the starting wage from 45s. to 80s. per thirty working days, in spite of employers' complaints that high wages would encourage Africans to settle permanently in towns.

While recognising the inevitability of urban growth, critics wished to have it discouraged in the interests of public morality threatened, they said, by the spread of prostitution, booze, crime and unemployment. Why incur these risks of urbanisation when labour was becoming stabilised without urbanisation? Miners, after long service, should be retired to their home villages, presumably with their children born and raised in town. 'The issue really turns on the question of housing,' said Sir Ronald Prain, chairman of Rhodesian Selection Trust, in 1956. 'The capital outlay required from employers in order to house a rapidly growing African population is frightening; it may tend to make the Copperbelt mines high-cost producers with all the dangers attendant on that, and it is actually inhibiting the development of secondary industries.'[17] He thought that home-ownership schemes for Africans would be more satisfactory, but did not explain how they could afford to buy or rent a suitable house of their own on a single man's wage.

The argument from cost concealed a racial bias. Colonial orthodoxy prescribed for black people a family structure and morality different from those considered normal in Western industrial society or in traditional agrarian systems. In the one, husbands produce incomes while wives control consumption; in the other, man and wife participate jointly in a production and consumption unit. The migratory labour system breached both codes, imposed a spatial separation between husbands and wives, weakened family ties and inhibited the emergence of a new family order attuned to changed conditions in town and country.

The conceit that towns were created by whites and belonged to them pervaded the debates on rural stabilisation, balanced stabilisation and stabilisation without urbanisation. The issue was settled not by cost accountants or social scientists but by the migrant workers. Brushing aside the white man's ideology and rules, they marched in to take possession of what was theirs by right of birth and by virtue of their labour.

To curb the flow, government agencies relied on penal constraints of a South African type: identification certificates *(citupa)*, tax receipts, visitor's permits, night passes, police raids and the repatriation under court order of women and children living without a male guardian. Convictions under the laws averaged nearly 10,000 a year. In spite of repeated and angry protests, this oppressive and discriminatory system of urban administration was repealed only in 1960 under the pressure of a militant movement for African rule and Zambian independence.

The shortage of good housing that snowballed under colonial rule left independent Zambia with an almost impossible task of providing homes for urban Africans. Of Lusaka's African population of 110,000 in 1963, 47 per cent lived in municipal townships, 22 per cent in domestic quarters on employers' premises, 10 per cent in government or private 'compounds', and

21 per cent in unauthorised settlements. Matero and Chilenje, two municipal townships built in the 1950s, had concrete block houses of two or three rooms and an outside kitchen. Two-thirds of the houses in other townships and the settlements were flimsy structures of sun-dried bricks or mud and poles.
Housing standards were better on the Copperbelt. The mining companies had the authority to contain squatting and resources for the construction of solid dwellings. Of the 40,000 company houses rented to African mineworkers in 1966, 15,000 were two or three roomed structures of burnt brick or concrete, with a floor area of about 400 square feet, individual toilets and washing facilities. But 10,000 houses, each consisting of a single habitable room (ten feet square) and a kitchen, were below minimum standards. Toilet and washing facilities were communal, 'squalid, humiliating and overcrowded'. More than 2000 rooms, euphemistically called 'single quarters', were largely occupied by married men, wives and children. 'In many cases married couples share a single room with one or more unmarried men.' Commenting on these conditions, the Brown Commission observed that the mining companies had only themselves to blame. 'Houses with one habitable room, without windows or separate ablutions, should never have been built at all, and it is important to realise that it is moral and not building standards which have improved with the passage of years.'[18]
The layout and design of major urban settlements followed the colonial pattern of racial segregation. Separate areas and schools were set aside for Africans, who usually had their own shops, government offices and even cemeteries. Houses and plots in white suburbs were three or four times the size of those in African townships. The visible differences accentuated the social gap between expatriates and Zambians, and, after Independence, between high and low income groups of all races.

Freedom of Movement
African patriots loathe and strenuously oppose the humiliations and injustices imposed by racists on black people. A major component of national movements for majority rule is therefore always a relentless struggle against white chauvinism, racial privilege and black disabilities. In Zambia, UNIP's programmes, before and after Independence, pledged the Party 'to abolish all forms of discrimination and segregation based on colour, tribe, clan and creed'. They 'rank among deadly vices', declared President Kaunda.[19] In keeping with the Party's objective, protection from discrimination is one of the fundamental rights and freedoms under the constitution. Article 25 of the Constitution Act, 1973 defines 'discriminatory' as differential treatment, imposing disabilities on some persons and according privileges to others by reason of their race, tribe, place of origin, political opinions, colour or creed.
There were other colonial institutions, however, that survived the transfer of power, often in a very different form. Colonial capitalism became Zambian capitalism; racial inequalities became class inequalities; and segregatory

arrangements persisted in the distinction between high and low density residential areas. A competitive, profit-making materialism offers valued rewards to ambitious persons with a taste for high living, big houses, expensive cars and other symbols of success. Zambian Humanism, the Leadership Code and a professed socialism provide a corrective of acquisitive tendencies but not to the extent of stopping the growth of a flourishing private sector. Independence brought new opportunities for success, new ways to freedom of choice, and most of them are to be found in cities and towns.

The constitution set the seal of legitimacy on what was virtually an accomplished fact, a social reality achieved through political struggle. Article 24 of the Constitution states that 'No person shall be deprived of his freedom of movement', defined as 'the right to move freely throughout Zambia, the right to reside in any part of Zambia, the right to enter Zambia and immunity from expulsion from Zambia'! Gone are the colonial pass laws, identification certificates, colour-bar covenants in title deeds, police raids and harassment of 'squatters' in unauthorised settlements.

Some people question the wisdom of this freedom. A majority of those giving evidence before the Chona Commission of 1972 on the Constitution 'expressed grave concern about the presence of squatter compounds and the concentration of unemployed persons in urban areas' which, they said, was responsible for the high incidence of crime. Placing the blame for urban instability on the uncontrolled movement of people from rural areas, they urged that unemployed persons of both sexes should be returned to their villages. 'Some further proposed that people should leave rural areas for urban areas only with the express permission of their chiefs.'[20]

The Commission approved of measures to repatriate 'illegal immigrants' and abolish 'illegal dwellings' in squatter compounds but felt that restrictions on movement would infringe fundamental rights. Critics of the open door policy have not failed to note the apparent inconsistency in these recommendations. If migration to the towns is free, it cannot be illegal, and coercive attempts to stop the growth of squatter areas is not only tantamount to infringing the constitutional right of the citizen to reside where he wishes but is also like using a sieve to bail water out of a leaking boat.

Influx controls, besides being oppressive, are ineffective when the urban economy grows faster than the rural economy. That lesson can be drawn from Zambia's colonial experience and South Africa's far more oppressive pass laws. The large increase in Zambia's rural migration since Independence must be attributed to uneven development. Schools, health centres, services and roads were spread at great cost throughout the countryside, but more than 80 per cent of productive capital went to the Copperbelt and towns along the railway line. National development plans confirm these trends. In the projections of the second plan, covering the period 1972-76, mines and industries were to absorb 33.5 per cent of total investment while only 7.8 per cent was allocated to the improvement of crop production, livestock, forestry, fishing and game. The conventional thinking behind the plan is that accelerated growth in the advanced sectors of the economy will generate more income, tax revenue, employment, social services and markets for Zambian products. A corollary of this development is an accelerated movement of men and women from the villages.

Though substantial gains have been made in the production of maize, sugar, sunflower seed, poultry and eggs, the 65 per cent of the population which depend mainly on agriculture contribute only 13 per cent of the gross domestic product. The bulk of marketed produce comes from a mere twenty or thirty thousand commercial farmers. Three-quarters of rural households rely for cash mainly on non-agricultural activities such as beer-brewing, charcoal burning, fishing and wood carving. Their biggest handicap is a shortage of labour, the result of small-size households. Those in the largest and poorest group of family farmers average only 3.5 persons each. One out of three adult members is older than fifty-five. The predominance of old people and women imposes a very narrow limit on the area cultivated and the type of crop grown by farmers using only hoes and axes.[21]

Large households and those with ox-drawn ploughs fare better. They probably doubled their real incomes in the past ten years. Small-scale farmers in this higher bracket are able to take advantage of such aids to farmers as subsidised fertilisers and seeds, credit facilities, extension services and state marketing, but little of this assistance trickles down to the bulk of small family farmers away from the line of rail. It is likely that their average household income, including the value of own produce consumed in the household, amounts to no more than K200 a year, which is one-third of the urban family's median income and well below the K345 required to maintain a rural family of five at a minimum subsistence level. One-fifth of urban families, who receive less than K480 a year, also live below bare subsistence levels. Yet young people, hopeful of finding jobs or working on their own account, continue to leave their villages for the towns. This exodus, which seems to be the consequence of rural poverty, must be regarded as a major cause of economic stagnation among small family farmers.

The rate of urban growth measures, among other things, the disparities between rural and urban living standards, perceived opportunities and aspirations. This is one significance of the steep rise in the population of administratively defined urban areas. Its share of the total population increased from 20 per cent in 1963 to 35 per cent in 1974. Towns in the railway zone absorbed over 70 per cent of the national increase in 1963-69, while of forty-three administrative districts, twenty-eight lost population through migration. On the assumption that the natural rate of increase was constant and uniform, a comparison of population distributions in 1963 and 1969 shows that the Copperbelt Province had a net gain of 183,000 persons from migration and Central Province a net gain of 129,000. The migrants added 30 per cent and 20 per cent respectively to the provincial populations that would have resulted in 1969 from the natural rate of increase alone.

One further point should be made to indicate the nature and effects of the movement. In proportion to their share of urban populations, more women than men migrate to the towns, thereby reducing the excess of males.

For example, in the Copperbelt's urban districts the average number of males per 100 females dropped from 127 in 1963 to 114 in 1969. This tendency towards balanced sex ratios in the towns is accompanied by a growing excess of females in rural districts with a high rate of male migration, as in those of Northern and Eastern Provinces. As has been mentioned, villages in areas far removed from the railway zone have a preponderance of old people, women and young children, whereas urban populations include a big proportion of men and women aged 15 to 40 years.[22]

Freedom of Residence

The Constitution, as we have seen, guarantees freedom of movement and the right 'to reside in any part of Zambia'. Men and women who invaded the towns after Independence in search of opportunities for better living were exercising their constitutional rights. In so doing, however, they placed heavy burdens on local authorities and created conditions that resulted in far-reaching reforms of laws and housing policies.

Freedom of residence is qualified by two sets of rules, one stemming from traditional systems of land tenure, the other from the capitalist system of private property. In customary law, every Zambian African has a right to occupy and use land in the home area of his mother, father or more remote ancestors. He cannot, however, settle elsewhere on land held communally unless he has the permission of the local headman, chief or other competent authority.

The law of private property, which gives a landowner exclusive control of his property, regulated the ownership of land and buildings in urban areas before Independence. There was no statutory ban on African land owner-ship, though title deeds to certain housing estates included a discriminatory clause of dubious validity that prohibited the sale or lease of plots to persons other than Europeans. Yet, according to Helmuth Heisler, hardly any Africans wished to own a house in approved residential areas, in spite of assistance available from local authorities and mining companies. He cites evidence showing that in 1964 no Africans employed by the companies owned their urban houses and only seventy-eight occupied their own permanent houses in high density municipal townships.[23]

A plausible explanation is that workers expected employers to house them or pay a housing allowance in compliance with the Employment of Natives Ordinance, 1929, and the African Housing Ordinance, 1948. Most wage earn-ers became dependent on accommodation provided for them in one way or another by employers, while others (the unemployed, self-employed and persons unable to obtain a house in municipal townships) built their own houses in labour compounds or 'squatted' on vacant land in and around the towns. Unauthorised squatter settlements expanded and proliferated after Independence. Lusaka's squatter population increased tenfold from 16,000 in 1957 to 160,000 in 1975, or from 22 per cent to 42 per cent of the city's total population. Of every 100 housing units recorded in 1974, in the main urban centres, squatters occupied 46 in Lusaka, 42 in Kabwe, 36 in Kafue and 32 in the combined areas of Kitwe, Luanshya, Chingola and Mufulira exclusive of houses in mine townships. J. T. Robertson, who compiled these figures, comments that 'the majority of urban requirements, 60 per cent or more, are met by construction in unauthorised areas.'[24]

'Squatter' and 'unauthorised', when applied to urban settlements, are colonial hangovers that no longer fit. The proper meaning of 'squatter' is a settler without right of title, or, more rarely, a person who settles on public land with a view to acquiring title under government regulation. Thus, when colonialists expropriated African-owned land, the original inhabitants of the alienated land were transformed into illegal squatters. Squatters in urban areas were Africans who settled without lawful permission on vacant land belonging to the State, local authority or individual proprietor.

A settlement is 'unauthorised' if formed without the approval of the appropriate municipal council and town planner. The settlers are not squatters if they rent their plots from the landowner even though he may be in breach of town planning regulations. But they are 'unauthorised squatters' if they occupy land without the consent of both the land owner and the planning authority. In that case they may be said to have expropriated the land.

Colonial authorities strongly disapproved of informal urban settlements, though they flinched from the repressive measures of white minority regimes farther south, which harry squatters, demolish their homes, expel people from towns or force them to live under bureaucratic surveillance in segregated towns. Several years of anxious debate went by before Zambia rejected the colonial approach and decided to legitimate squatter settlements. The new policy was foreshadowed in the Second National Development Plan for 1972-76. Squatters' areas, the planners observed, represented social and financial assets. Since the demolition of houses, whether bad or good, was not a practical solution, the recommended remedy was to re-plan the settlements and give them essential services.

The decision to legitimate the occupation of land expropriated by urban settlers is in keeping with President Kaunda's 'Watershed' announcement of 30 June 1975 to the National Council on land nationalisation. Almost immediately after the announcement, there followed the Land (Conversion of Titles) Act, 1975, vesting all land in the President and converting every piece of land held as a freehold to a statutory leasehold as from 1 July 1975. An earlier measure, the Housing (Statutory and Improvement Areas) Act, promises plot-holders in formerly unauthorised areas security against demolition and certificates of title. Thus equipped, the settlers cease to be squatters and become tenants of the State like other primary occupiers of land.

It is a realistic policy that acknowledges the failure of public authorities to provide housing of an approved standard for two-fifths of the urban population. Those affected build their homes without loans from banks, building societies or government funds. Ignoring the law of private property, they extend the traditional system of land tenure to the towns, make do with meagre resources, improve their dwellings as best they can, and, in village style, cultivate large gardens on nearby vacant land. By introducing an element of rural living, the shanty dwellers strike more of a balance between town and country than the policy makers are able to achieve. This display of fortitude, self-reliance and capacity to adapt is not enough, however, to reduce the social inequalities inherent in a system that sanctions sub-standard housing for a large section of the working people.

Homes for Workers
Shanty towns are self-help suburbs whose residents, of necessity, have responded to the government's home ownership policy. They look like slums, and in fact are unplanned settlements crowded with small, flimsy cottages, irregularly spaced along winding, uneven dirt roads and alleys, dependent on pit latrines and water drawn from wells or streams, and without electricity. What makes a slum, however, is less the physical condition of its inhabitants than their feelings of deprivation and alienation, of being outcasts and at war with people of property. That is hardly the mood of shanty dwellers. Up to one-third are lodgers or tenants, many of whom are mobile workseekers unable to find accommodation in municipal townships; but most, as house owners, have reason to improve their dwellings and neighbourhood. With little aid from public agencies, and dependent on their individual and collective efforts, they acquire a community spirit and are more integrated than the tenants of municipal housing schemes.

Housing standards in self-help suburbs fall below the officially presented standards. Most shanties, however, are superior in size and quality to the traditional dwellings of villagers, of whom four out of five live in one or two roomed houses built of mud-packed poles or sun-dried bricks with roofs of grass or thatch. Comparable figures for shanty areas alone are not available. But in 1969 56% of rural and 9% of urban dwellings had pole and dagga walls; 70% of rural and 6% of urban had grass roofs; 59% (rural) and 23% (urban) had only one room. Overcrowding is also greater in rural areas. In rooms occupied by over 3 persons, 56% of rural occupants lived at an average of 6.2 per room, while 46% of urban occupants lived 4.7 to a room. Migrating villagers who settle in self-help suburbs have a reasonable prospect of improving their housing standards, the more so in towns whose councils allocate funds to servicing and upgrading shanty settlements. Houses built by owners on planned and serviced plots contributed one-third of all approved urban dwellings constructed since 1966, when site and service schemes were first introduced. The councils of Lusaka, Kabwe and Copperbelt towns, more affluent than the rest, are upgrading settlements by introducing planned roads, piped water and latrines. Lusaka, aided by a World Bank loan, is adding clinics, primary schools and community centres. Upgrading projects will benefit about 25,000 households, one-third of the estimated number of shanty houses in December 1974.

Improved services may stimulate shanty owners to build bigger and better houses but can hardly reduce significantly the great disparities between high-cost suburbs and high density low-cost settlements. The inequalities, we have seen, stem from the colonial system of racial discrimination and residential segregation. In 1964, few Zambians held senior positions in public services and private firms, or lived, except as servants, in low density housing areas. As expatriates moved out of offices and homes after Independence, Zambians took their place. Though high-cost suburbs ceased to be white enclaves, they remained select residential areas inhabited by upper and middle income families of varied ethnic origins and segregated from high density settlements peopled by less prosperous Zambians.

Zambia's housing market has never been wholly competitive because of the practice, dating from the colonial period, whereby the government, mining companies and other big employers provide employees with housing at sub-economic rents or pay them a housing allowance. The subsidy is a labour cost and part of the worker's wage but it gives some protection against inflation in the property market. It also accustoms public officers and other subsidised tenants to a higher standard of housing than they could afford if obliged to buy their homes or pay an economic rent.

An officer occupying a government house in a low density area pays 12½ per cent of his salary as rent, and this amount is well below the market rate for housing of a comparable standard. To encourage home ownership, the government pays a housing allowance to officers who occupy their own homes. The allowances were doubled in 1975 and currently range from K40 a month for a house valued at K5,000 or less to K150 for one valued at K30,000 and above. It is doubtful whether the allowance is sufficient in most cases to bridge the gap between subsidised rents and the monthly cost to the owner of a mortgaged house on which he pays interest, redemption, rates, insurance and maintenance. Most officers and parastatal employees consequently prefer to live in rented houses, and expect employers to supply these by building new houses if old ones are not available. 'Even today, new high cost dwellings are being built to satisfy the expectations created by employer's subsidised housing. The effect is a distortion in the investment pattern with little or no relationship between the cost of new dwellings and the incomes of the occupants.'[25]

Expensive houses built for the emergent elite swallow up the bulk of urban housing investments. Thus the construction of 1710 high- and medium-cost dwellings and 1307 servants' quarters absorbed 77.2 per cent of the amount spent on urban housing in 1974. Another 13.4 per cent went into the building of 1266 low cost units, 4.7 per cent into 2000 houses on serviced plots, and the remaining 4.7 per cent into 9905 shanty houses. J. T. Robertson observes that the shanties accounted for 61 per cent of all new urban dwellings in 1974 and 'were probably financed by less than 5 per cent of the total investment and entirely from non-public funds.'[26]

Average unit costs ranged from K200 for a shanty to K18,000 for a house at the top of the scale. Low cost houses averaged K4,500 and servants' quarters K1,500 each. If the K30 million spent on high- and medium-cost dwellings had been utilised to build houses of an average value of K3,000 each, the addition to housing stock would have been 10,000 units instead of the 1,710 for the well-to-do. The shortage of good homes for working people must be attributed to the uneven distribution of resources and not only to their scarcity. Housing policies and practices involve conflicting social objectives. Existing institutions favour investment in high-quality houses for the favoured few. On the other hand, Humanist conceptions of social justice give priority to essential services for the deprived majority. The choice depends partly on what people can afford and partly on social forces that determine the method of allocating funds, materials and labour.

The determining factor in a competitive capitalist economy is the relation between supply and demand on the property market. It continues to operate in spite of the national objective of socialist ownership. Property values rise with urban growth and development; scarce plots are exchanged at many times their original cost; and landlords, both in shanty towns and authorised settlements, are in a position to extract high rents from homeless people. Newcomers and newly married couples have great difficulty in obtaining accommodation at rents which they can afford, and may be forced to erect unauthorised dwellings, the nucleus of new shanty communities, in the peri-urban area.

Nationalisation of Land
Against this background of land speculation, rising costs and squatters' towns, President Kaunda announced on 30 June 1975 far-reaching changes in land laws and property ownership. These include the conversion of freehold titles into leasehold for 100 years, the nationalisation of vacant and undeveloped plots; and a ban on building society loans to private companies and individuals for the construction of buildings for renting. Local authorities are to acquire blocks of flats belonging to non-Zambians, and landlords will be expected to sell to the Government at reasonable prices before the end of 1978 properties used for renting. Rented buildings in private hands will be taken over by public agencies when the value or cost has been recovered in rent.

There is a measure of continuity between the public ownership of land and traditional land tenure systems which combine communal ownership with individual family farming. In its pre-independence programme, UNIP derived its land policy from custom, and urged the government to accept the fundamental principle that all land was ultimately vested in chiefs and the people. President Kaunda has further expanded and refined this concept in his expositions of Humanism. Speculation in land is morally wrong and economically deplorable since it helps to raise the cost of living. Landlordism, 'one of the worst forms of exploitation of man by man in a capitalist system' is evil and must be wiped out.[27]

A landowner who does not develop his land or who leases it for a definite period benefits from a general rise in land values and, in the second case, from improvements made by the tenant. This aspect of private ownership figures prominently in Karl Marx's critique of landed property. It is 'the basis of the capitalist mode of production' and yet, at a certain stage of social development, appears superfluous and even harmful to capitalism. The contradiction occurs because the landlord, by exacting tribute in the form of ground rent, diminishes the tenant's stock of productive capital, and by holding the title to land, limits the tenant's productive investments which in the final analysis benefit the landlord. Private landowning is therefore a barrier to production and the 'conscious rational cultivation of the soil as eternal communal property.'[28]

On this plane of reasoning, it would seem that capitalism might be better off without landlords. Lenin thought as much. 'Theoretically,' he wrote in 1899, 'it is possible for capitalist production to exist in the absence of private property in land, i.e. with the land nationalised.'[29] Following the 1905 revolution, he urged his Social Democratic Party to tell the peasants, frankly and emphatically, that land nationalisation was 'a bourgeois measure', useful only in definite political circumstances. For Marxism 'has very definitely established that nationalisation of the land is possible and conceivable even in bourgeois society; that it will not retard, but stimulate, the development of capitalism.'[30]

The Marxist-Leninist position, in summary, is that the relationship between the owners of production resources and the actual producers determines the nature of a social structure and the form of the State. If nationalised land is leased to individual producers who sell their commodities on an open market the result is capitalism. If production is carried on collectively by co-operatives or State enterprises in a planned economy the result is socialism. By these criteria the preponderance of individual family farmers and individual homeowners in Zambia's 'mixed' economy gives it a pronounced capitalist orientation.

The effects of the 1975 land reforms will depend largely on the way in which they are administered and can be assessed only provisionally at this early stage. The Land Act, as we have seen, vests all land in the President and converts freehold to leasehold for 100 years. As the universal landlord, he regulates all land transactions. No person may sell, transfer, sublet, subdivide or mortgage any part of his land without the President's consent. In giving consent, he may fix the maximum amount of the price or rent to be paid and will presumably use this authority to reduce speculation and curb inflation in the property market.

These procedures have provoked two kinds of criticisms. One complaint is that delays in processing applications tend to hold up the construction of urgently needed buildings. The other, which is more basic, challenges the principle of price control or its application. In fixing the maximum price or rent, the government follows the advice of its officers who inspect and assess the value of improvements on the land. Difficulties arise when the consent-price is less than the vendor's price and perhaps less than the cost of construction. The owner may then refuse to sell or lease his property at the lower figure or force the buyer to pay more, illegally, than the approved sum. Faced with such uncertainties, contractors and other developers of real estate may well be reluctant to build houses for prospective buyers.

Government spokesmen, in reply, claim that official price adjustments since January 1976 have saved some 6,000 buyers an amount of K2 million. It seems, therefore, that the controls do counteract inflation and, for that reason, tend to reduce the volume of new housing. The resulting scarcity may encourage clandestine dealings between sellers and buyers who have the means and disposition to evade price controls. Since the market remains competitive, it favours buyers who have more money or power and fewer scruples than their rivals.

Regrettably, and no doubt without intent, the land reforms appear likely to substitute one source of inequality for another, as in the system of statutory leases of residential plots in urban areas. The rents are fixed at a flat rate of K20 a year for a hectare or part of hectare for all plots, no matter where they are situated. Leaseholders, being relieved of the necessity to invest in the purchase of plots, can add the sum so saved to their expenditure on dwellings. The saving is greatest on the most favoured plots which, if sold on an open market, would fetch the highest prices. It is likely, therefore, that the payment of rents at a constant rate will increase, rather than reduce, inequalities in housing standards.

Shanty owners anticipated the reforms by settling on vacant, unimproved land. They will benefit from the security of tenancy contemplated under the Housing (Statutory and Improvement Areas) Act, 1974. It authorises councils to subdivide housing areas and improvement areas, allocate building plots and issue certificates of title or, in improvement areas, occupancy licences for a maximum of thirty years. Leaseholders and occupants may with the council's approval, sell or mortgage their improvements on the land; and will pay fees in lieu of rates and as a service charge. Leaseholders and occupants in the declared areas will continue to construct their own dwellings, for which moderate council loans are available.

Land nationalisation is presumably irrelevant to the housing conditions of wage workers living in subsidised houses, rented council houses, or shanties built on rent-free plots. Shanty owners in upgraded settlements and on serviced sites receive certain basic services but remain dependent on their own resources for building and improving their dwellings. Sub-standard housing will therefore persist for a large proportion of urban workers who manage to live on low incomes because of their low, sub-standard housing costs. So regarded, the shanty settlements are seen as having a depressing effect on the urban wage structure.

The complement to public ownership of land in a socialist society is public ownership of housing in town and country. This is the indicated remedy for housing inequalities and deficiencies. The common objection that public housing absorbs capital needed for production reproduces the argument used by colonial capitalism to support its policy of sacrificing workers' welfare to promote the export of minerals. The argument is flawed in two dimensions of production. Investments in housing have a multiplier effect on the domestic manufacture of building materials and household goods; and, by raising housing standards, improve the health of workers and their efficiency.

Investments in workers' homes, education and health services are productively consumed inasmuch as their effect is to raise standards of living, fitness and efficiency. By the same criteria, poor housing is economically counter-productive. There are also social costs, broadly of two kinds, one associated with individual deviance, the other with class antagonism. As regards the former, bad housing is said to breed bad morals. But police reports and crime statistics do not support the notion, held, for instance, by witnesses before the Chona Commission of 1972, that shanty settlements harbour more than their proportionate share of thieves, prostitutes and vagabonds. The proposition must be doubted also on other grounds. Shanty dwellers are much the same kind of people as the tenants of council houses. Most heads of households are wage earners, odd-jobbers, self-employed craftsmen or small traders. Perhaps one in ten is out of work at any time. Trade unions, churches and UNIP are well represented in shanty settlements, where the Party is often an acknowledged authority and defender of the peace. The residents, loosely organised in Party units, do much of their own policing and have a fairly intimate knowledge, such as villagers possess, of what goes on in their immediate neighbourhood. Being houseowners, they have an incentive to disapprove of hoodlums, idlers and thieves. If the facts are otherwise, however, if 'squatting' sustains a deviant sub-culture, that condition would strengthen the case for comprehensive programmes of public housing.

The class aspect may be more significant. It is seen as such by the anthropologist Peter Gutkind in a general comment on urbanisation in poor countries. 'But as migration to the towns increases, as unemployment rises at an ever accelerated rate, inequity, poverty and misery steadily increase. Squatter settlements rise faster than they can be removed by governments offended by urban blight, and under these conditions the towns become tinder boxes of discontent.' Flexible social structures that integrate the poor in approved institutions may dissipate the discontent but, he warns, the safety valves will not operate for ever.[31]

The safety valves are presumably education, job opportunities, rising incomes and political participation — the package promised at independence and delivered in varying degrees of fulfilment in succeeding years. Given a reasonable prospect of upward mobility, working people may accept assurances that social inequalities will not last, but in the absence of visible attempts to close the gaps, new generations of shanty dwellers are less likely to tolerate arrangements acceptable to their parents. An urban proletariat, born and bred in squalor and deprived of opportunities open to more prosperous citizens, will have reason to insist on fulfilment of the Humanist principle of transferring power from capitalists, elitists and technocrats to the people as a whole.

The elite live mainly in cities and provincial capitals: the seats of government, headquarters of UNIP, the ZCTU and mass media, centres of financial institutions, and the location of major mining, industrial and commercial enterprises. These power centres attract people as honey attracts bees. Operating from them, decision-makers acquire urban habits and perspectives. Under their influence investments are channelled into urban projects and high-cost suburbs. Current trends run contrary to President Kaunda's solution, which is to introduce socialist planning, make human needs the criterion of investments, vest decision-making in producers and adopt the socialist mode of production.

References

This essay was first published in H. J. Simons *et al*, *Slums or Self-Reliance? Urban Growth in Zambia* (University of Zambia, Institute of African Studies Communications No. 12, 1976).

1. G. Breeze, *Urbanization in Newly Developing Countries* (Englewood Cliffs, 1966), p. 137.
2. Adam Smith, *The Wealth of Nations* (London 1776), p. 357. The citations are from the Modern Library edition (New York, 1937).
3. K. Marx, *Capital, I* (London, 1887), p. 716. Citations are from the Foreign Languages Publishing House edition (Moscow, 1962).
4. J. A. Hobson, *Imperialism* (London, 1938), p. 85.
5. G. Kay, *A Social Geography of Zambia* (London, 1967), p. 76.
6. C. S. Lombard and A. H. C. Tweedie, *Agriculture in Zambia since Independence* (Lusaka, 1974), p. 56.
7. J. M. Davis (ed.), *Modern Industry and the African* (London, 1933), p. 188.
8. I. Henderson, 'The growth of a wage-earning labour force in colonial Zambia' (Lusaka, 1974), p. 10. Mimeographed.
9. Davis, *op. cit.*, p. 199.
10. *Ibid.*, p. 135.
11. H. Heisler, *Urbanisation and the Government of Migration* (London, 1974), p. 133.
12. A. L. Safferey, *A Report on Some Aspects of African Living Conditions on the Copperbelt of Northern Rhodesia* (Lusaka, 1943).
13. Davis, *op. cit.*, p. 80.
14. Heisler, *op. cit.*, p. 92.
15. Lord Hailey, *An African Survey* (London, 1956), p. 1392.
16. Heisler, *op. cit.*, p. 64
17. R. L. Prain, 'The stabilization of Labour in the Rhodesian Copperbelt', *African Affairs*, 55 (October, 1956), p. 308.
18. Republic of Zambia (Roland Brown), *Commission of Inquiry into the Mining Industry* (Lusaka, 1966), p. 60.
19. K. D. Kaunda, *Humanism in Zambia* (Lusaka, 1967), p. 11.
20. Republic of Zambia (M. Maina Chona), *National Commission on the Establishment of a One-Party Democracy in Zambia* (Lusaka, 1972), pp. 9-10.
21. D. Honeybone and A. Marter, *An Evaluation Study of Zambia's Farm Institutes and Farmer Trading Centres* (Lusaka, 1975), pp. 47-52.

22. M. E. Jackman, *Recent Population Movements in Zambia* (Lusaka, 1973).
23. Heisler, *op. cit.*, p. 118.
24. J. T. Robertson, 'The Urban Situation: Shelter', in *Human Settlements in Zambia* (Lusaka, 1975), p. 45.
25. *Ibid.*, p. 58.
26. *Ibid.*, p. 44.
27. K. D. Kaunda, *Humanism in Zambia, Part II* (Lusaka, 1974), pp. 73-5.
28. K. Marx, *Capital, III* (London, 1894), pp. 608, 743, 792.
29. V. I. Lenin, *Collected Works, IV* (Moscow, 1964-5), p. 147.
30. V. I. Lenin, *Collected Works, X* (Moscow, 1964-5), p. 171.
31. P. C. Gutkind, *Urban Anthropology* (Asser, 1974), p. 38.

Study Questions

1. Why is Zambia's rate of industrialisation among the highest in Africa?
2. What pressures were applied by the colonial administration to supply workers for commercial farmers and the mining industry?
3. Account for the housing shortage for urban workers before and after Independence?
4. In what way did housing policy in the post-colonial period contribute to the formation of a class structure?
5. Is the nationalisation of land under the Watershed reforms an anti-capitalist measure? What are its advantages and disadvantages?
6. Discuss the relationship between agrarian reform and urban growth.

2. Jacob M. Mwanza

Rural-Urban Migration and Urban Employment in Zambia

Zambia manifests typical features of a developing country. Its economy can be characterized as a dual one, comprising a relatively small modern sector and a large, predominantly subsistence, rural sector. In such a dualistic setting one of the crucial problems lies in achieving the effective shift of the centre of economic activities from the subsistence sector to the modern sector through reallocation of labour. In such a process the subsistence sector is expected to be modernized in order to increase its productivity to the level that will generate adequate income of those engaged in this sector and at the same time produce sufficient food and raw materials to support the entire economy. The subsistence sector should then be able to release surplus labour. On the other hand the modern sector should grow and expand at the rate that should create adequate employment opportunities to absorb both released workers from the subsistence sector and the natural growth of the urban labour force.

The experience of Zambia over the first fourteen years of independence has shown that its path of development diverges significantly from the ideal type described above. There has been no significant productivity improvement in the subsistence sector. This has perpetuated very low incomes for the rural areas and has widened the rural-urban gap as well as accelerated rural-urban migration. The growth of the modern sector has not created enough jobs to meet the demand of those who have left the traditional sector. In fact, the expansion of the modern sector has not been accompanied by similar growth in employment. The result of this phenomenon has been the emergence of explosive urban population growth accompanied by widespread open unemployment and the growth of the informal sector with disguised unemployment.

This essay will attempt to analyse the factors which may have contributed to rural-urban migration, the constraints on the growth of wage employment in the modern sector and the consequences of this state of affairs on the distribution of income. We will then suggest possible policy measures that ought to be taken to tackle the serious problems outlined.

Zambia has a population density of only about 6 persons per km^2 as of 1976. Because of the low population density there has not been population pressure on agricultural land and this is unlikely to arise for decades to come. Between 1963 and 1977 Zambia experienced a very rapid growth of the urban population as Table I shows.

Table I
Growth of Rural and Urban Population, 1963-77

	Population Growth (millions)				Annual Growth Rate	
	1963	1969	1974	1977	1963-69	1969-74
Rural	2.8	2.9	3.0	3.3	0.5	1.2
Urban	0.7	1.2	1.7	2.0	8.9	6.8
Total	3.5	4.1	4.7	5.3	2.5	3.0
% Urban	20.5	29.4	35.3	38.3		

Source: 1963, 1964, 1969 Population Census; 1970, 1974 Sample Census of Population; 1977 Estimates (Lusaka: Central Statistical Office)

On the basis of the census of 1963 and 1969 the growth rate of the population was 2.5%. During the same period the annual growth rate of the urban population reached 8.9%. The annual growth rate of the population rose to 3% between 1969 and 1974. This may be attributed to improvement in the supply and delivery of health services. It should also be noted that the rate of growth of the rural population between 1963 and 1969 was only .5% — well below the natural rate of growth of the total population. The rural rate of growth of the population increased to 1.2% between 1969 and 1974, while the urban growth rate of the population declined to 6.8%. The trend may be explained by declining employment opportunities in the urban centres, which has been evident in the economy during this period.

The massive increase in the urban population cannot only be attributed to natural growth as can be observed from the data. The main factor that explains this rapid urban population growth is rural-urban migration. To demonstrate this fact we shall analyse the changes in regional population data. Zambia has five provinces which are predominantly rural and two which are predominantly urban. We shall examine the movements of the population from the rural provinces to urban provinces between 1963 and 1974. To derive the net migration over this period, we shall measure the difference between the change in regional population that actually occurred and the change that would have occurred had the provinces' population grown at the annual natural rate as that for the nation as a whole.

Table 2 shows that there was a net out-migration from the predominantly rural provinces of the magnitude of 20.8% of the 1963 population between 1963 and 1974. This trend was particularly serious in Luapula and Northern Provinces where the population actually dropped over the period 1963-1969.

Luapula Province has experienced population decline over the whole period of 1963-1974. The predominantly urban provinces experienced

Table 2
Rural-Urban Net Migration, 1963-74

Province	Population (in thousands)			Net Migration as % of 1963 Population	
Rural	1963	1969	1974	1963-1969	1969-1974
Luapula	357.0	335.6	321.0	− 22.0	− 19
Northern	564.0	545.0	580.0	− 19.6	− 9.0
Eastern	480.0	509.5	568.0	− 10.1	− 4.5
Northwestern	211.2	232.0	256.0	− 6.5	− 5.7
Western	362.5	410.0	463.0	− 3.1	− 3.2
Southern	466.3	496.0	540.0	− 10.0	− 7.3
Sub-total	2,441.0	2,528.0	2,728.0	− 12.7	− 8.1
Urban					
Central	505.0	713.0	920.0	+ 25.0	+ 19.0
Copperbelt	544.0	816.0	1,046.0	+ 34.0	+ 19.0
Sub-total	1,049.0	1,529.0	1,966.0	+ 29.5	+ 19.0
Total	3,490.0	4,057.0	4,694.0		

Source: 1963 and 1969 Population Census; 1974 Sample of Population Statistics (Lusaka: Central Statistical Office).[1]

massive net immigration from the rural areas. Between 1963 and 1974, 48.5% of the 1963% population of the urban provinces is attributable to net migration. This means that about 48.5% of the growth of the urban population resulted from rural-urban migration over this period.

From the data we have examined, it can be observed that migration to the urban centres was very high between 1963 and 1969. In the subsequent period of 1970-74 it continued to be high but the growth rate declined slightly. It is further evident that the proportion of the urban population has grown very rapidly rising from about 20% of the total population in 1963 to 29% in 1969, 35% in 1974 and 38% in 1977. This makes Zambia one of the most highly urbanized countries in Africa. The variables which have acted as stimulants to rural-urban migration will be analysed below. Zambia is a very thinly populated country. The push factors such as shortage of land for cultivation or a negligible income from share-cropping are not likely to have significantly affected migration. Land belongs to the State in all urban centres and can only be leased for use by individuals or organisations. In the rural areas land belongs to the communities and all members of the communities have access to its use. We shall therefore limit our discussion to pull factors. Rural-urban economic models of migration postulate that migration is dependent on differences in expected incomes that can be derived from participation in economic activities of the two sectors.[2] The higher the expected income differentials between the rural and urban sectors, the more likely will migration accelerate. We shall demonstrate here with available data

28

that the rural-urban income gap has widened in Zambia and consequently migration to urban areas has accelerated.

Available data suggests that there was a significant increase in both nominal and real wages for urban workers between 1965 and 1972 but there was fall in real wages for two subsequent years up to 1974. The nominal wages however rose even during these two years. The decline resulted from very high inflation rate experienced during the period and wage freeze which the government imposed in order to combat inflation. The rural sector which is predominantly subsistence, increased its income only marginally barely adequate to keep in line with the growth of the rural population. Table 3 shows the distribution of wage increase on sectoral basis while Table 4 shows the growth of real income of the various sectors including the subsistence one.

Table 3
Annual % Growth Rate of Nominal and Real Wages, 1965-74

Sector	Nominal (1965-72)	Real (1965-72)	Nominal (1972-74)	Real (1972-74)
Agriculture	11	5	1	− 0
Mining	9	22	3	− 4
Manufacturing	10	4	6	− 5
Construction	11	4	1	− 4
Transport	14	8	3	− 2
Services	8	2	5	− 2
Aggregate	10.5	4	3	− 4

Source: Monthly Digest of Statistics (Lusaka: Central Statistical Office, October 1977); Economic Report 1977 (Lusaka: National Commission for Development Planning, 1978).[3]

For the period of seven years there was a steady increase of both nominal and real wages. The growth rate of money wages averaged about 10.5% p.a. while real wages grow at an average of about 4% p.a. with inflation running at about 6.5% p.a. on the average. The last two years up to 1974 a decline in real wages of the rate of 4% was experienced by urban workers. While the real income of wage earners who are predominantly urban dwellers improved significantly over the period, the subsistence sector experienced no similar gains in real income as can be observed from Table 4.

The sectoral growth rates of the GDP give us an indication of the extent to which subsistence growth rate has lagged behind the modern sector's growth. The subsistence sector's growth rate was only 0.9% p.a. between 1965 and 1976, which is less than half of the overall annual growth of the GDP. The sectors based within or around the urban centres experienced much higher rates of growth. The manufacturing sector grew at the rate of 11.2% in real terms between 1965 and 1970, slowed to 4.8% between 1970

Table 4
Annual Percentage Growth Rate of Real GDP, 1975-76

Sector	1965-1970	1970-1976	1965-1976
Agricultural			
Subsistence	0.7	1.0	0.9
Commercial	6.9	9.1	7.7
Mining	− 4.8	0.3	− 2.0
Manufacturing	11.2	4.8	7.7
Construction	− 2.4	4.5	1.4
Transport	2.7	1.1	1.8
Services	9.3	4.5	6.7
GDP	2.0	3.0	2.4

Source: Monthly Digest of Statistics (Lusaka: Central Statistical Office, November/December 1977); National Accounts, Input/Output tables 1971-1975); 1977 Economic Report (Lusaka: National Commission for Development Planning, 1978).

and 1976, and averaged 7.7% over the whole period. Relatively high growth rates were also achieved in the commercial agricultural and service sectors, both of which are predominantly located in the urban or peri-urban areas. The mining sector's growth rate was negative due to serious technical problems which arose after the Mufulira Mine disaster, which resulted in temporary closure of one of the largest mines in the country. From the previous analysis we have established that the real wages of the predominantly urban workers increased and the urban sectors of the economy, particularly manufacturing, achieved high growth rate while the subsistence sector achieved negligible rate of growth. From this we can deduce that the rural-urban income differentials have widened in Zambia and that this factor has acted as a stimulant to rural-urban migration. This conclusion is only suggestive in view of the inadequate statistical information.

The high rate of migration to urban areas has serious repercussions for both the subsistence and the urban sectors. Migration deprives the subsistence sector of the most productive category of manpower. It has been established that the people who tend to migrate are the educated, the young and the most enterprising. In Zambia 90%[4] of secondary school leavers in rural areas migrate to cities within the first year of graduation. Similar evidence has been established in Ghana.[5] For the urban sector the immigrants increase the supply of labour to levels that cannot be absorbed resulting in rising open unemployment and rapid growth of the informal sector and growing urban poverty.

Labour Force and Urban Employment

On the basis of the 1969 Population and Households census, the total labour force amounted to 1.14 million. Some 610 thousand were classified as subsistence workers, 37 thousand were employed in the commercial agricultural sector and 291 thousand were recorded as employed in the industrial, mining, construction, transport and service sectors, the remaining 201 thousand were either unemployed or partly absorbed in the informal sector. By 1974, when a Sample Population Census was conducted, the informal sector showed the largest increase.

Table 5
Distribution of the Labour Force, 1969-74

| | Labour Force (in thousands) | | Growth (in %) | |
	1969	1974	1969-1974	
Subsistence	610	655	45	7.4
In wage employment	328	368	40	12.2
Urban unemployed and informal sector	201	298	97	48.3
Total	1,139	1,321	182	

Source: 1969 Population Census; 1974 Sample Population Census (Lusaka: Central Statistical Office).

For the period for which data is available, i.e. 1969 to 1974, the subsistence labour force increased by only 45 thousand or about 7.4% in five years. During the same period wage employment increased by 40 thousand or 12.2% in five years. The urban unemployed or disguised unemployed or engaged in the informal sector grew by 48.3% or 97 thousand from 201 thousand to 298 thousand. The proportion of the informal sector has increased from 17.6% of the total labour force in 1969 to about 23% of the total labour force in 1974. We can infer from the rapid growth of the informal sector that migration to the urban sector has greatly increased the problem of unemployment, underemployment and urban poverty in Zambia. The other fact that flows from the situation is that the informal sector has become so important that no meaningful social and economic planning can take place without taking it into full consideration.

The rate at which wage employment grew between 1965 and 1974 lagged behind the demand for employment as can be evidenced by rapid growth of the labour force engaged in the informal sector. We shall now examine some of the factors that may explain the failure of wage employment to grow at a high enough level to absorb the excess labour. We shall suggest that technological dependence resulted in the utilisation of capital-intensive production methods which yield few jobs for any additional investment. This was the main constraint on the growth of wage employment. Government artificially reduced price of capital by subsidies. Before we examine the main constraints on employment growth, we shall evaluate the performance of the economy in the field of job creation.

Table 6
Annual Percentage Growth of Wage Employment 1965-1974

Sector	1965-1970	1970-1974	1965-1974
Commercial Agriculture	1.4	− 4.4	− 1.1
Mining	1.7	2.6	2.1
Manufacturing	5.6	1.0	4.1
Construction	5.6	0.7	2.9
Transport	6.8	2.7	3.9
Services	7.6	2.6	6.0
Total	5.1	1.4	3.6

Source: Monthly Digest of Statistics, Oct. 1977; Employment and Earnings, 1969-70; Economic Reports, and First National Development Plan.

The data has been split into two periods; the first phase covers the First National Development Plan. During this period wage employment grew in all sectors. The largest growth rate was in the services sector, reflecting the fast-growing bureaucracy of the new state which had first achieved independence in 1964. The high growth in transport and construction is the result of large investments in infrastructure which was the dominant feature of the first National Development Plan. The manufacturing sector was the fastest growing sector, reflecting the short-term success of import substitution policy during the early stages of development. The overall growth rate of wage employment was 5.1% p.a. between 1965-1970. This was fairly impressive. Between 1970 and 1974 the growth rate dropped to only 1.4, and there are indications that the declining trend continued even further in subsequent years. The falling growth rate of wage employment was evident in all sectors although the GDP growth rate between 1970 and 1976 was higher than during 1965 to 1970. (See Table 3). This phenomenon may be attributed to increasing capital intensity in the production process. To probe this assumption we shall examine the behaviour of capital-labour ratios for the whole modern sector and a selected number of industrial projects which have been implemented during the post-independence period.

The overall capital-labour ratio rose from 4.5 thousand kwacha per worker in 1965 to about 6.1 thousand kwacha per worker in 1973, an increase of approximately 35% in real terms. This implies that the cost of creating a single job in the economy had gone up by 35%. The commercial agricultural sector experienced the highest rise in capital-labour ratio indicating intensive mechanisation of the production system. Capital-labour ratio increased from

Table 7
Capital-Labour Ratio 1965-73 (in constant 1965 Kwacha per worker)

Sector	1965	1973
Commercial Agriculture	826.0	2,914.0
Mining	9,970.0	10,747.0
Transport	8,955.0	10,454.0
Construction	336.0	783.0
Manufacturing	944.0	3,658.0
Services	6,213.0	8,037.0
Total	4,541.0	6,099.0

Source: Census of Industrial Production 1966, 1969; Employment and Earning 1966-1972; Statistical Year Book 1969; and Monthly Digest of Statistics, October, 1977 (Lusaka: Central Statistical Office)

.83 thousand kwacha to 2.9 thousand kwacha in real terms. This represents an increase in capital intensity of about 250% in eight years. Reference to Table 6 will show that the commercial agricultural sector experienced

Table 8
Selected Development Projects since 1964

Industry	Capital Investment (thousand K)	Employment at full Operation	Capital Cost per worker (thousand K)
Textile mill	8,000	960	8.3
Chemical fertilizer plant	18,000	600	30.0
Civil explosives plant	8,000	400	20.0
Petroleum refinery	24,000	350	68.6
Car assembly plant	2,500	250	10.0
Metal fabrication plant	2,300	80	28.8
Industrial fabrics	2,200	570	3.9
Oil pipeline	32,000	200	160.0
Tire and tubes plant	4,000	435	9.2
Sugar estate and refinery	14,000	2,500	5.6
Trucking	10,000	2,000	5.0
Breweries	7,000	600	11.7
Total	132,000	8,945	14.8

Source: *Enterprise*, Vol. 1, (1970) pp. 20-21; Industrial Development Corporation of Zambia Limited, *Annual Report* (1969-1970) pp. 6-7.

negative growth of employment. For all sectors there is a significant increase in capital-labour ratio. Small increases are observable in the mining and transport sectors which are traditionally capital-intensive.

We may now examine some of the major industrial development projects which have been undertaken since Independence to illustrate the use of capital-intensive production methods. Table 8 shows the type of industry, actual capital invested, number of jobs created and capital cost per worker. The total investment of about K132 million created only 8945 permanent jobs. The average capital cost of creating a single job amounted to about K14.8 thousand. For a surplus labour economy this amount represents high capital intensity. Increasing capital intensity was encouraged by policies that were biased in favour of capital importation such as exemption from payment of customs duties on all capital goods, investments credits on income tax and generous depreciation allowances. Increasing use of capital intensive production methods contributed significantly to the slower expansion of wage employment.

We have so far established that modern sector income increased much faster than subsistence income and that this has contributed to the acceleration of migration to the modern sector. The consequences of this development for income distribution have been very negative. First, we have moved further from bridging the gap between rural and urban incomes. Instead the income disparity between the two sectors has increased. On the urban scene, high immigration from the rural sector has not been accompanied by similar growth in employment opportunities resulting in the very fast spread of the informal sector which means increasing the number of people at the bottom decile of income bracket in the urban sector. On the basis of Central Statistics Office's Households Surveys of 1972/1973 the computation of the Gini-coefficient reveals a very skewed distribution of income. In fact the distribution of income has slighly worsened compared to what it was in 1959. The Gini-coefficient in 1959 was about .526 as compared to .55 in 1972/ 1973 period.

The situation revealed by this analysis calls for immediate policy orientation to reverse the present trend. It should however be appreciated that Zambia is a small country very unfavourably located both economically and politically.

The policy measures recommended here are aimed at improving the status of the poorest segment of the population, which still constitutes the vast majority. The policy package we recommend focuses on three areas:

a. Measures that will contribute to increasing productivity of the subsistence sector and thus raise the rural income and reduce the gap between the rural and the urban areas.

b. The introduction of innovations in the informal sector to raise its performance and increase the income of those engaged in it.

c. The introduction of changes in production pattern to increase the job creation capacity of future investments in the formal sector.

The subsistence sector has experienced no significant improvement in productivity. This may be explained partly by the fact that the organisation of both community and production has not been fundamentally changed. The first step to achieve improvement in economic performance of this sector is to introduce new forms of village organisation. At the moment villages are scattered over vast areas and they are in most cases too small to form a viable economic unit. The villages should be regrouped into larger units to facilitate easy delivery of infrastructure, agricultural inputs and other services. The form of organisation should be based on cooperative effort and self-management.

The new units should be settled in areas with high agricultural potential. The next step should be to create basic social and economic infrastructure in the new settlements. This should consist of feeder roads, schools and medical services. Some of these facilities already exist in some rural areas. In addition to formal education, extensive agricultural extension services should be developed and provided to the new organisations. The other innovation necessary is the provision of credit facilities for such rural units. The existing agricultural financing organisation should devote most of its resources to financing the new rural production units. To ensure that the production of the rural sector is properly marketed, there is need for establishing effective marketing organisations, possibly on a cooperative basis to distribute inputs such as seeds, fertilizers and equipment, and to buy the produce. The present marketing organisation is too large and too centralised to cope with effective buying of produce. It should be broken into small rural marketing organisations which should be self-managed. Similar decentralisations of the agricultural financing organisation would be appropriate. The policy makers should also introduce favourable agricultural prices to correct the current adverse terms of trade between the rural and urban sectors.

A similar programme is required for the informal sector. There is a need to introduce or extend the cooperative organisation of production and marketing in the informal sector. As we have established in our analysis, the informal sector is currently the fastest growing source of livelihood in Zambia. The informal sector needs to be provided with education which will provide the usable skills within the sector. There is therefore need to provide more technical and trade training for the sector to improve both the level of production and the quality of products. Access to financial institutions for the cooperatives or individuals engaged in self-employment in the informal sector should be forthcoming. The main objective for providing resources to this sector is to improve productivity so that the income of those engaged in it may be increased. In addition to the measures we have suggested economic incentives should be provided to encourage some of the people in the informal sector to go back to the land.

To implement the package for both subsistence sector and the informal sector, it will be necessary to change the whole investment pattern. Currently more than 80% of all investable resources have been to the benefit of the formal urban sector. To meet the new approach, the government should use its dominance in the economy to direct more resources to the subsistence and informal sectors.

The present pattern of investment in the formal modern sector encouraged capital-intensive methods of production which created relatively fewer jobs per unit of investment. Most of post-independence projects were large and capital intensive. In order to increase future job creation capacity, deliberate efforts should be undertaken to select the type of industries which are labour-intensive. Further encouragement should be given to small-scale industries which tend to be capital-saving and are labour intensive.

It is hoped that this approach to the development programme will create a more desirable balanced development. We need to divert more resources and pay more attention to the improvement of the economic status of the poorest in both urban and rural sectors while at the same time the modern formal sector should be restructured in order to generate growth and yield high employment using appropriate technology.

References

1. See M. E. Jackman, *Recent Population Movements in Zambia,* (Lusaka, 1972).
2. See W. A. Lewis, *Economic Development with Unlimited Supply of Labour,* (Manchester, 1954); R. E. Beals, M. B. Levy and L. N. Moses, 'Rationality and Migration in Ghana', *The Review of Economics and Statistics* (1967).
3. The growth rates have been rounded and do not include the trend of growth rates of Non-Zambian Employees' wages.
4. See *Tracer Project,* University of Zambia.
5. Beals, Levy, Moses, *op. cit.* Also J. B. Knight, *Rural-Urban Income Comparisons and Migration in Ghana.*
6. See R. E. Baldwin, *Economic Development and Export Growth: A Study of Northern Rhodesia, 1920-1960.* (Berkeley, 1966).

Study Questions

1. What factors contributed to the rapid growth of urban population in Zambia between 1964 and 1974?
2. What would have been the population of Luapula Province in 1974 had there been no rural-urban migration?
3. Why did the growth in wage employment lag behind the growth of real output in the Zambian manufacturing sector between 1964 and 1974?
4. What effect has the high rate of rural-urban migration on rural development, and what consequences has it on the urban areas?
5. Between 1972 and 1974 nominal wages increased in all sectors but real wages decreased in all sectors. Why do you think this was possible?
6. What policies should Zambia pursue in order to achieve balanced growth and development in both rural and urban areas?

3. Ann Seidman
The Economics of Eliminating Rural Poverty

The Problem: Development of Underdevelopment

Almost every one of the more than forty African states that have attained political independence in the last two decades has pledged major efforts to stimulate 'rural development'. Unfortunately, the consequences of these efforts have tended in most cases to augment the growing gap between the so-called 'modern' and 'productive' growth of the export economy and the poverty of the masses in the rural areas. Schemes to extend marketing facilities, to provide rural credit, to mechanize agriculture, to build co-operatives, have barely altered the fact that the vast majority of Africans still struggle to survive on the threshold of hunger. Increasing numbers of peasants drift annually into the cities, crowding into urban squatter compounds, swelling the ranks of the tens of thousands of unemployed. This is as true among the more recently independent countries of Central and Southern Africa as it is of those farther north.

Extensive debate has emerged among development theorists as to the nature of the inter-relationship between the rapid growth of the export enclaves and the persistent rural poverty of the masses. The significance of this debate rests in the fact that the effectiveness of the solutions to the problems of underdevelopment depends on the validity of the explanations given for them. If the explanation of the growing gap between the 'haves' and 'have nots' in Central and Southern Africa is inadequate, the proposed solutions will inevitably fail to improve life for the masses.

Traditional Western economic theory has argued that export growth should serve as an engine of development, stimulating the spread of modern productive activities to the countryside through a 'multiplier' effect. The cause of the obvious failure of this approach in independent Africa, these theorists maintain, is to be found in the characteristics of the rural population: their attitudes and traditional institutions hinder the emergence of the necessary entrepreneurial behaviour required to take advantage of the new opportunities created by the expansion of the export sector.[1]

South Africa is held by some conventional economists, despite its oppressive racist rule, to be the paradigm of success. Building on the export of gold to world capitalist markets, a determined white minority government has, in the post-Second World War years, successfully fostered manufacturing growth at one of the highest rates in the Western world. Multinational firms have enthusiastically contributed capital and technology. South African investment in the 1960s was the largest single source of British profits from overseas. American investment there has more than doubled in the last seven years. Over 80 per cent of all American manufacturing investment in Africa is located in South Africa.[2] South Africa's outreach to the north is conceived as a form of 'multiplier' to stimulate economic growth there. Over time, some still insist, this growth will ultimately trickle down to the masses of impoverished Africans.

Other Western theorists, repelled by South Africa's racist doctrines, argue that the failure of export-oriented growth to spread development to African populations in the independent states reflects the failure to create the appropriate institutions to provide them with the necessary market incentives. Once these are created, African peasants may be expected to behave like 'economic men' and augment output rapidly, setting the 'multiplier' effect into motion.[3]

Growing numbers of political economists have rejected both variants of this traditional Western explanation. The fundamental causes of the widespread rural underdevelopment still characteristic in Africa, they hold, are to be found not in traditional attitudes and institutions, not even in the lack of market incentives, but in the sets of institutions and class relationships shaped in the process of carving out the externally dependent export enclaves during the colonial era. Colonialism systematically undermined pre-existing agricultural and trading systems in order to coerce Africans into providing the low-cost labour needed to produce cheap raw materials for export to the factories of Europe.[4]

Most political economists espousing this explanation of underdevelopment have focused their analyses on the institutions and class relations which emerged in the export enclave itself, rather than starting such analyses from conditions in the rural areas. They have shown how the export enclave was geared to the production of one or a few raw materials for export. Simultaneously, the import of manufactured goods for the associated high-income group provided a market outlet for the surplus output of metropole factories in Europe and North America. The basic industries, foreign and internal wholesale trade and banks are dominated directly or indirectly by foreign firms, which mesh the export enclaves firmly into the external dependency network of the world capitalist system. The profits, interest, and high salaries drained from the continent by these foreign firms constitute a major loss of investible surpluses for national development. Moreover, since independence a newly emergent group of highly paid civil servants and politicians has become increasingly linked to the foreign firms in a variety of new ways. Together, these increasingly intertwined groups have tended to perpetuate and aggravate the lopsided, externally dependent growth initiated during the colonial period.

This is not to argue that theory must begin its analysis in the rural periphery rather than the export enclave, but that such theory needs more sophistication in relating itself to the specifics of rural poverty. It is essential to probe more deeply into the historical roots and continuing inter-relationships between the expansion of the export enclave and mounting rural and urban poverty in Africa today. This is the key to understanding the way the new institutions and class relationships, which dominate the export enclave, continue to distort and undermine development in widespread rural areas in Africa. The evidence needed to warrant this explanation cannot be uncovered by any one scholarly discipline alone. Neither the problems involved nor the explanations come in boxes neatly labelled 'economics', 'history', 'sociology', or 'political science'. What is required is systematic inter-disciplinary analysis employing a time scale.

Herein lies the value of *The Roots of Rural Poverty*.[5] This book sheds considerable light on the way the historical process of underdevelopment has taken place in Central and Southern Africa. It lays the basis for the articulation of a theoretical model exposing the causal nexus between the growth of the export enclaves and the deeply rooted poverty of the rural areas of the region.

The Explanation: Colonial Origins
Despite the obvious differences in the historical development and colonial-imposed ties of the various Central and Southern African countries into the world commercial system, the evidence in this book exposes the basic similarities in the process of the development of underdevelopment in the rural areas of the region. This postscript therefore seeks to set forth an explanatory model[6] of the origins of the problem, flexible enough to identify key variables while still accommodating the variety of the case studies presented in *The Roots of Rural Poverty*.

The imposition of export enclave production varied in detail from area to area, but the underlying pattern in all cases was that of carving out export production sectors as intermediate centres between the European metropole and the vast labour reserve of the Central and Southern African economies in the context of the world capitalist system.

The growth of the export enclaves contributed to the impoverishment of the rural areas in two ways. Directly, through the extraction of surpluses produced by the low-paid wage-labour generated out of the vast rural reservoir. Indirectly, in the form of surpluses accumulated from the sale of high-priced manufactured goods sold by the big trading firms and their agents in both rural and urban areas. A major share of these surpluses was shipped out of the country by the giant firms dominating the mines, trade, and finance.

The export enclaves of Central and Southern Africa therefore were developed at the expense of the rural African populations. In all the countries, laws and administrative controls had the cumulative effect of turning control and ownership of vast mines and estates over to foreign firms and settlers.

Initially in some areas the expanding labour force on the mines and plantations provided growing markets for food and crops produced by neighbouring peasants. Not a few Africans successfully expanded their food crop output, despite the almost universal failure of the colonial governments to provide funds or technical assistance. In some cases, disease and drought destroyed their crops or animal wealth. In almost all cases, the settler-dominated governments ultimately took steps to end this African peasant competition, especially when the Great Depression of the 1930s sharply reduced overall demand for agricultural produce. In effect, natural calamities combined with restrictive governmental policies deprived Africans of the opportunity of participating in the use of the new means of production introduced in the export enclaves, except as members of a low-wage labour force.

Sir Harry Johnston, an architect of British colonial policy, explained that the colonial goals of acquiring cheap raw materials and markets for European factories could be achieved 'if the European capitalist can be induced by proper security to invest his money in Africa and if native labour can be obtained by the requisite guarantees of fair play towards native rights'. He made quite clear what he meant by 'proper security' for European investment: 'The White capitalist . . . must have something conceded to him. The native must be prepared to guarantee a fairly handsome return for money hazardously invested.'[7] He had earlier spelt out what he considered 'fair play' to the African: 'A gentle insistence that the native should contribute his fair share to the revenue of the country by paying his hut-tax, is all that is necessary on our part to secure his taking that share of life's labour which no human being should evade.'[8]

The imposition of hut and poll taxes, requiring Africans to earn cash, was not the only means of 'gentle insistence' applied in Central and Southern Africa. Africans were typically forced off the best lands, particularly those located near roads and railway lines leading to cash markets. These lands were turned over to European settlers who received extensive technical and financial assistance from government agencies to expand their output. Complex marketing and quota arrangements excluded Africans from producing cash crops in competition with them. In those areas like Shaba/Katanga where Africans were permitted to continue to grow cash crops due to the settlers' failure to produce sufficient amounts, administrative coercion, reinforced by the violent impact of economic fluctuations emanating from the world market, destroyed peasant initiative. Foreign-owned import houses and their associated agents were encouraged to sell manufactured goods mass-produced in European factories throughout the colonies. Government licensing and other restrictions on local productive activities and trade completed the process of undermining and destroying traditional African handicraft industries. The money and banking system, created to finance the imposed system of production and trade, intertwined the export enclaves still more closely into the international commercial system. Africans were explicitly denied credit on the grounds that they were poor risks. In some cases, legislation was passed making it illegal for banks to lend them funds.

As a result of systematic policy decisions, then, Africans in many areas were given little opportunity to earn cash except by joining the vast migratory wage-labour force required to expand the production of the foreign-owned mines and plantations. The previous status of women as independent cultivators in some areas was undermined and destroyed. Tens of thousands of young African men were forced out of the villages to search for wage employment. Forty to sixty per cent of the men aged twenty to forty years old might be out of a village at any given time. The women, children, and older men who stayed at home had difficulty in maintaining the levels of agricultural productivity previously attained. As traditional irrigation and cultivation practices fell into disuse and the soils became increasingly eroded, the vast majority of the young men growing up in rural areas were even more narrowly restricted to seeking jobs on the large mines or plantations.

The wages paid to men who worked on the mines and plantations were actually subsidized by the rural areas. Women were expected to remain there, and to continue to provide housing and foodstuffs for the children. Cash wages were only expected to pay for the men's subsistence, with a little left over for taxes and perhaps a few 'extras', like a bicycle or a new suit of clothes. In other words, the colonialists did not even expect wages to cover the minimum defined by Marx as essential under capitalism: i.e. the socially necessary labour time required to maintain and reproduce the labour force. This system has been institutionalized by *apartheid* in South Africa and increasingly in Rhodesia, but it remains a dominant characteristic of the economies of the black-ruled states of Central and Southern Africa even today.

As the rural areas became meshed into the monetary sector through the sale of labour and the purchase of trade goods, the class relationships there became increasingly dependent on the dominant institutions of the export enclave. Chiefs were enticed or coerced into participating in extensive labour recruitment networks. A few entrepreneurial types, co-operating with the big trading firms, established small village stores or a bar. They gradually accumulated wealth. Those who benefited from the limited educational facilities available obtained posts as teachers or as clerks and petty officials in district offices north of the Zambezi, or in mines and private business south of the Zambezi. In a few areas, where cash-cropping was permitted, so-called 'emergent' or 'progressive' farmers expanded their output. They extended their land areas and hired their neighbours at a few pence per month, adding the resulting surpluses to their income. New class relationships gradually emerged in this way, with a clique of relatively well-to-do traders, farmers, and low-level civil servants benefiting from the extension of the commercial system from the enclaves into the provinces.

The Problem Today: Post-colonial Perpetuation
The attainment of political independence in Central and Southern Africa has done little to alter the fundamental institutions and class relationships which emerged during colonial rule. The new governments there, as elsewhere on the continent, began to expand their social and economic infrastructure. Zambia, with the highest per capita income and tax revenues in independent Africa,[9] was perhaps the most successful in building up a national network of schools,

roads and electric power facilities. In part, this was a response to the popular demand for 'development'. In part, it reflected orthodox economic theory that the establishment of infrastructure contributes to the creation of a 'hospitable investment climate', which will attract foreign firms to build manufacturing industries, thereby providing employment and stimulating development throughout the economy. It was assumed that, eventually, given the appropriate opportunities and market incentives, African entrepreneurs would begin to benefit from and contribute to the resulting 'multiplier' effects, spreading development into the rural areas.

But even where newly independent governments could afford to finance the rapid expansion of social and economic infrastructure—as in Zambia—this did not change the basic institutions which tied the allocation of resources to the export sector, dominated by European and South African interests. On the contrary, its impact tended to aggravate the inherited, externally dependent dualism.

Zambia's experience is typical. On the one hand, the civil service multiplied rapidly to provide personnel to man the new projects created. This required funding, which necessitated increased current tax revenues merely to cover operating costs. The immediate source of new revenues was perceived to be the expansion of copper exports, an added argument for further investment in mining. When the price of copper fell on the world market, the government was forced to borrow internally and externally. The former added to domestic inflationary pressures, the latter to future burdens on the balance of payments and ties to multinational banking interests. This still further aggravated external dependence.

On the one hand, the new foreign investment attracted into Zambia's (import substitution) manufacturing sector tended to produce more and more luxury items for the limited high-income elite associated with the export enclave, along with a few profitable mass-produced goods, like beer and cigarettes. This remained true even where government had purchased a majority of shares in the businesses, for government personnel adopted the same import substitution criteria as their foreign partners.[10] Beer and cigarette output, for example, expanded rapidly. By 1972, it had reached 40 per cent of the manufacturing value added in Zambia. Pharmaceuticals, radios, television sets, air conditioners, even private cars, are now being 'produced' locally in last-stage assembly and processing factories using imported parts and materials. The import of finished luxury items for high-income groups, in other words, is gradually being replaced by the import of some machinery and equipment and the continuing import of parts and materials, instead of developing local resources. The resulting finished products are often sold at higher than world prices in the tariff-protected markets. The fact is that the complex industries required to produce such luxury items cannot be established in the truncated markets of Zambia or any other African state for a long time to come. Typically, moreoever, the machinery and equipment imported for these kinds of industries are relatively capital-intensive, so that the number of new jobs created is limited. The new factories are generally built in the already developed export enclave to take advantage of existing external economies and the urban high income market. Few new job opportunities are spread into the rural areas. Peasants seeking to escape rural poverty still have little choice but to crowd into urban slums.

Although Zambia's greater per capita wealth may have facilitated the more rapid expansion of its social, economic and political infrastructure, as well as its manufacturing sector, the situation is different in degree rather than in kind in Zaire, Malawi, Botswana, Lesotho, and Swaziland.

In all of the ex-British and ex-Belgian states of Central and Southern Africa, a new class of Africans, termed by some the 'bureaucratic bourgeoisie', has emerged rapidly with the growth of the civil service and the upper echelons of the ruling political parties. Although at the outset its members did not control the major means of production—still owned outright by foreign firms and settlers—their positions in the government gave them a base from which they could attain a status of dependent participants in that control. They tended, from the beginning, to be linked with the more advantaged, well-to-do groups in the villages. Some used their high salaries and newly acquired facilities to obtain bank credit to invest in large estates, as well as in trade and speculative real estate in burgeoning urban communities. Government 'Africanization' policies combined with licensing powers rapidly endowed the 'bureaucratic bourgeoisie' with *oligopolistic* status as intermediaries between the firms dominating the export enclave and the impoverished populations. While they generally lacked the expertise and capital to acquire a significant share of the rapidly expanding (import substitution) manufacturing and mining sectors, selected individuals began to participate in the managements and as members of the boards of directors of newly formed parastatals in which governments had invested directly. Thus they became directly associated with the foreign firms and banking businesses which continue to handle the management, the marketing networks, and, in most cases, own a major share of the capital invested in the export enclave.

Widespread appeals for peasants to exert greater efforts to expand rural production have, as might be expected, been ineffective in such a context. Mere appeals cannot create new sets of institutions or contribute to expansion of new sectors of the economy in any way which might restructure the narrow choices of impoverished rural dwellers. New factories are not built to provide markets for local agricultural raw materials or to increase the productivity and living standards of the rural poor.

Marketing institutions designed to collect agricultural produce tend to purchase crops produced by the estate sector, in which the new dominant class now has a stake, and to pay premium prices for the produce. Government spokesmen argue that it is cheaper to purchase maize or tobacco by the ton than to buy a few bags from one small farmer here, a few more from another several miles away. But the fact remains that, as leading political figures and civil servants have become owners of large estates, their attention has become primarily focused on ensuring the profitability of their own operations.

The foreign private banks, still operating primarily in accord with traditional lending criteria, continue to finance larger farmers who can prove secure title to their land. Government civil servants and politicians may now have some access to bank credit, but the small peasant in remote rural areas is still excluded. The smaller African peasant, unable to expand his sales in competition with the larger estate farmers, inevitably finds himself squeezed out. His only remaining channel for escape from rural poverty is to flee the countryside, vainly hoping to share in the conspicuous consumption which political independence has bestowed on a lucky few of his compatriots.

The Implicit Solution: New Institutions and Class Relations
In short, the explanation of rural poverty in Central and Southern Africa lies in historically developed institutions and class relations. The white rulers of South Africa and Rhodesia will seek to perpetuate these institutions and class relationships, relying on racist policies to admit only a tiny minority of African collaborators to luxury consumption patterns, and to restrict the majority to underpaid labour. But it is becoming increasingly obvious that replacement of the white rulers by an emergent class of wealthy Africans in the context of the inherited sets of institutions has not fundamentally altered the situation in the black-ruled countries of Central and Southern Africa. It is true that more social and economic infrastructure has been built than ever before – but the *nouveau riche* has greater access to the benefits than the masses of rural poor. In fact, there appears to be some evidence that their own newly acquired comfortable status, combined with the pressures of the economic crisis currently engulfing the capitalist world, is rendering this emergent class increasingly hospitable to South Africa's outward-looking policies.

If the above model is valid, as the evidence accumulated in this book suggests, it indicates that the only way to uproot rural poverty in Central and Southern Africa is to implement fundamental changes in the inherited class relationships and institutions. This implies, in the first place, the necessity of carrying through the national liberation struggle until all the nations of the region are political independent under governments which represent all the people. The recent victories of the liberation movements of Mozambique and Angola have accelerated the timetable. South Africa remains the bastion of colonial minority domination, backed by extensive foreign investment. It seeks to consolidate and indeed to expand its position, though its domination of the region is increasingly threatened by guerrilla successes in Zimbabwe, by the struggle in Namibia, and by growing numbers of strikes by workers in South Africa itself.

The post-independence experience of Central and Southern African states, however, especially when viewed in the context of the explanations exposed above, suggests that African accession to political power is not in itself enough. Fundamental restructuring of the regional political economy is essential to end the continuing development of underdevelopment. Proposals along these lines, stemming logically from the explanations embodied above, are tentatively outlined here as possible guides for further investigation and evaluation in terms of their potential contribution to more effective attainment of 'rural development'.[11]

1. Rural focus: Every effort should be made to create new opportunities for the rural population to expand their productive activities and improve their living conditions. This requires creation of new rural institutions to encourage all peasants, not just the few wealthy ones, to participate in discovering new ways of increasing productivity and benefiting from new industrial and agricultural activities. Appropriate backwards and forwards linkages must be forged between these rural institutions and those controlling the 'commanding heights' to ensure that they supplement, rather than contradict, each others' efforts. Our model has shown how the development of underdevelopment in rural areas is the obverse side of the growth of the externally dependent export enclave dominated by foreign firms and settlers. Hence attainment of rural development requires that the institutions and class relations created in the rural areas be accompanied by fundamental measures to attain a balanced, nationally integrated, independent political economy capable of providing productive employment and higher living standards in every region.

2. The political arena: New political institutions need to be shaped to ensure the effective participation in government at all levels of those classes which would benefit from rural development, particularly the masses of low-income rural peasants, the wage-earners on plantations, in mines and factories, and the growing numbers of urban unemployed. Appropriate channels of communication and feedback should be shaped to enable these groups to take part in critical decisions relating to reallocation of resources and creation of new productive activities designed to stimulate rural development.

3. Government machinery: The inherited colonial sets of government ministries were designed primarily to facilitate the expansion of social and economic infrastructure to stimulate private investment in productive sectors. The entire structure of governmental administrative machinery and parastatals needs to be redesigned so that it is capable of coordinating measures to ensure the spread of *productive* industrial and agricultural activities into remote rural areas.

4. A long-term physical plan: Such a plan, covering, say, twenty years, should be formulated to create balanced industrial and agricultural sectors to increase productive employment opportunities and raise living standards in the countryside, while reducing external dependence. This does not imply that the economy should no longer produce exports. Rather, the export sector should be increasingly characterized by production of more finished products in place of low-cost raw materials. A greater share of the inputs and outputs of the export sector should come from and contribute to the expansion of employment and production in other sectors. New manufacturing industries created should be explicitly designed to increase productivity and improve the consumption patterns of the rural population. Poles of growth should be established to stimulate the spread of agricultural and industrial activity in each geographical region. Local resources should be developed and processed to contribute to the greatest possible local spread effect in the rural areas. Appropriate technologies, based on available labour and skills, should be introduced to advance overall productivity as skills and domestic investible surpluses are augmented in each stage of the plan.

5. *A long-term financial plan:* Such a plan should be formulated to ensure that all available investible surpluses are directed to fulfilment of the planned physical perspectives. This would require a national incomes policy – which co-ordinated taxes, profits, prices, wages and salary payments, as well as bank credit – to direct surpluses, previously accruing to the 'haves', to productive activities providing jobs and incomes for the 'have nots'.

6. *The 'commanding heights':* The government, involving the masses of the population at every step, would need to exert control of the 'commanding heights' – that is, basic industries, banks, and foreign and internal wholesale trade – to enable it to implement long-term physical and financial plans. Basic industries could then be directed to providing parts and materials for essential manufacturing and agricultural development, at appropriate levels of technology, in planned locations in all areas, as well as adding to national foreign exchange earnings and investible surpluses. The banks could facilitate check-ups on financial implementation of physical plans, as well as provision of credit to planned industries and agricultural development in rural areas. Foreign and internal wholesale trade could be reshaped to support planned expansion of domestic productive sectors. No goods would be imported in competition with planned local projects. New trade channels would be opened to bring domestic inputs to new factories and to spread their products at reasonable costs into the most remote local markets. Efforts could be made to expand foreign sales of new manufactured products.

7. *Regional co-operation between states:* Potential economic development in both industry and agriculture is severely limited at present by the inherited colonial borders which fragment Central and Southern Africa into coastal and landlocked states. Only South Africa has the wide array of natural resources and integrated infrastructure which has enabled it to practise economies of scale and benefit from modern technology to diversify production and expand its market. So long as the rest of Central and Southern Africa does not realize its great potentials through regional co-operation, especially to create basic industries that individual states could not attain alone, South Africa will retain its economic advantages over its northern neighbours.[11]

Conclusion
Pledges by independent governments in Central and Southern Africa to foster 'rural development' appear to have failed to achieve the promised goals. Analysis of the historical evidence presented throughout this book permits the formulation of a model which may help to explain why. The causes lie embedded in the institutions and class relationships which perpetuate and aggravate the inherited externally dependent dualism characteristic of Central and Southern African economies. If this explanation is valid, it

suggests specific areas for new policy measures to change those institutions and class relationships. These have been outlined here for further critical evaluation in the light of evidence as to the historical validity of the explanations which lie behind them, as well as possible consequences of their adoption. This, then, presents a new challenge to inter-disciplinary teams of researchers seeking to contribute to the formulation of more effective policies for rural development. Not only is further information required as to the historical development of the causes of underdevelopment. Systematic study is also needed, in the light of that essential historical background, of the consequences of policies adopted in efforts to restructure the political economy today.

References

This essay was first published in R. Palmer and N. Parsons (eds.), *The Roots of Rural Poverty* in *Central and Southern Africa* (London, 1977).

1. See, for example, D. C. McClelland, *The Achieving Society* (Princeton, 1961), especially pp. 36-106; E. E. Hagen, *On the Theory of Social Change: How Economic Growth Began* (London, 1964); B. F. Hoselitz (ed.), *Economies and the Idea of Mankind* (New York, 1965).

2. R. First, J. Steele, and C. Gurney, *The South African Connection* (Harmondsworth, 1973); United States Chamber of Commerce, *Survey of Current Business* (Washington), October 1969, October 1971, August 1974.

3. See W. O. Jones, 'Economic Man in Africa', *Food Research Institute Studies, I,* 1960, pp. 107-34; M. P. Miracle, Capitalism, Capital Markets, and Competition in West African Trade', in C. Meillassoux (ed.), *The Development of Indigenous Trade and Markets in West Africa* (London, 1971), pp. 399-410; P. Hill, *The Migrant Cocoa-Farmers of Southern Ghana: A Study in Rural Capitalism* (Cambridge, 1963).

4. Perhaps the best known is Samir Amin, head of the Institute for Development and Economic Planning, Economic Commission for Africa. See his 'Underdevelopment and Dependence in Black Africa — Origins and Contemporary Forms', *Journal of Modern African Studies, 10,* (1972), pp. 503-24.

5. R. Palmer and N. Parsons (eds.), *The Roots of Rural Poverty in Central and Southern Africa* (London, 1977).

6. There is a growing literature on model-building for the social sciences. The following have been found useful in formulating the model presented here: G. C. Homans, 'Contemporary Theory in Sociology', in R. E. Faris (ed.), *Handbook of Modern Sociology* (Chicago, 1964), pp. 951-77; M. Black, *Models and Metaphors: Studies in Language and Philosophy* (Ithaca, 1962); I. D. F. Bross, *Design for Decision* (New York, 1965); M. W. Riley, *Sociological Research, Vol. 1, A Case Approach* (New York, 1963).

7. H. H. Johnston, 'The Importance of Africa', *Journal of the African Society, 17,* (1918), pp. 186-7, 192.

8. Public Record Office, London, FO 2/106, Johnston to Salisbury, 29

April 1896, 'Report on the British Central Africa Protectorate from April 1st, 1895, to March 31st 1896'. Quoted in R. Oliver, *Sir Harry Johnston and the Scramble for Africa* (London, 1957), p. 270.

9. For data on Zambia's investible surplus, see A. Seidman, 'What To Do with the Copper Surplus', *African Development, 8,* (October 1974), Z.59-Z.61.

10. See, for example, A. Seidman, 'The Distorted Growth of Import-Substitution Industry: The Zambian Case', *Journal of Modern African Studies, 12,* (1974), pp. 601-31.

11. For more elaboration, see A. Seidman, *Planning for Development in Sub-Saharan Africa* (New York and Dar es Salaam, 1974).

12. R. H. Green and A. Seidman, *Unity or Poverty? The Economics of Pan-Africanism* (Harmondsworth, 1968).

Study Questions

1. How did the growth of the export enclaves during the colonial period contribute to the progressive impoverishment of the rural areas of Zambia?

2. In what way can the development of a 'bureaucratic bourgeoisie' be seen as impeding African peasant production?

3. What are some possible short- and long-term strategies for revitalizing the rural sector of the Zambian economy?

4. Muna Ndulo
Domestic Participation in Mining in Zambia

Background to the Policy

The Mines and Minerals Act[1] makes mandatory domestic participation a
precondition for the establishment of any mining enterprise by a foreign
investor and the law fixes the terms of the domestic capital participation
required. This article looks at the background to this policy decision, the
terms of participation, the objectives of the policy and the state's prospects
of realising these objectives in practice.

The policy of requiring domestic participation was announced in 1969[2]
and was subsequently incorporated in the Mines and Minerals Act in the same
year. It is not a novel provision in the context of the history of mining
activities in Zambia. In the early period of mining in Zambia the British
South Africa Company required every registered mining location to be held
by the registered holders on joint account with it in the proportion of two-
thirds to the registered holders and one-third to the British South Africa
Company.[3] It exercised this interest at the time formal permission was
requested to work for profit.[4]

The Zambian government, following the attainment of independence in
1964, virtually confined itself to increasing the tax revenues obtained from
the mining companies and demanding that the existing companies Zambianise
mining posts at all levels as rapidly as possible.[5] This was despite a 1963
United Nations Economic Commission recommendation that in view of the
significance of the industry in the economy of the country, the government
should have direct participation,[6] and also despite the fact that in 1964 the
existing mining companies had offered the government minority participation in their mining ventures.[7]

The government's attitude can be attributed to the fact that soon after
independence there was general insecurity on the part of mining companies
and their workers. As a result, it did not want to take measures which might
have increased the insecurity.[8] And not unnaturally, there was also lack of
confidence on the part of government in its own ability to manage such a
large enterprise.

This policy change in 1969 was in fact largely due to the behaviour of
foreign firms in Zambia, both mining and non-mining. While in 1953-63 the
country was still a British protectorate, and a member of the Federation of

Rhodesia and Nyasaland, the tendency was for secondary industry in the Federal industrial sector to be concentrated in Southern Rhodesia, while the North remained a supplier of revenue from the copper mining industry and a market for manufactured goods.[9] It was not only the Southern Rhodesia industries which served Northern Rhodesia, but also those of South Africa.[10] One of the major mining companies, for instance, is a subsidiary company of South African mining houses and the other, though controlled by American Metal-Climax, has South African interests. It had been the custom over many years for the Zambian subsidiaries to be administered from the South.

Most foreign firms, mining and non-mining, looked to South Africa for supplies and stock was brought up from Southern Rhodesia or South Africa as needed. After the Unilateral Declaration of Independence in Rhodesia the companies went on as before, although it became increasingly contrary to government policy, especially as Zambia responded to the United Nations call to impose sanctions on Rhodesia.[11] She has also been committed to reducing her dependence upon imports from South Africa. But many companies appeared unwilling to seek alternative sources of supply of goods in East Africa and elsewhere despite government requests. A marked reluctance to set up genuinely separate company structures in Zambia was also apparent; indeed some branches had little more than a nominal existence and were used to order imports from Britain which were off-loaded en route in Rhodesia to circumvent sanctions.[12]

Allied to these economic consequences were political side effects. Africans could find little opportunity to acquire managerial or technical expertise. During the colonial period it was impossible for them to obtain loan capital on the terms granted to Europeans, and various legal restrictions prevented them from advancing beyond certain levels. For example, until 1960 Africans were barred from becoming apprentices.[13] Academic limitations were also severe; at the time of independence, Zambia had only 960 Africans with school certificates and fewer than 100 graduates.[14]

As a result, the mines were staffed at senior levels totally by expatriates. In 1969, of the employees of the mining companies operating in the country, 40,000 were Zambians (mostly unskilled) and about 7,000 expatriates were in skilled jobs. On the board of the mining companies, there were two Zambians, one indigenous Zambian and one expatriate who had taken Zambian nationality.[15] Efforts to Zambianise in the five years since independence had been largely unsuccessful.[16]

Table 1
Expatriate Labour Strength in Mining Industry, 1965-69

Year	Average strength	Engagements	Resignations	Displaced by Zambianisation
1965	7,035	902	1,131	247
1966	5,981	1,213	1,403	360
1967	5,378	1,011	1,058	292

| 1968 | 4,845 | 1,088 | 1,124 | 178 |
| 1969 | 4,727 | 947 | 1,127 | 100 |

Source: *Mining Year Book of Zambia*, 1969. Most replacement of expatriates was in the personnel divisions of the mining companies and not at operational levels. E.g., in 1965 there were only nine Zambian shift bosses out of 823, see *Prospects of Zambian Mining Industry*, p.18.

In the years 1964-69, the Zambian economy expanded rapidly. With the end of Federation, the return of control over the country's revenue made possible a great increase in government spending.

Manufacturing developed at a fair pace and its contribution to the gross domestic product rose significantly.[17] But this rapid expansion was inevitably accompanied by inflationary pressures and these were made dangerous by the desire of some companies to extract high profits from a relatively small capital investment. Some companies committed the smallest possible paid up capital and exported most of any profits while relying extensively on local borrowing. Quite apart from the fact that local borrowing is in conflict with the interests of the host state, it also means there will be less credit available for domestic entrepreneurs.

There was no exchange control for the first few years after independence and the absolute freedom to export profits was used to the full.[18] Some resident companies purchasing merchandise from parent organisations abroad added as much as a third on the cost price when making payments. This allowed them to remove capital at a still higher rate while at the same time increasing Zambia's cost of living. This behaviour did much to whip up feeling against foreign companies within the country. The major reason for the introduction of the policy of government participation is therefore to ensure that mining-right holders operate within the framework of the overall economic and social goals of the country.

The policy is also borne out of a desire to ensure that the mining industry is not completely foreign owned and controlled, a desire widespread among developing countries, particularly in relation to extractive industries.[19] In these countries the ordinary man in the street sees no value in theoretical political independence, if most of the decisions relating to employment, inflation, pricing and basic economic consideration which affect his ability to work and look after himself and bring up his family are in the final analysis dependent upon decisions made in other countries. The need for this domestic involvement can best be understood when it is realised that before 1969, there was no direct indigenous financial participation in mining activities as such, although some local capital had been invested in the big mining companies and there were a few local companies exploiting minerals such as mica and limestone.[20]

The policy was first implemented in 1968 with regard to non-mining activities.[21] This had as its precedent the Tanzanian Arusha declaration.

Two other precedents could be said to have been relied on. Zaire, a neighbour and a fellow member of the International Copper Organisation, had taken similar moves in relation to its mining industry in 1966, as had Chile, another fellow member of the Copper Conference.[22]

This desire for economic independence should be distinguished from a desire to cut off all foreign investment. In fact in the *Second National Development Plan* one aspect of the government's mineral policy is stated to be the creation of a favourable investment climate in order to encourage the private sector to increase its level of interest in exploiting the mineral potential of the country.[23] It emphasises that legislation must always reflect this objective. There is a general realisation of the need for foreign capital in the development of the country's mineral resources. Throughout its history the industry has been developed by foreign capital.[24] In the early part it was largely British, American and South African capital which put mining on a sound footing and has, to this day, a significant interest in the existing mines, although now control rests in the state. And even if foreign investment were not to take the form of financial investment, at least in the beginning 'know-how' would have to be contracted from abroad and financing arranged by borrowing from abroad if new mining projects were to be generated and successfully realised. Because of these and other benefits discussed later which the country derives from foreign capital, the Government does not wish to nationalise the mines completely.

The Terms of Participation

Various ways exist of enforcing domestic participation. One such way, which has been adopted in Botswana, is for the government to be issued with a certain percentage of all equity stock free of charge to itself. Another, of which the operations of the government of Ghana in relation to that country's gold and diamond mines provide one of many examples, involves enunciating a policy that a certain proportion of the equity of all major mining companies should be owned by the government and then inviting the companies concerned to enter negotiations with a view to giving effect to this policy.

The Zambian mining legislation follows neither of the two above but instead legislates a government option to participate up to the extent of 51 per cent of the equity shares on terms fixed by it. This option is in practice held by the Mines Industrial Development Corporation, whose issued capital is held 100 per cent by the State. This condition is imposed by section 20 of the Mines and Minerals Act, and the granting of a prospecting licence is made dependent on the applicant agreeing to this condition being included in the licence. So far all prospecting licences that have been issued have carried this condition and no licence has been refused on the grounds that the applicant does not wish this condition to be included though one cannot tell the number of firms that might otherwise have applied for prospecting licences, but did not bother to do so because they knew that the participation option would be made a condition of the licence. The relevant part of the section reads as follows: 'An application for a prospecting licence may be granted subject to conditions, including, in particular (a) a condition requiring the applicant to agree to the Republic or any person nominated on behalf of the Republic, having an option to acquire an interest in any mining venture which might be carried on by the applicant or by any person to whom he transfers his mining right, in the proposed prospecting area.'[25]

The decision to participate: The State does not have to participate, and has in fact refused participation in one case,[26] although the case in point is not a very good example of government's non-exercise of the option, since it was an existing mine and the mine was operating at a loss. It may also indicate that the State will not exercise its option in the case of projects of doubtful viability. It makes a decision whether to participate or not and the extent to which it will participate within the limits of 51 per cent. It may also ask another person to participate on its behalf.

The procedure for the implementation of the policy where a condition as to participation has been included in a prospecting licence or carried over into an exploitation licence is that, prior to applying for a mining licence, the holder of a prospecting licence or an exploitation licence must notify the State and the holder of the option that he intends to apply for a mining licence and requires the holder to exercise his option.[27]

An application for a mining licence may only be granted if the holder of the option exercises the option or informs the holder of the licence in writing that the option will not be exercised, or fails to act within six months of being required to exercise his option.[28]

Should the option not be exercised at the time of the granting of the mining licence, it is not exercised thereafter except upon the invitation of the mining-right holder. This stipulation appears in an annexure attached to prospecting licences. The provision is generally interpreted by miners and mining officials as meaning that once the government does not exercise its option at this time the mining-right holder can operate without any fear of government participation as any such measure would be a breach of the prospecting licence. Any other interpretation would be contrary to the concept of vested rights which is an essential element in the encouragement of mining investment in that it would be eroded if negotiations relating to participation by government, or its nominee, were to take place after the issue of prospecting or exploration licences.

Objectives of the State
The country aims to derive from this policy the well known advantages of local equity participation in foreign ventures in developing countries as cited by several writers on foreign investment.[29] Government participation reduces deeply ingrained suspicions of foreign economic domination. This is particularly important in mining operations because usually their size is large in comparison with other industries. Whether such suspicions are justified in a particular case or not, they have been recognised to be a real and important aspect of that national sensitiveness which characterises many emancipated peoples

who were formerly held in a state of political and economic dependency. It stimulates the engagement of responsible local capital in productive enterprises where the option is exercised in favour of a private local company.[30] It may even help to develop a nucleus of experienced managerial personnel in the public and private sectors in proportion to the participation of public authorities and private capital in joint ventures, in that local labour becomes directly involved in the industry through the equity participation.[31] This in fact has been the result in the other spheres of the economy where the State has participated. These companies have made the deliberate choice of hiring local talent, which has paid off in the sense that several former employees of the State-owned companies have gone into business for themselves, providing an indirect benefit to the economy. In addition to the skills which the inhabitants of the country acquire from employment in these enterprises, equity participation is also simply a mechanism for the transfer of technology from the developed countries.

But the overriding consideration for this policy is control of mining activities so that they operate within the overall economic and social policy of the country. There are many areas of conflict between the State and the mining-right holders in their mining operations; one was the rate of development in the 1960s, when the mining-right holders were keeping the minerals in the ground while the State was concerned to increase the speed of extraction. Another major area of conflict which has often emerged is the use to which investible resources should be put. In the past, for instance, the miners have wanted the reinvestible profits confined to mining activities whereas the State wanted them applied to other spheres of the economy. There is also the problem of how much of the profits should be reinvested at all.

Sometimes the conflicts arise because of a conflict of interest between the State and the mining companies. A case in point arose over the use of 'formed coke' in processing lead and zinc at Broken Hill Mine. The government, mindful of its obligations to the international community in relation to sanctions against the Rhodesian regime, proposed that Waelz kilns should be constructed to produce 'coke' locally which should be used in the reprocessing of slag. This, it was anticipated, could prolong the life of Broken Hill mine by eight years, since the reserves were diminishing. The process cost approximately K70 to produce a ton of coke, whereas the cost of importing a ton of coke from the Rhodesian Wankie coal mines was about K27 per ton. Anglo-American Corporation Ltd favoured leaving the Wankie market still open. In the first place they argued that it was cheaper to do so, but at the same time one must remember that the Anglo-American Corporation owns equity interests in the Wankie Collieries.

There are conflicts about sources of equipment and other resources. The State, mindful of its duty to develop the country, would prefer local sources even if it means a small sacrifice in performance, whereas the mining-right holders tend to insist on the best and cheapeast sources of supply. This was the problem over the development and the exploitation of Zambia's coal resources for use in the mining industry, although the problem was also partly due to the fact that the coal is not as good in quality as the Wankie coal.

In theory participation of domestic capital in foreign enterprises is acknowledged to have positive advantages in the possibility of fair policy decisions by the enterprise. Government directors sitting on the board are in a better position to scrutinise the activities of the business and to deduce its intentions correctly than would an external group of officials to whom the miners otherwise have to report in its absence.

The State has financial interests also by way of participation. Its equity participation in the existing mines has proved to have overall benefits in the area of profits in that it has effectively increased government revenues from mining activities.[32] It has also reduced the concern that any immediate benefit to the balance of payments arising from the inflow of foreign capital would be more than offset in the long run by the outflow of dividends. The burden of dividend transfers and repatriation of foreign capital is thereby reduced, while still achieving the gains in acquisition of techniques and management skills as well as in industrial activity, that a solo venture would have provided.

State participation also gives the State an opportunity to control the extent to which companies allow their parent bodies to profit from their relationship with their subsidiaries. This in certain circumstances is important particularly with regard to the fact that most of the mining companies in Zambia are worldwide. It has been established that multinational corporations develop a planned and global strategy in their foreign operations and that sometimes, through transfer of products within a vertically integrated company, the prices which are used for these transfers are a major avenue for a subsidiary or to the head office. Participation affords the government directors an opportunity to scrutinise purchasing and marketing arrangements, the fees for provision of technical and consultancy services and investment of surplus funds, all of which can be used by companies to make hidden or disguised profits outside the host country.

Reaction of miners to government participation: There has been a change in attitudes from ten years ago, so much so that now there is no doubt that the great majority of mining-right holders within the country welcome and are prepared to undertake joint ventures with the government[33] in mine development and exploration, although, given a choice, they would prefer minority rather than majority participation. So far there has not been any case in which mining capital has had to withdraw because of the government's insistence on acquiring equity in a new mining venture and there are no mines that have been discovered but are not in production because of this policy.

In some cases the mining-right holders consider that there is an absolute advantage in the association of the State with their enterprise. They may be short of capital, as in the case of Mkushi Copper Mines, which several times invited government to take an interest in it, as a solution to its liquidity problems.[34]

Also the country presents certain political and economic risks, such as nationalisation, devaluation, foreign exchange controls, depreciating currency, and excessive taxation, so that some mining-right holders are often willing to accept domestic participation in order to reduce the financial risk involved in mining investment. Their reaction to risk is to ask themselves whether the company is able to absorb a possible loss before proceeding and then inquire into the possibilities of diminishing its exposure to risk. This was partly the reason why Anglo-American Corporation Ltd and Roan Selection Trust Ltd in the early 1960s invited the State to take minority interest in their mining activities. Financially they could have gone on without difficulty on their own.

More recently this attitude has been particularly noticeable in the new companies; the larger the capacity for investment in relation to the amount of the pre-discovery investment, the better able the company is to absorb a possible loss. It must be realised that new mines are expensive to bring into production. For instance, any investment in exploration must be backed by a determination to follow up, by further investments of ever-increasing amounts, the indications proved by initial prospecting efforts.

An example of this is that an aerial geophysical survey generally requires an additional expenditure of the order of ten times its costs on follow-up checking of indications provided by the survey. Thus an investment of K1 million on a large aerial survey will require an investment of an additional K10 million for follow-up on the ground, and unless these follow-up works are carried out the purpose of conducting the survey is negated. The follow-up will in turn lead to the development of one or more mines involving the expenditure of millions of kwacha.

One way of reducing the impact of risk is by reducing the amount of capital invested. From this point of view, the availability of government or any other local currency loans is a very important incentive. It minimises the amount of equity capital committed by the mining company and therefore reduces the impact of risk. There is a good example in the case of Lumwana prospecting area, which is supposed to come into production in two or three years time. The prospecting was done jointly by Anglo-American Corporation and Amax, the prospecting wing of Roan Selection Trust Ltd. When they reached the stage of exploration the two companies indicated that they would not go on unless the State joined them. Although it contains one of the largest ore bodies Lumwana has very low copper content but the State has decided to join the companies. Anglo-American Corporation Ltd seems to be coming to nearly the same position over the recently discovered nickel deposits in its Munali prospecting area. The company seems to be particularly worried over infrastructure costs.

Other positive benefits derived from such associations by the mining companies are that local voting control causes the State to feel a greater sense of responsibility for the success of the enterprise. For some it provides ready access to know-how, manpower, knowledge of the geology of the country. The government, through its geological survey department, has the most complete information about the geology of the country.

Writers on foreign investment recognise that a joint enterprise provides a bulwark against government interference or greater government participation,[35] as the State will be more reluctant to impose profit restrictions, import controls, or even expropriation measures where local investors or itself is involved. And in that participation in most cases sufficiently satisfies nationalistic aspirations to forestall any need for greater participation by the government itself by deflecting harmful emotional charges which the foreign venture may attract when it is big and successful and still remains completely foreign.

State participation provides a helpful liaison with local government authorities and financial institutions as the local officials, particularly the directors, are able to influence government action by private negotiations with government officials and politicians. This is especially true in a small country such as Zambia, where the limited population means that the individuals sharing power will often have much of their life experience in common. It is true that the foreign officials can do the same but the function is better performed by local partners than by the investor company because they know the local situation better. In any case it is obvious that reports about the companies in which the State has participation will be given more credence if they are made by government officials than when they are made by the foreign company's men.

It appears also that since the State began taking equity participation in the mining companies greater local interest has been generated in their operations. The companies themselves have also become more interested in local programmes such as education, sport, and the like though in fact they can now afford to take less interest. Friedmann suggests that there is an important managerial advantage of a relatively intangible kind which could result from this. He suggests that it has a favourable effect on the morale of the local employees, since it is a major step in the process of localisation by which a foreign investment assumes a local character and status. Which, when it is achieved, makes it easier for the local employee to integrate his loyalties, with a consequent reduction in tension and improved work performance.[36]
Participation as a disincentive to investment: Some international mining companies dislike the requirement of participation and try to avoid areas in which it is an established policy. To this extent it is a disincentive to investment. It has been cited as the reason why, for instance, low-grade minerals of porphyries are being mined in the United States while exceptionally fine deposits of the same minerals are being neglected in Chile and Peru.[37] Several reasons have been suggested by writers on foreign investment for the companies' dislike of such requirements.

Friedmann suggests that local participation can seriously inhibit an internationally integrated company in its operations. What might otherwise be complete freedom to fix transfer prices marketing areas, and so forth, may be substantially circumscribed in the case of a joint venture with local equity participation. And that to some, political and psychological conditions militate against joint ventures, so that when difficult and unstable conditions prevail in a country, the association of a foreign investor with local interest may increase the precariousness of the situation.[38]

Yet perhaps the most widespread discouraging factor to a foreign investor is what has been widely acknowledged to exist — the disparity of outlook between the foreign investor and the local partners. In the business activities of developed countries there is a certain community not only of tradition but also of scientific, technical, and legal standards, and there has also been more experience with responsible investment practices and legal supervision.[39]

In a country like Zambia, this stage has not yet been reached. Power and wealth are concentrated in relatively few hands, and are not matched by a corresponding sense of responsibility. For instance, the partner from an industrialised country, usually a large corporation with world-wide experience, generally takes a long-term view of profits, placing the development of the enterprise before quick dividends.

Some of the investors, it is stated, resent direct participation by the government or a government-owned corporation in a capital-importing country.[40] This is particularly so in American mining circles, where it is felt that there is something inherently unsuitable about mixed government-private enterprise, since the government 'wears two hats' as regulator and partner. Others fear government partnerships because they feel they would be subjecting themselves to the dangers of frequent changes in government policy and government-appointed personnel in their companies. But it cannot be denied that in a country like Zambia the only alternative to initial participation by government is no local participation at all. There simply is no body big enough to form a mining concern.

Some writers have suggested that the policy of requiring domestic participation in foreign ventures is somewhat inconsistent with a declared policy of attracting maximum foreign investment. The government option, when exercised, utilises local capital that could have financed alternative development and thus would have enhanced the development of other sectors of the economy.[41] Further.it has been argued that the inconsistency between the two sets of motives stands out sharply when it is realised that through government participation outside investors may be forced to divest themselves of their equity to make room for local interests, resulting in true disinvestment, with the foreign investor repatriating part of the capital he would otherwise have used.

If this happened it would be unfortunate in that this is capital that would already have been attracted into the country. It is unlikely to happen in Zambia, since section 20 of the Mines and Minerals Act ensures that prospecting licences, the very first mining rights, are granted to those who accept the principle of State participation should minerals be discovered.

It must also be realised, as has been demonstrated by the examples of Lumwana and Mokambo licence areas, that the reverse is equally possible, that is, that lack of government participation may discourage some investors who do not want to take a greater risk in searching for minerals and would prefer to share their risks with the State.

The arguments also make a basic assumption that all mining companies that start or wish to start a mining venture have adequate financial resources to engage in such a venture. Mining being an expensive and risky business, this is not always so. It is not necessary to go further than Mkushi Mine, which closed after the government turned down its invitation to take equity participation, to prove that not all mining companies have enough money to complete their ventures.

Even when they do have the money they may not be willing to use it because of the size of the risk its use entails without government participation. As observed earlier, in Lumwana licence area, for instance, the companies have indicated that they might not have gone ahead without government equity participation. And more recently, as pointed out earlier, Anglo-American Corporation Ltd has invited government participation in respect of its Munali nickel prospect and has indicated that it might not go on if this is not forthcoming.

It has been suggested that since the government, in the event of it deciding to participate, would have to get its money from some other source, it is open to question precisely what the State receives for the percentage of the development costs that it subscribes. Since the funds would readily have been provided by others, the State money would not be optionally allocated[42] quite apart from the fact that the argument need not follow if the State can borrow from abroad to cover its share of investment costs.

Where the government indemnifies the company to the total amount spent on prospecting and exploration it still gains, it is submitted. In the first instance, it cuts out the risk part and anyway the recoverable value of the mineral discovered will always be far in excess of the prospecting and exploration expenses. In that sense the money is optionally allocated. And as has already been stated, money is not readily available once a deposit has been found.

The disincentive impact of government participation is nowadays minimal, since direct government participation in mining ventures has spread both among developed[43] and developing mining countries, so that its disincentive impact can no longer be as serious as when its practice was limited, quite apart from the fact that there are fewer alternatives available. In fact among developing countries recent demands for a new international economic order have led to an ever-increasing number of governments, in these countries, demanding participation in the mining sector of their economies.

Its disincentive impact is definitely not placed very high on the list of disincentives by most mining-right holders currently operating in the country. Several others are considered as more discouraging, such as the threat of outright nationalisation at undefined compensation levels, the political environment, which may threaten the validity of contracts or result in the imposition of onerous controls, costs of services, legal complexities which make it difficult to know what the law is, foreign exchange restrictions, taxation and the sheer magnitude of the investment required where the mine to be brought into production is on a large scale.

It may be questioned whether it is wise at all to have any measure which has the least prospect of discouraging any amount of much needed capital. In the final analysis, the answer to this problem is a question of balancing two evils. The cost of discouraging some mining investment may not be too high a price to pay for the control of the industry the government acquires, the direct government participation in profits which results, and the consequent reaction in the outflow of profits. It is as important for Zambia to attract mining investment as it is for her to regulate the repatriation of profits which considerably reduce the investment resources in the country and limit its positive effects within the country and could well be greater than the amount of investment discouraged.[44] The key to the government policy should be fair play with the private sector over its term of participation to minimise the disincentive effects of the policy.

The Level of Equity Participation
As stated earlier, the State is at liberty to acquire any amount of shares up to a maximum of 51 per cent in any new mining venture. A decision whether to take minority or majority shares in a venture must depend on which of the two levels is more likely to reflect effective control.

The desire to make mining-right holders operate within the wider terms of government's economic and social policy rather than in their own narrower terms can be achieved to some extent by limited participation of, say, 15 to 30 per cent with two or three directors on the board, but in reality this achieves little more than increasing the information available to the State about the company. State-appointed directors sitting in at board meetings receive reports and schedules, but the real decisions continue to be made at the head office of the parent company. Further than that it would only have the advantage that State directors could ensure that a company board was fully apprised of government's policies in respect to matters which came up for discussion.

Majority participation by a foreign company will entitle it to a virtual power of veto in respect of a wide range of actions and decisions of the joint venture, since its equity holding would entitle it to a majority of the seats on the board. Several major corporate actions would require the approval of the foreign firm, with the result that the State would not have effective legal control of the source of all executive functions of the mining company, the board of directors and over matters which it is necessary to have a say in if government control of the industry is to be effective.

All decisions relating to finance and including the development of new mines would be subject to the majority veto. Thus if the State wanted the company to engage in further exploration which did not appeal to the foreign partner, then it could not push forward its views very forcefully. The area of finance and planning of capital programmes of mining companies is one in which the State must exercise some control or have the opportunity to exercise meaningful control if any appreciable influence is to be exercised over the activities of mining companies in which it participates. For as a United Nations study on multinational companies[45] has noted, even in the most loosely knit international firm the minimal control or restriction which is exercised is control over the capital budget.

Where the State participated only to the extent of less than 50 per cent, it would also not be in control of the general meeting. Under the Companies Act of Zambia only three resolutions can be passed, a simple resolution, an extraordinary resolution, and a special resolution. The first one requires a simple majority and the other two require much higher majorities in order for them to be passed.[46] Free voting at these meetings is out of the question in that in practice only two people attend a general meeting of a joint venture, since its members are the two holding companies of the equity participation.

Admittedly the same limitations apply to the foreign mining companies, in that with their equity participation they too may not be in control of the board of directors when they take less than 50 per cent and they cannot change any major areas of policy in general meeting without the consent of the State should it take an amount of shares which makes it impossible to pass a resolution without its co-operation. These limitations, however, are likely to hurt the government more than the private miner in that it is the government that is interested in changing certain attitudes of private investors, be they mining or non-mining, such as the control of the profit motive.

If the government is to have a chance of a real say in the decision-making of a mining company in which it wishes to participate, it must acquire majority equity participation. This will then entitle it to have half the directors, as in Mokambo Development Company and Mindeco Noranda, so that its directors on the board have a real sanction to apply in terms of voting numbers. The State in Zambia is insisting on at least 51 per cent participation and there is at present no indication that it will exercise its option in a mining venture for any share less than this.

A large number of mining-right holders hesitate to agree to participation at over 50 per cent without a management agreement. This was the case in the 1969 partial nationalisation of the then existing mines. The experience of the State has been that these demands should be resisted, as they go a long way towards negating government control and influence on mining activities; indeed it has recently terminated in previous management agreements.[47]

The control of the board of directors is not sufficient in itself. The board does not run a company, its affairs are manned by executives, who are charged with implementing the board's policies. It is therefore important to have some control over the executives. This in fact sometimes explains why although foreign investors are not concerned with staffing at the operational levels and encourage it because of the political pressures in favour of localisation and the lower cost of local labour, they have a strong interest in controlling decisions with regard to the staffing of the management functions.

It must be acknowledged, however, that it is also because it is not easy to get expatriates on hire except on secondment and under management agreements. It is preferable that the joint ventures should be self managing. The employment of management agreements could only be justified if there were such a thing as the 'neutrality' of management, i.e. management systems were capable of universal application regardless of the social-political context and the ideological basis of the economic system. This of course is not the case. Management agents have their own values and their judgements on policy matters are going to be influenced by these values, and their employees owe their loyalty to them.[48]

It may be argued that their recommendations are not imposed on their principals and that their job is only to offer a possible solution to the organisation. This argument assumes a technocratic board capable of perceiving alternatives, which, as will be pointed out later in this paper, are lacking in Zambia. In addition they are extremely expensive (sometimes deliberately so that their advice will be regarded as pre-eminent), as they proved in the case of those concluded in 1969 between Anglo-American Corporation Ltd and Roan Selection Trust Ltd, on the one hand, and the Government of Zambia on the other.

Table 2
Management and Consultancy Fees Paid to Roan Selection Trust Ltd by Roan Consolidated Mines Ltd, 1970-73

Elements of Fees	Fees Paid (million kwacha)			
	1970	1971	1972	1973
¾% of sales proceeds	1.335	1.461	1.434	1.779
2% consolidated profits before income tax but after Mineral Tax	1.045	0.82	0.526	0.742
Total	2.380	2.221	1.960	2.521

Note: This is disregarding the recruitment fee of 15 per cent gross emoluments of a recruit in the first year of duty, if in service not less than six months.
Source: Calculated from figures of gross sales and profits in the company's *Annual Reports*.

The employees of management agents tend to stay for short periods of time and thus make themselves open to the criticism that the agents frequently use developing countries as a training ground for young staff fresh out of business schools. There is some truth too in the criticism, that most expatriate employees, particularly at the high levels, tend to be largely concerned with furthering their careers with the foreign company that is employing them.[49]
Factors affecting control: The distinction between majority and minority

participation may of course in certain circumstances be rather artificial as equity alone, even when accompanied by joint management, can not lead to effective control.

Participation needs to be backed up by government insistence on formalised planning. Only if management techniques such as corporate planning and management by objectives are used will the board be consulted on all major matters. These techniques are designed to see that a company has a policy clearly defined, after careful thought and consultation, for each facet of its operation, and that this policy is known throughout the company and related to each employee's job. These techniques are particularly relevant in that they will show up the areas in which there is a conflict of interest between the partners and see that an explicit policy is laid down to cover them. At the moment the existing joint ventures have a very poor working relationship with government. There are no accepted policy guide lines for State officials who have become members, for instance.

The State must appoint directors and executives who are capable of looking after its interest to represent it on the board. Its nominees must have a general knowledge of mining and of finance and management in order that thy can withstand any arguments from their fellow directors from abroad when pressing for the carrying out of government objectives such as localisation and reinvestment of profits. The effectiveness of the control government-appointed directors can exercise on a mining venture will depend on their being a capable, alert, astute and qualified team, so that together with the foreign directors they can supervise the activities of management. Care must be taken to see that people appointed to these posts understand and sympathise with government's objectives, for some local people, because of their training, are very sympathetic to the point of view of foreign companies.[50]

The Zambian government is faring rather badly in this regard. Owing to the relative youth of the country and the colonial neglect of education, there is no local stock of retired executives on which the government can draw to strengthen the technical knowledge of the government side of these boards. The paucity of available technical management is also a result of the disproportion established at the university level between the student population in technical faculties and other faculties, and is reinforced by the high percentage of failures in the technical faculties.

But the problem is more complex. Board appointments are usually a contentious question, as political and other factors such as ethnic considerations seem to play significant roles.[51] Even in the cases where reasonably able people have been given such positions they have been transferred from company to company and also in and out of companies far too often, frequently for political rather than technical reasons. Several cases can be cited of managing directors being moved three times in a year,[52] with the result that few of them have the opportunity to become familiar with their management tasks or conversant with the industry and its difficulties, and consequently they are rarely able to make rational judgements based on time tested operations. Their difficulties are increased, too, by regular reorganisation of companies.

In one or two cases the government has appointed civil servants to the boards of directors of some mining companies.[53] In practice this is unwise, because they simply do not have the time to do the work effectively without sacrificing efficiency in their real jobs, and this problem is exemplified by the fact that they are usually unable to attend board meetings, being either on tour or busy in another way.

All these factors combine to produce board members without the necessary knowledge and ability. And the scarcity of available people produces a situation in which it is common practice to find one person being a member of several boards, many more than he can cope with. Consequently his supervision and control diminish considerably and his contribution becomes weak.

The need for directors who have mining experience cannot be overemphasised. After all, management is largely a question of decision, and decisions cannot be properly taken unless the mind is clear about objectives and priorities. It is not being suggested that a director needs to possess a huge intellect to do his job properly. What he needs far more urgently is a clear comprehension of what he is aiming at, the object of the exercise from which he is able to issue clear and unequivocal instructions because he is in no doubt about the purpose of his management task. In a highly technological industry like mining, there are very few management tasks that do not call for a general understanding of technological operations.

Additional measures towards effective control: Zambianisation is not only an important instrument in the transfer of technology to one's nationals, it is also an important way of increasing control over foreign ventures. Therefore the State should ensure that it operates efficiently but reasonably. The well intentioned policy of Zambianisation can create management difficulties which can endanger the performance of the industry where haste results in people with little or no knowledge at all of the operations they are supposed to manage being placed in management positions.

Although it is the policy of the government to increase local employment, the measures employed to implement it do not seem to be very effective. The main check on the rate at which the industry is being localised is through the control on the immigration of expatriates. The Immigration Department will not grant any entry permit to an expatriate unless the Ministry of Labour certifies that there are no local citizens with the necessary qualifications and experience to fill the job he is to take up, and further that adequate steps have been taken to train local personnel.[54]

The problem with this provision is that the Labour Ministry acts mostly on the recommendations of senior mining officials who are themselves expatriates, for after all only they are well placed to judge on questions of qualifications and experience as the local people at the Ministry of Labour are unable to grasp fully the scope and extent of the expertise that is required by the people to fill the jobs.

The other check could be the application of the tax on expatriates,[55] now applied to other categories of industry, to the mining industry. But this

may be unsuitable, as it operates as a cost on production.
It is suggested that a measure additional to the one pertaining to control of immigration could be taken. This could be done by creating a financial incentive to localisation of a different nature and one which does not create the same problem as the one above, by providing that when a company has Zambianised to a given percentage, a level to be determined by the educational standard of the country, it can deduct a fixed percentage of its net income free of taxes to reinvest in the activities of its own firm or in other mining activities.

Foreign investors draw their special strength from their ability and opportunity to think in terms that extend beyond any single country and the use of resources that are located in more than one jurisdiction,[56] and sometimes try to end up making the largest profit in the lowest tax country by transfer of pricing. It is important to start thinking in terms of devising measures which can assist in the control of this phenomenon where it exists. This can be done by regulations through which the State can get hold of the total accounts of a company to supplement the present limited regulations in the Companies Act, which were originally devised for national companies.[57]

An example of what is suggested is the recent agreement among the members of the Organisation for Economic Co-operation and Development establishing a code of conduct among multinationals. Among other things, the code outlaws transfer pricing methods and requires multinational companies to give wide-ranging information about themselves including annual financial statements of profits and sales, investments, and numbers of employees on a geographical basis and the disclosure of a consolidated profit and loss account.[58] Although this can best be undertaken on an international basis, a start can be made with some measures on an individual basis.

In the final analysis, however, the ultimate source of power of foreign companies is in their control over the process of technological change.[59] Even if Zambia purchased advanced machinery, it might well find itself backward in a space of ten years. This is also the primary vehicle, as observed earlier, for the acquisition of abnormal profits where they exist. They keep this power by keeping research and development at home. Zambian legislation should encourage foreign companies to conduct research in Zambia concerning their projects. This could be done by creating incentives such as exempting profits to be spent on research studies from any form of taxation.[60]

Conclusion

In the preceding pages the current legislation concerning government participation in mining rights in Zambia has been examined. From the colonial days the country inherited a system of mining rights and a system over which it had no control. This has been corrected by the fairly enlightened and progressive provisions of the 1969 legislation. With the exception of certain reservations indicated in the paper, and although their effectiveness will largely depend on the efficiency of Zambian managerial and technical manpower, the provisions relating to domestic participation have laid in law a proper framework within which to secure control of mining activities.

References

This essay was first published in *African Social Research* 25 (June, 1978).
1. Mines and Minerals Act, No. 33 of 1976, s. 20.
2. Kaunda, *Towards Complete Independence*, 1969, p. 36.
3. See Letter from Secretary of the Company to the Colonial Secretary, 5 May, 1911, C. O. 417-507. Later this could be substituted for royalty payments; see Imperial Institute, *The Mining Laws of the British Empire and of Foreign Countries, Northern Rhodesia*, 1930, p. 17.
4. The requirement was unpopular among miners, who complained that it made it impossible to procure capital for many propositions which would otherwise attract capital by their intrinsic merit, and that, where investors were prepared to invest their capital subject to the condition, it resulted in an undue inflation of the capital and in a consequent repetition of mining propositions. See letter of High Commissioner to the Colonial Secretary, 5 November 1906, C. O. 417-24.
5. The year after Independence, export tax was introduced and the income tax rate was increased. See Copper Export Tax Act, 1966, and Taxes Charging and Amendment Act, 1965, s. 19 (2).
6. U.N.E.C.A./F.A.O., *Economic Survey Mission of the Economic Development of Zambia*, 1964, p. 39.
7. Prain, Address to the National Affairs Association, Lusaka, 1964.
8. The government attributed its lack of action to the fact that the mines were too big. See Kaunda, *Zambia's Economic Revolution*, 1968, p. 50.
9. The scale on which this was done was massive and it is estimated that Zambia lost well over K84 million over the ten year period of federation. See U.N.E.C.A./F.A.O., *Economic Survey Mission on the Economic Development of Zambia*, 1964, p. 36.
10. In 1964 Southern Rhodesia supplied 39 per cent of all imports and South Africa a further 21 per cent. See Central African Research – 4, *The Significance of Zambia's New Economic Programme*, 1968, p. 1.
11. *Ibid.*, p. 2; for example coke from Wankie had to be replaced for mining use at great cost with supplies from Germany. See Zambian Economic Survey, *African Development*, 1973, p. 13.
12. Republic of Zambia, Commission of Inquiry, *Report of the Tribunal on Detainees*, 1967. This report revealed many practices that were going on and showed that there was general sympathy among the white population to Rhodesia's point of view.
13. Central African Research – 4, *op. cit.*, p. 2.
14. U.N.E.C.A./F.A.O., *Economic Survey Mission on the Economic Development of Zambia, op. cit.*, p. 34.
15. Central African Research – 4, *op. cit.*, p. 2. The situation has not changed much with government participation in existing mines. Of the over 30,224 workers only 107 Zambians held senior positions in 1974 (see Nchanga Consolidated Copper Mines Ltd, *Annual Report*,

1974), and yet the government target was much higher; see Zambianisation Committee, *Report Progress of Zambianisation,* 1972.

16. An official enquiry in 1966, however, found no reason to doubt the sincerity of the companies with respect to their programmes for the training and promotion of Zambians; *Report of the Commission of Inquiry into the Mining Industry,* 1966, pp. 73-4. But there is contrary view, e.g. Burawoy, *The Colour of Class on the Copper Mines: from African Advancement to Zambianisation,* Zambian Paper No. 7, 1972. The local employees seem to believe that the companies are to blame. See *Times of Zambia,* 11 February 1974, p. 1.

17. The contribution of manufacturing to gross domestic product rose from K14,100,000 in 1964 to K30,000,000 in 1967. Its volume rose by 25 per cent per year on average. This was despite the limitations imposed by the Rhodesian situation; see Central African Research – 4, *op. cit.,* p. 2.

18. This led the government to limit the amount of dividends that could be externalised to 50 per cent of profits. See Kaunda, *Zambia's Economic Revolution,* 1968, p. 7.

19. This desire though widespread among developing countries is not confined to them. Such rich countries as France and Canada have been concerned about the limitations on their independence created by large-scale American investments, and Britain is frequently worried by the loss of freedom that arises out of running a reserve currency with inadequate backing. Canada's concern has been so great that in 1973 the government passed the New Foreign Investment Review Act which in clause 2 states, 'This Act is enacted by the Parliament of Canada in recognition by Parliament that the extent to which control of Canadian industry, trade and commerce has become acquired by persons other than Canadians and the effect thereof on the ability of Canadians to maintain effective control over their economic environment is a matter of national concern.' See also Wahn, 'Towards Canadian identity: the significance of foreign investment' (1973), 11 *Osgoode Hall Law Journal,* p. 517.

20. United Nations, *Report of the Commission of Permanent Sovereignty over Natural Wealth and Resources,* 1962, p. 170.

21. Kaunda, *Zambia's Economic Revolution,* 1968, p. 11. See also Arusha Declaration, 1967.

22. Members of the C.I.P.E.C. have undertaken to keep each other informed of important developments in their own mining industries and to cooperate in matters of mutual interest. For instance, they sometimes cooperate on measures aimed at improving the price of copper, e.g. cutbacks on production; see *Chairman's Statement,* Nchanga Consolidated Copper Mines Ltd, 1975.

23. *Second National Development Plan,* 1972, p. 91. See also Kaunda in Industrial and Mining Corporation Ltd, *Annual Report,* 1974.

24. Basic sources on the history of the industry include Bradley, *Copper Venture,* 1952; Bancroft, *Mining in Northern Rhodesia,* 1962; and Coleman, *The Northern Rhodesia Copperbelt, 1899-1962,* 1971.

25. This is carried on in the exploration licence in s. 31 (1) (g), which provides that 'An application for an exploration licence may be rejected

where the applicant is unable or unwilling to comply with any terms
or conditions on which the relevant prospecting licence was granted
and which are applicable to the granting of the exploration licence';
see Mines and Minerals Act, *op. cit.*

26. This is the case of Mkushi Copper Mines Ltd.
27. See s. 46 (1) (b) of Mines and Minerals Act, *op. cit.*
28 Notification takes the form of a notice which states the percentage of
the ordinary shares in the company to be acquired and signed on
behalf of the government and sent by registered post to the registered
office of the company. Notification is given, where the option is held
by any person on behalf of the Republic, to that person, and, where it
is held by the State, to the Minister of Mines.
29. Friedmann and Beguin, *Joint International Business Ventures in
Developing Countries,* 1971, p. 2.
30. *Ibid.*
31. Nwogugu, *The Legal Problems of Foreign Investment in Developing
Countries,* 1965, p. 12.
32. In 1974, quite apart from its tax receipts, a dividend of K43.2 million
was declared by the holding company to the State. See Zambia Industrial and Mining Corporation Ltd, *Directors' Report,* 1974.
33. Mr Oppenheimer has recently given some indication of the thinking of
his group. In the course of his *Statement to Shareholders* at the 1974
Annual General Meeting he said, 'No government likes its basic industries to be entirely foreign owned and yet in many developing countries
individual members of the public either do not have the resources to
invest in industry or, for ideological reasons, are prevented from doing
so. The only alternative in such cases to full foreign ownership is for
government to take a direct interest. In these circumstances we willingly
accept a partnership between the government as owners of the mineral
rights and private companies that can provide the necessary financial
resources and technical know how.'
34. Mkushi Mine has since closed. See *Mining Mirror,* 3 October 1975, p. 7.
35. Friedmann and Beguin, *op. cit.,* p. 385.
36. Friedmann and Beguin, *op. cit.,* p. 385.
37. Carman, 'Notes on impediments to mining investment in the developing
world' (1975), 14 *Bagaunda Paper.*
38. Friedmann and Beguin, *op. cit.,* p. 388.
39. *Ibid.*
40. *Ibid.*
41. Nwogugu, *op. cit.,* p. 13.
42. Bostock and Harvey, *op. cit.,* p. 203.
43. Britain is now, for instance, insisting on participation before issuing oil
prospecting licences. See *The Guardian,* 28 May 1976, p. 1. Canada has
government participation; see Drolet, *Mining Legislation and Responsible Authorities,* paper presented at the International Symposium of
Technical Research in Mineralogy and Management of Mineral Patri-
mony, Orleans-Lasource, 1975, p. 11.
44. The Organisation of African Unity Conference of Heads of State at its
1973 meeting recognised this problem and resolved among other things
to defend vigorously, continually and jointly the African countries' in-

alienable sovereign rights and take concrete measures to regulate the repatriation of profits which considerably reduce the investment resources of African Countries; see *Organisation of African Unity, Declaration on African Co-operation Development and Economic Independence,* 28 May 1973.

45. United Nations, *Report on Multinational Corporations in World Development,* 1976, p. 46.

46. Companies Act, chapter 686 of the Laws of Zambia, ss. 12, 14, 15 and 112.

47. For the announcement cancelling the management agreements, see *Times of Zambia,* 31 August 1973.

48. Sklar, *op. cit.,* quoted some mining executives of Anglo-American Corporation as saying, 'I feel as though I belong to the Company more than any country,' and 'My first loyalty is to Anglo; Harry Oppenheimer sent me here and there is something I can do for the group in this place' (at p. 203).

49. For instance, since the termination of the management agreements the mines have experienced loss of senior staff; see *Chairman's Report,* Nchanga Consolidated Copper Mines Ltd, 1975.

50. This is particularly so if they have been trained by one of the companies involved as such companies teach them how to approach problems from their own point of view.

51. Complaints by members of parliament are frequently that appointments are made on political grounds; see *Times of Zambia,* 28 January 1976.

52. For instance, Mines Industrial Development Corporation's managing directorship changed hands three times in 1975 alone.

53. See Mines Industrial Development Corporation Ltd, Directorate of 1974, and Roan Consolidated Mines Ltd, Directorate of 1974. Both in Mines Industrial Development Corporation, *Zambia Mining Year Book,* 1974.

54. Immigration and Deportation Act, chapter 122 of the Laws of Zambia, ss. 18, 19 and 20.

55. See Selective Employment Tax Act, No. 9 of 1975.

56. For detailed discussion of this, see Vernon, *Sovereignty at Bay; the Multinational Spread of United States Enterprises,* 1971, p. 265.

57. Companies Act, *op. cit.* All information relates to a company's domestic activities; see ss. 120, 29 and 90.

58. *The Guardian,* 22 June 1976, p. 14.

59. The problem of technology is discussed at length in Kapalinky, 'Accumulation and the transfer of technology; issues of conflict and mechanisms for the exercise of control' (1974), 80 *Institute of Development Studies Discussion Paper,* Sussex.

60. A limited incentive exists but one has to spend the money first, as it is allowed in ascertaining the gains or profits of a business; see Income Tax Act, *op. cit.,* s. 43.

Development in Zambia: A Reader

Study Questions

1. What are the problems which have been encountered in establishing domestic control of mining in Zambia?
2. Explain the various attitudes of foreign companies to government participation.
3. Is the lack of Zambian trained personnel a factor which hampers the state control of mining?

5. Ben Turok

The Penalties of Zambia's Mixed Economy

In the first few years of Zambia's indepdence the economy made striking progress. With a GDP per capita that was among the healthiest in Africa and just below half that of South Africa, and a copper mining industry large even by world standards, the forecast was for rapid growth and development.

But the early promise has not been realised. It is commonly accepted that the weaknesses of the economy, which levelled off in 1972 and then began to decline, cannot be solely ascribed to falling copper prices, though this has indeed been a major factor. This is shown by the fact that even by 1974, before the collapse of copper prices, foreign exchange was becoming a serious constraint on development. The problem seems to lie deep within the system itself and to have its basis in the ambiguities and lack of direction in national development goals and the structural contradictions this has caused.

Despite its inheritance of a highly concentrated and dominant foreign-owned mining enclave, the Zambian government soon showed a determination to use the state for development. As a result, there is now a preponderant state sector, at least at the formal institutional level, though it operates in the context of a mixed economy. By 1972 the state sector share of manufacturing output was 53% of the total, and it was concentrated on the essential consumer goods required by Zambia.

However, despite its size and scope, the state sector (which formally includes the parastatals) has not established a commanding position so that the government might effectively determine what should happen in the economy. Stated social goals are pursued spasmodically as though there were insufficient power to press forward rigorously. There is also evidence of periodic failures of political will resulting in ambivalent public policies. Despite the seemingly overwhelming public ownership of the means of production, the influence of private interests, both local and foreign, remains substantial, seeming to block tendencies to a centrally-planned economy. Clearly, in the Zambian case, public ownership is not socialism. Instead, there is a form of state capitalism in which interests and policies frequently collide to the detriment of the smooth running of the system. Van Arkadie's conception of frustrated state sector development in a dependent economy seems apt in relation to Zambia.[1]

This essay will try to show that the failure of the state to take full command of the economy and to provide clear direction to each of the sectors (which does not mean the total elimination of the private sector) has been responsible for many of the economic problems and for the continuing uncertainty about which development path the country is to follow. This failure is partly due to the fact that though Zambians now occupy most top positions in the economy, public and private, it is not always evident that they share the government's socialist perspectives. On the contrary, there is evidence that some would like to sustain the existing private sector and even open the doors wider to the emergence of private enterprise based on Zambian capital.

The ambivalences of official policies are well known. In the private sector, there has been considerable government intervention and restriction, though this falls short of complete control. In the parastatals, the presence of Ministers and political leaders on boards of directors has often constituted political interference without amounting to direction by the state. Interventions in pricing policy seem to be more concerned with social welfare than mobilization for development. (Low prices for basic foods may help consumers but do not in themselves fuel economic development.) The inadequacies of state initiatives are nowhere more glaring than in the persistence of Zambia's dependence on foreign capital, expertise, technology, supplies and markets. There has been a marked failure to ground the economy in Zambia's own human and material resources.

What causes most concern is that increasing public ownership has been accompanied by economic stagnation. Symptoms of the malaise may be found in the levelling off of government development capital expenditures in 1970. Growth seems to have ceilinged in 1973 when value added in manufacturing was 106 million kwacha rising to only 107.5 million kwacha in 1976. This has to compare with the earlier sharp rise from 48.0 million kwacha in 1965. A similar levelling off in 1972 may be seen in the quantities of marketed agricultural production. (GRZ Economic Report, 1976). More recently, value added by manufacturing in 1978 was, in real terms, 15% lower than in 1974, and the contribution of construction to GDP in 1978 was 30% less than in 1976. There has been 'a precipitous drop in real gross fixed capital formation'. (GRZ Economic Report, 1978). Capital expenditure in 1979 was the lowest in real terms since Independence.

Since the state owns the major share of key industries the reasons for the decline must be sought in this area. Many Zambians now believe that the state sector has become a great burden on the society and that 'it doesn't pay its way'. Undoubtedly, even if one disregards the conventional notions of profitability as applied to private enterprise, it is apparent that the state sector is not performing adequately. It often seems to provide neither profits nor services commensurate with the country's requirements.[2] While it is difficult to assess profitability of an individual state enterprise (because of government subsidies or because of compulsory low product prices which hold down profit levels) the picture is fairly clear in relation to a whole sector. For instance the Indeco Group had a pre-tax profit of only 9.2

million kwacha for a turnover of 397.9 million kwacha in 1977-8. Glaring cases of failure in individual companies are however also available. Zambia Clay had a loss of K3.7 million against a turnover of a mere K764,000 in 1977-8, while Zambesi Sawmills suffered a loss of K1.8 million on a turnover of K844,000. (GRZ Economic Report 1978). Finally, in 1976 when no government subsidy was accorded to Indeco, it reported net losses amounting to 3% of total assets.

It can be seen therefore, that Indeco, one of the main pillars of state intervention has often performed poorly, casting grave doubts on the government's policies in relation to the state sector and the parastatals in particular. Yet, in an age of giant state corporations in most countries, capitalist and socialist, many of them successful, it would be churlish to question the effectiveness of this type of organisation in itself. There is no reason why large state corporations cannot be successful in Zambia and current weaknesses cannot be attributed to factors like state ownership and size. More to the point is the lack of a clear direction for the state sector in the context of a mixed economy as will be elaborated below.

The State Sector

At Independence Zambia's economy was highly skewed with the dominant copper mining enclave being supported by a fairly small industrial and service industry on the Copperbelt. The sector as a whole was not integrated with the rest cf the economy in any productive way.[3] Instead, the mining industry, like most of the rest of the modern economy, was geared to the economies of South Africa and Southern Rhodesia, which treated Zambia as a labour reserve. The new government found that there was very little to build upon in non-mining related industry. Domestic production supplied less than one third of the local market for manufactured goods while total manufacturing accounted for only 6 per cent of GDP.

The government first sought to establish its political power at the level of the state by establishing an indigenous administration and various public corporations. The state bought out the private shareholders in the Industrial Development Corporation (Indeco) in 1965 and it obtained a larger share of the profits from copper by means of higher taxation which was then used for public investment. Subsequently, the state also acquired an interest in private firms by the acquisition of shares, not by nationalisation. They acquired derived control by means of Articles of Association leading to control of the boards of companies and thus the companies themselves.[4] Even today there are no statutory provisions giving the government explicit control over non-statutory enterprises, which means that outright nationalisation is not possible in Zambia. This method of proceeding piecemeal had important consequences for the government's efforts to establish itself in a commanding position in the economy.

In the copper mining industry the government moved cautiously, clearly reluctant for political reasons to take drastic measures against the powerful foreign interests. But there were practical reasons too. Since copper was the heart of the whole modern economy the government treated it gingerly. The industry was managed and manned by Europeans at all higher levels and it was feared that early outright nationalisation would antagonise them irrevocably. The government therefore proceeded to gain increasing authority by degrees so that white management and skills could be retained. Similarly in other enterprises, the state bought its way in, paying for its share out of the substantial profits from copper or from future profits in the firms themselves. Thus arose the parastatals, Zambia's formula for enlarging the state's powers while capitalising on the foreign skills and capital which Zambia itself lacked.

Nevertheless, the rate of acquisition was on the whole quite rapid. From 1965 to 1967 Indeco's total assets increased seven-fold. By 1971 the Zambia Mining Corporation (Zimco), the major parastatal corporation, had total assets of 713 million of which the copper mines constituted 75 per cent. This can be compared with the state controlled assets at Independence of K234 million. Total state controlled assets in 1971 were roughly K1,009 million. By 1975 Zimco assets alone stood at K1,468 million and total assets under government control were almost K2,000 million.

This growth in the state controlled sector was accompanied by Zambianisation of higher level posts in many industries. The purpose was to take over control from expatriates and give the government greater authority over decision-making. In a few years a new Zambian bureaucracy emerged which has since taken command of top positions in the civil service and parastatals. Over the whole public service the Mwanakatwe Commission of 1975 reported that the number of superscale posts rose from 184 in 1962, to 573 in 1967, to 865 in 1971, to 1,116 in 1974. That is, a six-fold increase over twelve years and double since 1967. (Personal emoluments as a part of government recurrent expenditures have increased from K61.5 million in 1969 to K155.8 million in 1977. This bureaucracy is now both large and influential and the way it perceives its role is crucial to the effectiveness of the public sector in relation to the economy as a whole. That the President had some anxieties on this score is indicated by the reasons given for allocating Ministers to lead parastatal boards. He said, 'I did so because of the urgent necessity then, to make parastatals an organic part of the body politic. The process of the re-education or de-colonisation of these organisations is now complete and all their chief executives now appreciate that they are an extension of the Party and its Government in the business sector.'[5] Perhaps it is for these reasons that the President has retained the right to make all major appointments including the members of the governing boards of directors of all parastatals including Zimco, Indeco, NCCM and RCM as well as other public enterprises.[6] However, in so doing he acts as an executive for the state in its capacity as shareholder, and not as head of state.[7]

One of the major reasons for state participation in existing enterprises in the early years was to get hold of policy-making at board level, to stop the repatriation of profits by foreign-owned firms and to re-orient their operations.[8] But new parastatals were also created, particularly after Rhodesia's

UDI in 1965 which led to Zambia's disengagement in trade from that direction and created gaps in Zambia's commodity supplies. There was a need for import substitution manufacturing and some joint ventures were started with multinationals. The local private sector did not have the capital for some of the larger operations required, nor did it wish to enter them because of political uncertainty. The field was therefore wide open for parastatals.

The creation of parastatals was seen as one of the most important achievements by the Zambian government.[9] Large investments were made in power, transport and roads. The parastatals were seen as engines for development, creating an infrastructure which would lay the basis for growth and development on a wide front. This would lead to steadily expanding employment . opportunities. During the decade after 1965 the expansion in manufacturing was indeed remarkable as total output rose from K48 million to K128 million. The power generated increased from 1,869 kwh in 1965 to 8,563 kwh in 1976. In the face of it, the intervention of the state in the economy seemed highly successful and the process of state control of the economy has continued. Gundar Frank's recent observation that in the Third World 'the state intervenes more directly and visibly in the organisation of the economic, social, cultural – in a word – political processes than in the developed capitalist countries,' obviously applies to Zambia in this period.[10]

The parastatal sector is now preponderant in the economy as a whole. The parastatals number well over a hundred enterprises providing employment for almost 150,000 workers, which is about a third of the work force in the formal sector. They are involved in mining, energy, transport, toursim, finance, agriculture, service industries, commercial enterprises, trade, industry and construction. Total assets are estimated to be K3,500 million, while Indeco alone declared net assets of K358 million in 1978.[11] Altogether, the parastatals contribute about half of GDP. It is clear therefore, that the parastatals have performed a substantial *accumulation* function for the state. This has certainly brought considerable benefits to the management and the bureaucracy as a whole.

But the parastatals have also performed a *legitimation* function in the sense that the government seems to be intervening in the economy to place curbs on the private sector and to enhance the state's overall control in the public interest. There have certainly been increases in employment and many basic commodities are subsidised to keep prices down. (Low food prices have also of course assisted private employers to keep down wages.) Perhaps even more important in the current conditions of recession, state control of industry has helped cushion the labour force from the hazards of unemployment and closure of plants which have been much more pronounced in the private sector. The number of employees in private manufacturing fell from 27,370 in 1975 to 23,390 in 1977, while they remained constant in the parastatals over this period.

But in the last resort legitimacy must depend on performance, and it is evident that the parastatals are now a focus for much criticism. There are continuing reports of inefficiency, mismanagement and corruption.[12] The report of the Committee on Parastatal Bodies (the Kayope Commission) revealed catastrophic failures in major parastatals and widespread misappropriation of funds. But there are also structural problems which are perhaps more fundamental. The parastatals are grossly undercapitalised and the shortages of raw materials and spare parts due to the lack of foreign exchange have cut production drastically, in some cases to a bare 20% of capacity. Despite rescue operations within Indeco in the form of internal provision of loans from one company to another, it is likely that some will go to the wall unless substantial emergency aid is forthcoming. Even then it is difficult to absorb new capital because of a lack of managerial, professional and skilled manpower. Many firms also have a low efficiency of capital, with unit production costs rising against higher import costs. Yet capital intensity has been encouraged by low duties on capital goods, by investment credits and big depreciation allowances. It is favoured by those parastatals with multinational links since their parent companies want to sell their capital goods which are often made up of advanced technology. In a country where brick making was commonplace at low levels of technology, two large automated brick factories were built, one of which is now closed at an enormous loss of invested capital.

Capital intensity substitutes machines for labour, thereby cutting down on employment. It facilitates the retention of control of management in expatriate hands, allows major financial leakages abroad, and leaves the manipulative control of technology as an additionally important lever for foreign control. The effect of these policies has been to create a relatively high cost economy, greatly exacerbated by the increased costs of transport for imports and exports. Most important, even where the government is dominant on the board of a capital intensive parastatal, lack of experience in the industry leaves decision-making in the hands of the foreign corporations which are called in to run them. Such companies cannot be the basis for socialist policies nor can they even be seen as acting in the interests of the country itself.

As institutions, parastatals have exhibited many of the characteristics of state corporations in developed capitalist countries. There is a high degree of caution in production and planning due to the civil service mentality of managers who have much responsibility but little concrete accountability to any central body. As a result, they 'just keep things going'. The situation is confounded by seemingly frequent interference at the political level though this does not amount to state direction. The Party exercises a mainly supervisory presence which includes the appointment of officials and complaints are often heard that the frequent reshuffling of heads of corporations seriously undermines efficiency and self-confidence of managers. But basic management decisions remain within the province of managers whose profit orientation may well conflict with overall government policy in industry and more so with the social goals espoused by the government. The conflict is brought out in this statement by a parastatal chairman, who stated that Zimco companies, 'are expected to show greater consideration for social benefit than normally apply to privately-owned companies. They are nevertheless business organisations, and as such must operate in a business-like manner, become ever more efficient and profitable, and stand on their own in a ruthlessly competitive economy.' (Chairman's statement, 1970-1, Zimco company report.)

Profit making is certainly the declared *raison d'etre* of the parastatals and this was emphasised recently. Government-imposed price fixing is to be relaxed and subsidies are falling. In 1975 total subsidies amounted to K82.8 million while in 1979 only K30.4 million has been allowed, a reduction of 30 per cent. There is now an insistence that parastatals operate at a profit so that the state will gain some revenue.

The multinationals have certainly not found the existence of parastatals an insuperable obstacle to doing business. Parastatals are in a sense a rationalising mechanism since they provide a convenient outlet for bulk sales. Foreign capital is often willing to go into joint ventures with parastatals since they provide an umbrella against unfavourable government policies such as protective tariffs and even outright nationalisation.[13]

Most studies of parastatals show that ownership is but one of the mechanisms of control in the Third World. State ownership by no means ensures that profits will remain in the country or that other benefits will accrue locally. Dependence often persists, even where there is only a minority foreign shareholding. Dependence is most often tied to management needs, imported advanced technology and access to foreign markets. On the other hand, there has been a notable lack of determination in Zambia to create indigenous economic institutions which could reverse previous trends of dependency, seize hold of the parastatal enterprises and operate them autonomously. Hence the frustration of state sectoral development in conditions of dependency relations. Van Arcadie writes, 'Formally public institutions could easily become the means of continuing dependence on private foreign interests, operating in effect as a front for foreign managers, promoters and exploitation by foreign know-how, and continuation of dependent relationships in commodity markets.'[14]

Many of these factors might be minimised in an economy which had central planning and direction. It is not every expatriate expert or manager who acts against the interests of his Zambian employer and many try to and do make a serious contribution to their enterprises. As for the others, their more harmful activities could be contained by greater centralisation of control and greater attention to government guidelines. The lack of central planning in the Zambian economy has been often noted.[15] In part this is a manifestation of a lack of political will by the government and perhaps a reflection of weak ideological commitment to socialism at the higher levels of the state bureaucracy. But there is also a structural aspect. As long as a substantial private sector remains, and as long as parastatals are motivated by considerations of profit (in the capitalist sense) rather than a commitment to fulfil specific production targets, there will remain a lack of integration and planning which must undermine overall performance. Furthermore, where the parastatals enjoy a monopoly over the market (as is usually the case) in-

inefficiency causes little concern since price rises can be passed on to the consumer. In such circumstances the mixed economy suffers from the disadvantages of laissez-faire capitalism and of state monopoly control and the advantages of neither. Instead the state sector becomes parasitic and a burden on society without generating development benefits.

The lack of coordination and integration between public and private enterprises is partly a function of overlapping and competing interests, but it is also the result of resistance to centralised planning by parastatal managers and private entrepreneurs alike. It would seem that the kind of planning that development requires cannot be done in a mixed economy which lacks the necessary institutional structures to enforce targets and programmes.

The Private Sector
As previously indicated, Zambia's private sector at Independence was fairly small outside of the mining enclave. As the state began to harness the country's resources for development, the policy that emerged was to reserve the existing small and medium-sized enterprises for Zambian entrepreneurs while the state moved into a position to control the bigger concerns.[16] Following the Mulungushi Reforms of April 1968, the state entered retail trade, building supplies, transport and breweries. The Matero Reforms of August 1969 gave the state 51% participation in the mines. Subsequently the November 1970 reforms extended the policy of state participation by the 51% takeover of the banks, the establishment of the state monopoly in insurance and the acquisition of 51% shares in most big companies still in private hands.[17] The effect of all these measures was to create a mixed economy with a strong state presence which retained substantial capitalist elements and accepted individual profit-making to be legitimate, though within prescribed limits.

The terms of the 1970 measures are particularly important. Having stated that the programme of reforms was complete, President Kaunda added, 'The Party and Government have given Zambians the widest possible opportunity to grow in stature and to expand their area of participation in the growth of the Zambian economy, in the improvement of the economic and social welfare of all the people. *To many enterprising Zambians now the sky is the limit in terms of improving their position.*'[18]

Whatever the President's intention, an important consequence followed. The Zambianisation of posts in the public sector and the indigenisation of ownership in the private sector facilitated the emergence of a Zambian 'quasi-bourgeoisie' straddling the public and private sectors in a mutually reinforcing relationship which persists to the present day and which represents a powerful social force politically and economically. Martin foresaw this when he wrote in 1972 that 'a new black elite may take over all the privileges of the old white one, and that the new society Zambia is trying to develop may turn out no more egalitarian than the old . . .'[19] He saw the parastatals as becoming an 'elaborate machine for transferring wealth from certain sections of the Zambian society to others.'[20]

The mixed economy in Zambia does not however give free reign to the private sector. The 1973 Party Programme which defined state participation also laid down loose guidelines for the private sector. Only firms with less than K500,000 gross profit margins would be allowed. Each firm was expected to conform to the 'country's philosophy, social legislation and objectives'. The declared intention was to use the private sector as a major source of local capital. Local manufacturers and foreign investors would be encouraged and it was expected that their profits would 'to the largest extent possible [be] ploughed back into development.' However, private business was brought up sharply by the President's Watershed speech in 1975. He reminded the country that 'capitalism is not our political line . . . ' In a Humanist society there would be no private enterprise and 'the working people will control the means of production as well as distribution.'[21] The effect of the speech was to dampen private sectoral investment and activity as businessmen wondered whether Zambia might after all be seriously considering taking the socialist path. The size of the private sector in relation to the public sector may be gauged by the table below.

Table 1
Employees in Each Industry, June 1976

	Private Sector	Public Sector	Parastatals
Agriculture, forestry, fisheries	14,300	9,610	9,800
Mining and quarrying	1,230	–	64,650
Manufacturing	26,360	520	15,460
Electricity and water	–	1,220	4,720
Construction	29,400	24,940	170
Distribution, restaurants, hotels	19,020	2,160	12,180
Transport and communication	3,710	1,340	14,650
Finance, insurance, real estate, business	10,790	1,240	5,940
Commercial, social, personal services	8,010	86,820	120
Total	112,820	127,850	127,690

Source: Monthly Digest of Statistics, Vol. XIII, No. 11 and 12, Supplement.

Historically the private sector, especially on the Copperbelt, has been dependent on mining. The scale of activity on the Copperbelt is indicated by the fact that in 1972 there were 326 establishments with 22,553 employees, 50% of the total Zambian manufacturing.[22] For the rest, the manufacturing that developed was largely import substitution with a considerable dependence on imported inputs and a very low multiplier effect on the rest of the economy.

As a result of these two factors, mining relatedness and import dependency, the linkages between the private and public sectors are weak and there has been very little knock-on effect for the economy as a whole of the limited private sectoral activity. Furthermore, since the technology used has remained foreign based, it has not spread skills to the population. A possible exception is the construction industry which is still predominantly private and makes an important contribution as an employer of labour and user of local resources, though import content is still 30% of total construction costs. Manufacturing in the private sector is often carried on by firms with less than 50 employees with only 15% having more than 140 employees.[23] In 1972 private manufacturing produced 47% of manufacturing output employing 58% of the labour force in the industry, showing that the private sector is more labour intensive than the public. Most of the larger private firms remain foreign-owned though this is often difficult to identify since some have appointed Zambians to management and to the boards of directors. The most important multinational company in Zambia is Lonrho which has a nominal share capital of K2 million with a sales turnover in 1975 of K64 million for 50 subsidiaries.[24]

Despite a serious lack of local African capital and managerial know-how, there is a persisting drive to establish smallish private companies by Zambian interests with or without foreign support. A sense of the scale of these efforts can be gained from information published in the *Times of Zambia* (10 October, 1978). It was reported that 28 new companies were registered in the previous month with a total nominal capital of K5 million. The largest was for K100,000 for farmers and builders supplies (Asian-owned), the next for K50,000 for property agents (apparently African owned), followed by similar sized companies in trading, baking, milling foods and transport. Few indicated an interest in first stage production confirming a widely held view that Zambian entrepreneurs are not yet ready to initiate manufacturing and prefer the safer waters of transport, distribution and related industries. Many of these activities are marginal or parasitic and none can fuel genuine development. Loans for such firms are available from the Zambian Development Loan Scheme of Barclays Bank which offers loans from K500 to K10,000. The Development Bank of Zambia offers loans of over K25,000 only, indicating a surprising lack of concern for the small entrepreneur.

Private sectoral activity is thus generally small-scale, with the multinationals often maintaining only a minor presence to keep a foot in the door of opportunity in case the local market expands. On the other hand, the multinationals are very active selling technology, expertise and supplies to the parastatals and ministries. Local companies, however, have to be satisfied with those opportunities which become available in the interstices between the parastatals which are now preponderant in most of the major industries.

The private sector, once highly profitable, is now under severe strain due to the credit squeeze by the banks, restrictions on foreign exchange for imports, transport delays in bringing in supplies and the hold-up in the remittance of profits, which was about two years in February 1979. In 1978 only 15% of companies were paying corporate tax. The picture that emerges is that of a somewhat ailing private sector which is dwarfed by the scale of the parastatals, harassed by government restriction, and made insecure by frequent changes in direction and pace of official policy. At the same time, private enterprise ideology remains a strong current and there are plenty of champions for a resurgent private sector. The only qualification made is that this time it should be in Zambian hands.

A Mixed Economy of Uncertain Destination

Hard times have now come to Zambia and many of the economic indicators are negative. The 1979 Budget speech revealed that the real per capita GDP fell for the second year in succession. Some of the more pessimistic predictions of underdevelopment theorists have come true. Not even a significant increase in the price of copper will suffice to allow the economy to move ahead steadily since confidence has plummeted.

An important consequence of the failures of the economy is the growing pressure from many sources for a retreat from state intervention and hegemony over the economy. In 1978 the pressure was evident in the discussion on the draft Third National Development Plan in order to give greater prominence to the regeneration of the private sector with the parastatals relegated to a complementary rather than a leading role. It was also suggested by the President himself that they should no longer enjoy monopoly status and that central political controls should be relaxed.[25] A sign of the times may be the creation of Zimco as a powerful centralized body with greater powers over investment policies and greater freedom to fix economic rather than subsidised prices. Freeing prices to float upwards would satisfy private enterprise too since their prices cannot be controlled if the parastatals are allowed to charge uneconomic prices (firms like Coca Cola have had their prices fixed for several years). In respect of pricing Zimco is bound to act as a pace-setter for the economy as a whole.

The restructuring of Zimco may be seen as a step which will encourage private enterprise generally. Zimco can now better evade national planning guidelines, its management can more readily march in step with the private sector. Profit considerations will become even more pronounced.

The parastatals will be free to allocate business areas to the private sector and facilitate their operations. There will also be greater interaction between parastatal officials and private business, a process which is already encouraged by virtue of their joint membership of the Zambia Federation of Employers, a body which often espouses the cause of private enterprise. We can also expect greater job mobility of managers from parastatals to private firms and they may be invited to sit on private boards of directors. Much depends on the degree of 'respectability' accorded to private enterprise by government spokesmen and on the relaxation of the Leadership Code which has been a major obstacle in the past. If government follows through some of the proposals of the Third National Development Plan, it will provide state loans to private firms when the national financial squeeze is lifted. Many Zambians are waiting for a more favourable climate to emerge when they will seize the opportunity to go into business.

Because Zambia experienced a settler brand of colonialism there was no room for an indigenous African bourgeoisie. It was only after Independence that an embryonic class began to emerge with its main concentration in the state bureaucracy and parastatals. Those Africans who tried to establish themselves in private business found themselves sorely constrained by a lack of capital and expertise and apart from a few individuals who have indeed accumulated substantial capital, it cannot be said that there is now a full-fledged African bourgeoisie based in the private sector. Even the bureaucracy, with all the power of the state behind it, cannot be said to have consolidated itself into a class proper. For one thing, it does not own, in its own right, either capital or means of production. It can only ensure its privileged position by 'regulating the distribution relations by non-economic (political) exogenous means contradicting the actual production relations.'[26] It is also under the perennial constraint of having to hold the ring at the level of the state between a range of conflicting interests, local and foreign, private and public, elite and masses. While individual bureaucrats are able to find opportunities for personal enrichment, the bureaucratic class is limited in its acquisitiveness by its public role. But this does not mean that the hunger for greater individual wealth cannot find other outlets. There are signs that the bureaucracy is finding the manipulation of the state apparatus inadequate for its purposes. Some officials are carrying out their duties with decreasing conviction and commitment, and there is an obvious loss of confidence in the possibility of state-sponsored development succeeding in Zambia. Thus self-interest is legitimated by the external evidence of failures in the domain of state activity.

If the bureaucracy continues to press for greater access to private business, it will represent a distinct departure from the model of state capitalism which has been the dominant one in Zambia to date. Szentes has defined state capitalism as 'the restriction and regulation of economic spontaneity stemming from the existence of private capital . . . '[27] While I. Sachs says, 'in underdeveloped countries state capitalism substitutes for the non-existing capitalists, performing actually the function of "collective capitalism".'[28] Clearly both elements have been present in Zambia with the state confronting private (foreign and settler) capital, and the state serving as the principal means of accumulation. But now a reverse tendency is manifesting itself and is bound to create embarrassment to the Party and the Government. The new tendency amounts to a rejection of the socialist path, the stated goal of the President and the Party. Whereas the President acknowledged in *Humanism in Zambia* (Part Two) that Zambia was state capitalist in form, he has not renounced socialism as the preferred road. On the other hand it is also evident that Party and its Government have not been able to develop a state form and style of ruling which would curb capitalist tendencies and provide alternative channels for the fulfilment of individual aspirations and a wider vision and prospect of success for the country. Furthermore, having allowed private interests to prevail and been seemingly unable to create a clearly socialist party and state system, any further concessions to capitalism now will make a subsequent reversal very difficult.

This is not to say that Zambia would find it easy to forsake the path of state predominance in the economy. Such a move would necessarily lead to massive unemployment and serious distortions unacceptable in the Party and the country at large. The bureaucracy itself would not deny the importance of maintaining a substantial public sector as a national base for the economy. There is recognition that there is no likelihood of a capital goods industry emerging in the private sector, which must remain based on distribution or, at best, on the manufacture of consumer goods. There is therefore an acceptance that the basic industries must remain in national, i.e. state, hands. The mines, as the backbone of the economy and the major earner of foreign exchange must clearly remain a parastatal, and few Zambians would object to the increasing equity interest taken up by the state (now 60%).

Control by the state is also seen as necessary to limit the repatriation of profits abroad and to oversee Zambia's other interests in the economic field based on the lessons of the decolonization exercises after independence. For instance state control is accepted over money and lending institutions. (It also enables the bureaucracy itself to use their state positions to make capital and resources available from state banks and parastatals to lubricate private enterprise.)

What seems to be suggested therefore is that the respective roles of private and public sectors should be left somewhat ambiguous, leaving the door open to a transition by stealth to the Kenya model.[29] This compromise must be pleasing to the bureaucratic bourgeoisie which in any case lacks the capital, expertise and self-confidence to make a clean break into the private sector. Perversely, such tendencies away from a predominant state would be the reverse of those now setting in in Kenya itself where the already substantial bourgeoisie based in the private sector is now seeking to manipulate the state apparatus to strengthen its position against multinational interests.[30]

However, within Zambia itself, the encouragement of entrepreneurial activities by the bureaucracy could well undermine the remaining coherence of the parastatal system. As indicated earlier the method of state participation rather than nationalization chosen in Zambia, the continuation of minority interests within the parastatals, and the considerable influence of foreign personnel and interests within the institutions of the parastatal sector means that they are already far from being engines of socialist construction and development. Any further facilitation of private enterprise ideology and practices can only further erode the state's role.

The ground has already been prepared for a dual role for the bureaucracy by the example of many leading figures who combine public office with private business. While much of this activity is hidden from public scrutiny, enough is revealed from time to time to indicate that the practice is not uncommon and that it has been the seedbed for much corruption. It has also led to a substantial degree of demoralization of lower ranks who resent the abuse of public office by their seniors. Furthermore, while it may be wrong to ascribe the malfunctioning of the economy to abuse of office and corruption, it must be recognised that the public sector is large in relation to the rest of the economy and that malpractices there must therefore account for a great deal of malfunction generally.

It is, however, fair to say that the discovery of corruption in Zambia is likely to receive publicity and official displeasure. Top people have been suspended and this must create great personal difficulties in a country where non-state jobs are hard to come by.

But we must distinguish between efforts by individuals to make small private gains and the thrust of a class-in-potential which grows daily more visible. When this is combined with the promptings of foreign capital for greater permissiveness for private enterprise, then the government is placed under considerable pressure. The major lesson of the Third World is that the growth of private business in the conditions of peripheral capitalism has only led to greater dependence on foreign capital since so little is available within. Similarly the Zambian experience indicates that local capitalists are by themselves not able to mount a substantial programme of capitalist enterprise. Only in combination with foreign interests, as junior partners of multinationals, have Zambians been able to join the world of industry and finance. While this may benefit them individually, it cannot but reinforce Zambia's already substantial dependency and this would be in direct contradition with its hopes for autonomous development. As other contributions to this book show, overcoming dependence is a prerequisite for genuine development. It is essential that dependence relations must be broken in order to retain surpluses within the country, to commence a genuine process of accumulation and promote integrated and coherent development policies on a wide front.

It could be argued quite convincingly that although Zambia achieved political independence, economic independence has remained largely elusive. But it is certain that whatever gains have been made in this area will certainly be lost if a private sector is allowed to grow much beyond existing levels, for such a development can only be achieved by the influx of much foreign capital and its accompanying problems. If state sectoral development is frustrated in a dependent economy, the strengthening of private enterprise can only lead to greater restriction on development as a whole. It could well make Zambia's long road from independence an exercise in futility.

References

1. B. Van Arkadie, 'Development of the State Sector and Economic Independence' in D. Ghai (ed.), *Economic Independence in Africa.*

(Nairobi, 1973).

2. A distinction must be drawn between profits in the conventional capitalist sense and profitability in a socialist or publicly owned enterprise. The latter is an indicator of efficiency, the proper utilisation of resources and the capacity to generate a surplus. This may then be taxed off, redirected by the state, reinvested for greater productivity, paid out in bonuses to the staff, or used for social benefits. It is primarily a yardstick of successful operation.

3. UNDP, *A Profile of the Zambian Economy* (Lusaka, 1976), p. 3.

4. G. K. Simwinga, 'Corporate Autonomy and Government Control of State Enterprises in Zambia.' Unpublished Ph.D thesis, University of Pittsburgh.

5. President Kaunda, Speech at UNIP Conference, 11 September 1978.

6. Simwinga, *op. cit.,* p. 166.

7. *Ibid.,* p. 163.

8. *Ibid.,* p. 163.

9. President Kaunda *Humanism in Zambia, Part Two* (Lusaka, 1974), p. 80.

10. A. G. Frank, 'Economic Crisis and the State in the Third World', (mimeo, 1978).

11. Indeco Annual Report 1977/8.

12. Speech by Mr J. Lumina, Minister of Finance, at a seminar at the University of Zambia on 17 February, 1979.

13. A case in point is Zamefa, the copper wire manufacturing plant which is a parastatal but which is managed by staff seconded from Reid International. Even though the actual working machinery is not very sophisticated, the production process (and much of the marketing) is in the hands of this US-based multinational corporation.

14. Van Arkadie, *op. cit.,* p. 91.

15. Lumina, *op. cit.*

16. A. Martin, *Minding Their Own Business* (Harmondsworth, 1975), p. 267.

17. *Ibid.,* p. 252.

18. President Kaunda. Closing Speech at the UNIP National Council Meeting, November 10, 1970. Quoted in Martin, *op. cit.,* p. 252. (Emphasis added).

19. Martin, *op. cit.,* p. 219.

20. *Ibid.,* p. 216.

21. President Kaunda, 'Watershed Speech'. Address to the UNIP Council, 30 June 1975.

22. UNDP (1976), *op. cit.,* p. 61.

23. Data supplied by officials at the ILO Management Development and Advisory Service, Lusaka.

24. Phillips Electrical Zambia Ltd has a nominal capital of K1,250,000, while Barclays Bank has a nominal capital of K3 million.

25. Speech by President Kaunda, UNIP National Council Meeting at Mulungushi Hall, 12 June 1978.

26. T. Szentes, *The Political Economy of Underdevelopment* (Budapest, 1977), p. 275.

27. *Ibid.,* p. 311.

28. *Ibid.,* p. 312.

29.   R. Sklar, *Corporate Power in an African State* (Los Angeles, 1975), pp. 207, 209.
30.   N. Swainson, 'The rise of a National Bourgeoisie in Kenya', *Review of African Political Economy* (January, 1977).

Study Questions

1.   What were the principle reasons for state intervention in the economy after Independence?
2.   Give some of the reasons for continuing foreign influence in Zambian state enterprises.
3.   Why did Zambia not resort to outright nationalisation without compensation?
4.   Is it true that publicly owned enterprises must necessarily be inefficient? Can you give examples proving the contrary?
5.   Who does subsidised food benefit? (Be sure you have identified all possible beneficiaries.)
6.   Why does Zambia persist with its mixed economy when the party and the President seem to want socialism?

6. Edwin M. Koloko

Intermediate Technology for Economic Development: Problems of Implementation

Introduction

In the last few years there has been an increasing interest in what has been variously called 'intermediate' technology, 'low-cost' technology, 'appropriate' technology, or 'soft' technology.[1] There are a number of reasons for this interest. One major source has been the dissatisfaction on the part of both donors and recipients with the results of current approaches to development aid and technical assistance.[2] In addition to the criticisms of the low level of appropriations for aid, there have been increasing criticisms of the dependence of poor countries upon industrial countries for research and development, and dismay at rural stagnation and the resulting migration pressures on urban areas. Such criticisms and concern have led a number of donor countries to explore the concept of rural development.[3]

Discussions of rural development suggest not only a shift away from industrialization as the main thrust of development but also a concern with the scale of projects, whether industrial or agricultural. Questions relating to the appropriateness, real cost, and the social and environmental impact of projects and technologies become salient as soon as one seriously explores ways of trying to improve the overall condition of the rural masses. Interest in appropriate technologies has also been spurred by the various debates arising from the Club of Rome reports and the dissatisfaction of various groups with current large-scale industrial technologies, whether from an environmental, health, safety, or aesthetic point of view. The energy crisis has tended to give an added dimension of urgency, as well as a broader audience, to the discussion of alternative technologies and regulatory policies.[4]

Given the willingness of a wide range of groups to look seriously at alternative ways of dealing with technologies — whether in the industrial or the developing world — there is a need to examine the various cultural and institutional barriers which impede the development and spread of intermediate or appropriate technologies. This paper will attempt to show that to understand these barriers we need to re-examine what is meant by 'appropriateness' and by 'technologies'. While the basic idea that appropriate technologies are those that are adapted to their social and cultural environment (as well as being technically and economically viable) is fairly straightforward, it is difficult to apply in practice. Part of the difficulty relates to the difficulty of accurately assessing the characteristics of an 'environment' so that the correct adaptation can be applied. Another difficulty, however, relates to the Western cultural belief that technologies are essentially neutral as well as transferable. Section 1 of this paper critically examines this understanding of technology.

Another conceptual problem relates to the tendency for those concerned with intermediate technologies to focus only upon rather specific implements, tools, processes, and practices. This undoubtedly derives in large part from their concern with the small peasant and with the practicality of new technologies in rural settings, but tends to ignore questions of relationships to existing industrial and technological structures. It is only by understanding the linkages between industrial technologies and industrial institutions that we can fully appreciate the barriers created by the very structure of these institutions to the development and spread of intermediate technologies. The second section of the paper will attempt to outline these structures and barriers. Only then is one in a position to examine questions relating to the policy time-frame, which can be said to cover up to a decade.

The Cultural Bias of Technology

It will herein be argued that the most significant barriers to the development and spread of intermediate technologies exist on the donor side in the form of a number of peculiarly Western ideas regarding the nature of technology. These ideas have strong cultural and institutional underpinnings in Western industrial society, and it is these which will receive the greatest attention. Later in the essay, some of the cultural barriers on the recipient side will be outlined.

One of the most deeply-rooted attitudes towards technology present in Western industrial societies is the belief that technologies are value-free and transferable. They are seen as being associated with values only in the ways in which they are utilized. While there is some awareness that different technologies have different histories, this is normally seen to be a matter of interest only to historians, or as a matter of curiosity. Generally, technologies are seen to be transferable in space and time, and failure to successfully transfer and adopt a new technology is generally blamed upon the unwillingness of the recipients to change their ways in the face of 'progress'. Thus, cultural barriers to the spread of any new technology are normally associated with the recipient culture. This attitude, which permeates the business world as much as the developmental assistance establishments, is also the conventional wisdom of positivism in its various disciplinary modes.

There are two broad ways to attempt to show that this common Western understanding of technologies is culture-bound. One is to engage in theoretical work to show that logical systems cannot be built without explicit or implicit value assumptions.[5] Another approach is to look at a number of specific technologies to try to demonstrate that they can be understood only in terms of the physical and social environment in which they were developed. It is not by accident that much of the discussion of intermediate technologies relates to agricultural technologies — for many of the environmentally and culturally specific characteristics of currently-used technologies are most visible in the agricultural field. For example, any plough used in Manitoba (Canada) today has a long environmental and social history which makes its successful transfer very difficult without changing either the plough or — more often — changing the receiving environment. The Manitoba plough has been developed over a century for certain kinds of soil in a particular kind of climate with specific rainfall patterns. Also, it was developed in a society where labour was either scarce or expensive and where mechanical motive power became the dominant mode.

To try to 'transfer' such a plough to Asia or Africa (something which evidently has been tried) can only lead to serious difficulties. The soils are different and not as deep. The climate is different and monsoon rainfall pattern such that a deep plough becomes easily mired in the mud during the rainy season. Since a deep plough cannot be drawn by animals (at least not without changing local yokes and animal sharing arrangements), tractors have to be 'transferred' as well. These, of course, may be as inappropriate as the ploughs, not to mention very expensive and probably labour-displacing. The history of British, French, and Dutch colonial agriculture is replete with examples of animals, plants, implements, and cultivation techniques which were transferred from the mother countries to the colonies with little success, precisely because of a lack of awareness of their specific environmental and/or cultural characteristics.[6]

The various ways in which modern industrial technologies are culture-bound becomes even clearer when one examines them as an extensive and highly developed sub-culture. This sub-culture, like the larger culture of which it is a part, is largely urban in orientation, is highly specialized (in terms of personnel, equipment, and institutions), and is organised into hierarchic structures that tend to be centrally controlled. This technological sub-culture depends upon the availability of sophisticated equipment, research, and tools produced in the larger society and also depends upon extensive and sophisticated transportation, financial, and communications networks. The sub-culture has a series of rewards and sanctions related to current cultural and scientific paradigms and to maintenance of current operating practices.

It follows from the above that the various technologies produced by modern industrial societies can be 'transferred' with relative ease between individual industrial states, but that 'transfers' to the agrarian and non-Western countries of the world can be accomplished only through Procrustean measures, or by finally recognizing that to move the tip of the iceberg one will also have to move its largely hidden bulk as well. The history of foreign aid tends to reflect a gradual, but unfortunately still largely implicit, recognition of these problems. The success of the Marshall Plan — where technical assistance, equipment, aid, etc, were given to war-damaged industrial countries — led optimistic officials to think that equivalent results could be expected elsewhere in the world. The urban biases of foreign aid and technical assistance were reflected in the emphasis upon constructing industrial infrastructures and large-scale projects.

In the agricultural field, the emphasis until very recently has been upon introducting industrial agriculture into the tropical zones. The development of the high-yielding variety package (the 'green revolution') is a classic case of specialists from industrial countries operating without an awareness of the value assumptions built into their technologies. While there was a conscious attempt to recognise and deal with some of the fundamental physical dimensions which had prevented the 'transfer' of seeds from the temperate zones to the tropics, there was little cultural or social awareness. The 'miracle seeds' were promoted in the typical technological manner — that is to say, most other aspects of the receiving culture were expected to change to meet the demands of the new package.[7] A second general bias visible in the development of the high-yielding varieties relates to the fact that while hybrids can be employed successfully on a high percentage of temperate zone farms, irrigation is required for them in most tropical countries and generally only some 30% of the farmland is irrigated. Plant breeders and their supporting agencies have since recognized this and are starting work on improved varieties and practices for dryland farming.

Several other biases are visible in the programmes promoting high-yielding varieties. As with so many things technological and economic, they were developed without any consideration of questions of scale or of the receiving economic/social structures. It has been clearly demonstrated that when introduced into the real economic and social conditions of most developing countries the high-yielding varieties are clearly 'landlord-biased'.[8] Since the large landlords have better access to information and credit, the marginal utility of their using the new seeds is high, while the marginal utilities for small peasant farmers may be negative. A final — and very general bias — is visible here, that of assuming that economies of scale are very generally present in society. The idea of economies of scale is one which is being increasingly challenged on both practical and theoretical grounds. A large part of the practical challenge is visible in the literature on appropriate technologies. At a theoretical level the work of systems theorists, ecologists, energy analysts, etc, are all showing that the efficiencies of various enterprises look very different when one tries to consciously include their real environmental and social costs.

In the case of agriculture, even conventional agricultural economists will admit that above a certain minimum acreage level there are no economies of scale. Also, it is clear that the highest net food production tends to come from relatively small plots that are intensely cultivated — such as those in Japan, Taiwan, and the Netherlands. When one turns to the energy efficiency of modern agriculture as contrasted to more traditional agricultural systems, the energy inefficiency of the former is striking. The Steinharts have pointed out that the US food system (production, processing, transportation, and preparation) requires ten calories of energy input for every one food calorie produced.[9] And Pimental has demonstrated that at current US energy efficiencies, it would be physically impossible to feed the world's four billion a US diet.[10] Even though a serious re-thinking of industrial agriculture would seem to be called for (in line with the sort of re-evaluation that is going on in regard to rural development), the institutional support system and vested interests associated with the agri-business complex are such that any re-thinking will be a slow and painful process. As was demonstrated at the World Food Conference, there is still a great deal of momentum behind the idea that the only way for the developing countries to improve their agriculture is to adopt the industrial mode of agriculture.

In turning to cultural barriers on the recipient side, it must be emphasized that any full understanding of these is hampered and distorted by several common Western tendencies. First, there is a strong tendency to talk and think in universal terms about 'the peasant', 'underdeveloped countries', 'traditional societies', 'rural population', etc. The assumption behind any one of these concepts is that there are a series of common characteristics shared by all 'peasants'. While variations of place and culture are given lip service, it is commonalities that are stressed rather than the variations. Rarely is there an attempt to understand the complete context of culture — that is, to try to understand it in terms of a series of interactions between environment, institutions, and man taking place over time. Those who have tried to understand culture in these terms — anthropologists, some rural sociologists, and some area specialists — have generally had their work ignored by those promoting technical transfer.[11] The reasons are clear to anyone concerned about intermediate technologies — 'easy' technical transfer and the 'mobile' expert are hardly compatible with the task of adapting technologies to specific cultures and environments.

A second Western tendency is to communicate primarily with those who have either learned Western culture, values, and languages in the industrial countries or to communicate with those trained in the college preparatory schools of the Third World — schools that are still largely academic, urban, and Western in orientation and curricula content.[12] As a result, the underlying assumptions of the outside observer are often reinforced by those of the local elites. While there are clearly exceptions to these tendencies they have not, as yet, been able to overcome in any systematic way stereotypes regarding 'peasants' and 'rural folk'.

What is suggested from the above analysis of cultural barriers is that those interested in introducing technology will have a better chance of understanding the particular configuration of environmental and cultural influences in a specific locality if they are better aware of both their fairly well articulated development goals *and* the underlying value premises and functionally specialized modes of economic analysis which have led to the failure of many current programmes. Without a good deal of introspection about Western culture and institutions, the rural development and intermediate technology movements risk making many of the same mistakes — though in less environmentally and economically costly ways — that the 'high' technology advocates have made.[13]

Institutional Biases in Technology

As with the discussion on cultural barriers, Western institutional barriers will be examined first. To appreciate the complexity of the Western barriers, global, national, and local institutions and interrelationships need to be surveyed. At the global level one finds a series of international institutions (defined to include practices as well as organisations) which are based upon all of the functionally specialized assumptions and bureaucratically structured approaches of the industrial countries. Institutions in the realm of international trade, aid, and education are all so structured and tend to reinforce one another as well as create and maintain an international elite. International civil servants, technocrats, and experts may have basic political and economic disagreements depending upon whether they come from the industrial or developing countries. However, they generally share the same cultural attitudes towards science, technology, and modern economic and bureaucratic structures (those described in the preceding section). This international elite — which moves easily back and forth from national institutions (government, universities, and business) to international agencies — also generally shares the urban and academic orientations of Western societies.

The existence of this international elite is bolstered at the national level by the structure of the international economic system and also by the ways in which development aid has usually been given. The existence of basic differences about how the world's economic resources should be shared out and about the degree of 'leverage' which multilateral agencies like the World Bank should employ should not hide the more basic fact that the language and metaphors of international politics in the second half of the twentieth century are economic and bureaucratic and that the various forms of aid to create economic planning units and national development plans, but that they have strong foreign policy incentives to use these institutions and their vocabulary to 'fight fire with fire'.[14] This parallels the ways in which nationalist leaders seeking independence sought to learn the language of the dominant groups and institutions in order to better combat them.

The result of all this is a situation where economic and development plans are developed largely in the capital cities of the developing countries by Westernized elites who have every reason not to seriously consider rural development or intermediate technologies. Often they have psychologically rejected their own cultural/rural backgrounds.[15] Their training and socialization have encouraged acceptance of Western concepts of development and modernization. Positive reinforcements are available from international business, international aid and technical assistance programmes, and from bilateral assistance programmes from major powers. In addition, genuine rural development in many cases would upset the rural power structures upon which many urban politicians still depend.

Beyond this general international/national institutional setting, there are a

number of specific vested interests which have been created in the governments of many developing countries by the structuring of their research,
scientific, and technical policy-making bodies in ways which closely parallel
similar bodies in the industrial countries. There is often a national research
council which is supposed to determine the various research and development priorities. Usually there is some sort of agency which is supposed to
encourage small industry or small firms. Agriculture, to the degree that it
has been recognised as a priority, normally has its goals defined as part of
the overall development plan. In each of these areas there may well be a
number of regional or more often local offices or extension branches.
However, the structure is the typical Western functionally specialized and
centralized bureaucracy. These centralized agencies — whether in the fields of
research, small-scale industry, or agriculture — are staffed by the same
westernized elites that are found in the planning agencies, the military, and
the foreign offices. Also, the agencies which deal with areas or programmes
where intermediate technologies could be promoted tend to be lower in
status than the 'traditional' agencies — which means that in the competition
for resources there is a natural tendency for them not to challenge the underlying conceptions of modernization and development of the dominant
bureaus and departments.[16]

The vested interests of those agencies which should be locally focussed are
similar to those nationally oriented departments such as planning, defence,
and foreign affairs. That is to say, their training is urban and academically
oriented and the status systems to which they respond are closely linked to
those of Western scientists and agriculturists. Thus, *it is seen as more important to attend international meetings of fellow specialists and to have published papers in academic journals than to have devised a practical field
programme or to have provided years of useful service in some sort of
extension work.* Because of this, the phenomenon of large and impressive
'prestige' projects such as hydroelectric dams, national airlines, huge steel
plants, modern urban universities, etc. should not be viewed with surprise.
They are the logical outcome of a series of cultural orientations, imported
institutions, and international pressures which make them rather predictable.
The conclusion which is often drawn by Westerners 'shocked' at the waste
of these projects is one which is based upon the same sort of view of government and policy as they apply to technology: *that institutions are largely
neutral in terms of policy results and that one only needs to change the
'greed' or 'selfish' motives of the leadership to get policies which will help
the masses. They fail to realize that what is really needed is 'appropriate'
institutions to develop and implement 'appropriate' technologies.*

This need for 'appropriate' institutions is perhaps seen most clearly at
the local level and suggests that meaningful rural development will require
both the development of appropriate technologies *and* appropriate institutions. To appreciate this let us look at the major institutions that
heavily influence the quality of life for the rural masses: the political,
social, and economic systems, the educational system, the land tenure

system, and the infrastructural systems (irrigation, credit, roads, electrification, etc.). While there are degrees of variation, in most developing countries one finds that the traditional institutional systems tend to favour the small wealthy elites who exercise their influence through a combination of political and economic means. The traditional systems can, of course, be changed or modified by either technological or policy changes – which normally are introduced from the outside.

It is at this point that an understanding of the cultural and environmental elements of imported technologies becomes critical. For, as Keith Griffin has shown, if one introduces a new technology such as the high-yielding varieties which requires information, knowledge, credit, access to irrigation, etc. then, given the structure of the receiving institutions, it becomes strongly 'landlord-biased', as only the landlords have the necessary information, credit, etc., to take full advantage of the capabilities of the new seeds.[17] *This suggests that those concerned with rural development and intermediate technology have not only to try to find technologies which are 'peasant-biased', but that they need to work hard at trying to analyze, develop, and promote for specific situations institutional changes which will reinforce their technological efforts.* To ignore the local institutional patterns (and their relationship to national structures) is to risk having valuable islands of intermediate technological innovation gradually swallowed up by the persisting momentum of 'inappropriate' institutions.

Clearly, there is no simple way to transform these 'inappropriate' institutions, particularly since they often reinforce one another. Direct political, social, or economic change usually requires support of a broad-based popular reform or revolutionary movement. This, of course, is only a necessary, but not sufficient condition as demonstrated by the number of popular movements which have been crushed through external intervention. The situation is much the same for land reform. Short of land reform dictated by the military victors of a war – such as was the case in Japan – external pressures are not sufficient to induce significant land reform although it may well be sufficient to prevent or reverse it. The educational and the infrastructural systems remain as those where external development assistance – whether international, bilateral, or private – may have some institutional impact.

As mentioned earlier, the educational heritage of colonialism has been one of inappropriateness – at least as far as the rural masses are concerned. The education is urban and academically oriented and its main function has been to provide a means of social and geographical mobility for a lucky few. The vested interests therein are so great that some have concluded that the best approach for trying to make education relevant to the practical needs of the rural masses is to go outside of the existing structures to try to promote 'informal' modes of education – adult education, literacy programmes, programmes for drop-outs, etc. that would reach the people who would benefit from localized, practical programmes.[18] In addition, UNESCO recently started a series of international seminars and workshops to develop environmental education curricula which would redirect the current emphasis away from the academic to those skills appropriate to the rural environment. Whether this attempt at institutional reform will be any more successful than previous attempts remains to be seen, although the potential alliance of this reform with rural developmental programmes and intermediate technology programmes should not be neglected.

Infrastructural systems also offer quite a range of possibilities for institutional reform, although as with education one is still saddled with many large-scale and inappropriate structures inherited from the past. This is particularly true of the physical infrastructure where roads, dams, canals, railroads, ports, communication links, and power lines all tended to be designed to promote either the commercial or the security needs of the metropolitan countries. These pre-independence structures often combined with the early post-war development approach of rapid industrialization to further elaborate these highly urban- or export-skewed systems rather than seeking to diversify or disperse them. The emphasis has shifted in recent years as agricultural development has been seen to be more important. However the tendency to give top priority to the 'green revolution' has meant that the irrigated regions of the developing countries (usually less than 30% of the land area) have received the lion's share of infrastructural improvements.

As far as social or economic infrastructures are concerned, it has been most difficult to try to firmly establish credit cooperatives, agricultural extension services, local irrigation control districts, etc., which would promote appropriate technologies. There are several reasons for this as Jequier notes.[19] First, the administrative and management skills required for most of these units are clearly 'high-technology'. Often, they are formed at the behest of the government or of various development aid agencies, which means that the shared goals and values vital to the success of any communal activity are rarely present among the members. Finally, the government sponsorship is often met with suspicion and/or distrust. What all of this suggests is that the attempt from above to diffuse units which require 'high-technology' skills and values is hardly the way to promote appropriate technologies. Rather, an approach which draws heavily upon local concerns, values, and skills must be sought, though there is no reason why those from outside the local region cannot be of assistance. In essence, what is needed are 'appropriate' institutional structures and/or 'appropriate' governmental policies to encourage the local development of appropriate technologies.

Conclusion

There are several general implications which flow from what has been discussed. One is that those who are concerned with intermediate or appropriate technologies need to develop a better understanding of the longer-term and larger-scale aspects of technology, especially how these are linked to Western institutional structures. Only by becoming aware of these dimensions can the proponents of intermediate technology try to encourage sufficient institutional change so that they will not end up with a few small islands of successful intermediate technology development which are progressively swallowed up in a rising tide of centralized, 'high' technology.

Equally, those concerned with rural development need to recognise that they not only need the sort of local adaptiveness of appropriate technologies, but that the values they seek to promote require the same sort of 'appropriate' government policy and delivery systems that are required for any major implementation of the appropriate technology approach. The copying of Western institutional forms by many poor countries is certainly inappropriate for both intermediate technology and rural development.

This leads to an implicit questioning of the value of much of current development aid — whether bilateral or multilateral. Few aid-granting agencies are willing to consider projects like a national Cow Dung Commission as it lies outside both their world view and their competence.[20] Even less likely would be a serious backing of a multitude of decentralized projects and efforts. It would appear that Western development assistance will become 'appropriate' only to the degree that the industrial countries themselves become serious about decentralizing, adapting, and controlling their own technologies.

Finally, one can hope that attempts to understand in a more systematic manner the cultural and environmental elements that are built into every specific technology will assist not only in developing technologies which are genuinely appropriate for the poor countries of the world, but will also help the industrial countries recognize that their own 'high' technologies are not neutral and that there is as much or greater need for them to re-think and re-design their own technologies and supporting institutions. The world will neither support nor tolerate for much longer the squandering of resources associated with current industrial technologies.[21]

We have pointed out that the appropriateness of technology is, in effect, its adaptability to local conditions, its suitability for assimilation in existing socio-economic conditions, acceptability for existing workforce to handle it, and possibility of training locals (in a short period of time) in its use, its capacity to utilize local inputs and ultimately to reduce dependence. The importation of technology that does not fulfil these conditions will not be a real transfer qualifying for retention in the long run. If in the existing stock of technology there is none that fulfils these requirements, then there is more need to develop one that does. *Hence there is a dire necessity for institutions which can carry out research on techniques which are suitable for rural areas.* In this way assimilation of 'appropriate' technology becomes part and parcel of the development process and becomes acceptable to the rural areas.

It is clear from the foregoing remarks that no technology can be substantively absorbed in developing countries unless sweeping changes in the structure and functioning of the relevant institutional framework are brought about. For example, there are three areas in which such changes are required:

(a) Land-tenure system;

(b) Input and product marketing, and

(c) Research, extension and education.

Changes in land tenure should be designed to maximize resource mobility, that is, to promote development of new and re-allocation of existing resources along lines which facilitate growth in productivity. Moreoever, it should eliminate small farmers' risk inherent in transition from a low-productivity subsistence agriculture to a high-productivity commercial enterprise.

Inputs and product marketing should be so structured that the middleman's margin may be cut to reasonable size, and distribution of inputs and products may achieve greater efficiency and equity.

Research is needed for absorption of existing technology (in local conditions) as well as for development of new devices. For this a strengthening of scientifically trained manpower and physical assets is required. Along with this an efficient, committed and a fairly sizeable extension service is needed to achieve better results in a wider sphere of agricultural activities. Extended primary and secondary education facilities would also assist peasants to appreciate the benefits of new technology and better equip them to adopt new practices.

References

1. The term 'intermediate' technology has been used by E. F. Schumacher, *Small is Beautiful* (New York, 1973), to indicate technologies which are neither 'modern' nor 'traditional'. 'Low-cost' technologies relate to smaller operations where total investment costs are lower and/or employment opportunities are higher than modern large-scale technologies. 'Appropriate' technologies is a term developed by the Brace Research Institute of McGill University (Canada) to indicate technologies that are adapted to their social and cultural environment as well as being economically and technically viable. 'Soft' or 'low-impact' technologies refer to those technologies that have minimal long-term environmental impacts or costs. For a valuable discussion of both the terms and the whole range of problems associated with intermediate technologies see the interim report on OECD Development Center, *Low-Cost Technology: An Inquiry Into Outstanding Policy Issues* (Paris, 1975), especially the extensive synthesis of issues by Nicolas Jequier.

2. See for example the *World Plan of Action for the Application of Science and Technology to Development* (New York, 1971) and the resolutions on Science and Technology as well as on Food and Agriculture adopted at the Seventh Special Session of the United Nations Assembly.

3. Representative works include Edgar Owens and Robert Shaw, *Development Reconsidered* (Lexington, Mass., 1972); Laurence Rewes, *Rural Development: World Frontiers* (Ames, 1974); and *Rural Development: Sectoral Policy Paper* (Washington, D.C.: World Bank, 1975).

4. While this paper will focus on intermediate or alternative technologies for the 'developing' countries, many of the points are applicable to

industrial societies. There is a growing body of literature suggesting 'decentralist' strategies for the industrial countries. See especially Schumacher, *op. cit.*, and the 'Blueprint for Survival' originally published in *The Ecologist* (January, 1972).

5. This can also include efforts to delineate the implicit value assumptions intertwined with modern science and technology. See Kenneth A. Dahlberg, 'The Technological Ethic and the Spirit of International Relations' *International Studies Quarterly,* 17, (March 1973), pp. 55-88.

6. On certain valuable cash crops where profits were sufficient to finance a total transformation of local agricultural infrastructures and practices metropolitan approaches were sometimes economically successful. See G. B. Masefield, *A History of the Colonial Agricultural Service* (Oxford, 1972); the social and political costs of large scale plantation systems are described in George L. Beckford's *Persistent Poverty* (New York, 1972).

7. Egbert de Vries, 'Alternative Approaches to Rural Development', a paper delivered at the Development forum of GSPIA, University of Pittsburgh, July 1976.

8. Keith Griffin, *The Green Revolution: An Economic Analysis* (Geneva: U. N. Research Institute for Social Development Report No. 72. 6, 1972).

9. John S. and Carol Steinhart, 'Energy Use in the U. S. Food System', *Science,* 184 (19 April 1974), pp. 307-316.

10. David Pimentel *et al.,* 'Energy and Land Constraints in Food Protein Production', *Science,* 190 (21 Nov. 1975), pp. 754-761.

11. For an example, see Everett M. Rogers, *Modernization Among Peasants* (New York, 1969). While Rogers does list ten common characteristics, he has a good section on the risks and dangers of cross-cultural research and the ways Western researchers may misread the responses they receive (pp. 364 ff.).

12. For a detailed description of these aspects in Asia see Gunnar Mydal, *Asian Drama* (New York, 1968).

13. The above discussion should not be read to mean that there are no real cultural barriers among recipient groups to the introduction of appropriate technologies. The main point is that the real cultural barriers can be appreciated only after (1) Western biases are accounted for, and (2) one has developed a good deal of specific local expertise on environmental/cultural/institutional interactions.

14. For different views on 'leverage' see Teresa Hayter, *Aid as Imperialism* (Baltimore, 1971), and E. S. Mason and R. E. Asher, *The World Bank since Bretton Woods* (Washington, 1973).

15. Theodore Geiger, *The Conflicted Relationship* (New York, 1967), pp. 84-124.

16. Most of these problems and tendencies are visible in the detailed case study of bureaucratic competition in India over the question of whether India should import or build a small tractor. On the questions of importation there were divisions on whether to import from the 'free' world (the US) or the socialist world (Czechoslovakia). On local construction, questions on ideology (state ownership vs. private owner-

ship) and national vs. state or regional management and control came up. See G. S. Aurora and Ward Morehouse, 'The Dilemma of Technological Choice: The Case of the Small Tractor', *Minerva*, 10 (Oct. 1974), pp. 433-458.

17. Griffin, *op. cit.*
18. See the UNICEF sponsored study by Phillip H. Coombs, *et al.*, *New Paths to Learning: Nonformed Education for Rural Development* (New York).
19. OECD Development Center, *op. cit.*, pp. 48-50.
20. *Ibid.*, p. 63.
21. E. F. Schumacher, *op. cit.*

Study Questions

1. It has been said that 'Technology is a foreign resource under local control.' Discuss.
2. What should guide policy for technology and its transfer to developing countries?
3. What constitutes appropriate technology and which are the appropriate institutions? Do you see another way of expressing these categories?
4. The problems arising from developing countries on imported technology can be conveniently grouped into broad categories: short-term tactical problems and long-term strategic problems. The first relates to symptoms of technological underdevelopment and dependence; the second relates to problems arising from efforts to change the basic conditions of technological dependence and underdevelopment. Discuss.

7. Ann Seidman

The Distorted Growth of Import Substitution: The Zambian Case

The importance of industrial growth is widely agreed in Zambia, as elsewhere.[1] In the post-independence era, Zambia's manufacturing sector did grow at a rate exceeding that suggested by the UN experts as critical for attainment of the goals of the 'Development Decade' of the 1960s.[2] But the rapid expansion of manufacturing industry did not contribute significantly to the spread of increased productivity in all sectors of the Zambian economy.

The Problem: Zambia's Distorted Manufacturing Sector
This article seeks to explain what has happened and why, and to suggest an alternative industrial strategy for a more balanced, integrated national economy, capable of spreading productive employment opportunities and increasing the levels of living of the population in all sectors.

The Inherited Manufacturing Sector
At the time of independence, Zambia inherited an archetypical dual economy. Its small export enclave was devoted almost entirely to crude copper, which constituted 90-95% of its exports. It imported almost all the manufactured goods consumed. Outside the limited enclave built around the Copper Belt and about 1,000 line-of settler estates, the rural areas stagnated.[3] The drains of tens of thousands of young men, forced to seek wage employment by colonial taxes and by regulations which hindered other forms of African participation in the so-called 'modern' sector, disrupted and undermined the existing systems of production in these regions.[4]

Table 1
Value-Added in Manufacturing in Zambia, 1965 and 1972[5]

	1965		1972	
Manufacturing industries	Million Kwacha	Per cent of total	Million Kwacha	Per cent of total
Food	6.6	13.7	23.6	14.3
Beverages and tobacco	13.0	27.0	67.9	40.7
Textiles and wearing apparel	3.9	8.1	12.6	7.6

Wood and wood products,				
including furniture	2.4	5.0	3.3	2.0
Paper, paper products,				
publishing and printing	2.1	4.4	6.5	3.9
Rubber products	0.8	1.6	5.4	3.2
Chemicals, chemical petroleum				
and plastic products	2.8	5.8	7.6	4.6
Non-metallic mineral products	6.1	12.7	10.6	6.4
Basic metal products	5.8	12.0	2.3	1.3
Fabricated metal products,				
machinery and equipment	4.4	9.1	24.4	14.8
Other manufacturing	0.1	0.2	0.3	0.2
Total	48.0	100.0	164.5	100.0

Zambia's manufacturing sector at independence contributed less than 7% of the total Gross Domestic Product,[6] about half as much as was typical of other countries with the same income *per capita*.[7] It was dominated by the beverages and tobacco industries, which produced almost a third of total manufacturing value-added.[8]

Post-Independence Expansion

Several factors combined to stimulate a rapid expansion of Zambia's manufacturing industry after independence.[9] The Rhodesian UDI in 1965 brought a new sense of urgency to the development of local manufacturing industry. The oil pipeline from Dar es Salaam, and a major expansion in road haulage, stimulated the establishment of repair shops and associated activities. The high copper price of the 1960s expanded government revenues, permitting expenditures to double from 1965 to 1970. They consumed a third of the GDP in the latter.year. This contributed to expanded purchases of materials and supplies for infrastructural development and, indirectly, to increased demand for consumer goods for growing numbers of government employees. Wages and salaries rose in all sectors: to the extent that they were not offset by rising prices, they contributed to expanding consumer demand for a range of items. Most of this growing demand was satisfied through imports, which roughly doubled from K156 million to K340 million in 1970. The manufacturing sector also expanded: its estimated contribution to GDP in money terms had almost quadrupled by 1972.[10]

Despite this rapid growth, closer examination reveals several disturbing features of the manufacturing sector.[11] First, it became increasingly dependent on certain imported parts and materials. Local value-added actually declined from half to about a third of the gross output of manufacturing industry. Intermediate parts and materials for manufacturing constituted about 16% of all manufactured imports in 1970. Only about 5.3% of total imports contributed to fixed capital for manufacturing.

Secondly, the composition of manufacturing remained much as it had been before independence, except that beverages and tobacco became increasingly predominant. The output of these industries increased to 40% of total value-added by manufacturing — but they were the only ones in which domestic value-added exceeded the value of finished products. In the other industries for which comparable data may be easily calculated, imports still exceeded local value-added by a minimum of 1.8 times (textiles) up to 7.9 times (machinery and equipment).

Thirdly, the number of establishments reported by the census of industrial production dropped by a third from 1966 to 1969, while the number of workers per establishment, and the average amount of fixed capital invested per employee, just about doubled in the same period. This suggests that immediately after independence a large number of would-be entrepreneurs tried to establish simple manufacturing shops, but that many of them went out of business quickly. Only the larger establishments with greater amounts of invested capital continued to expand. The average value-added per establishment multiplied over 3 times, from about K90,000 to over K300,000. In the competitiveness of the post-independence boom, the larger firms with more capital and larger output — mostly foreign-owned — appeared able to survive.

Fourthly, Zambia's rapid post-independence expansion of manufacturing industry remained concentrated in the export enclave. A few exceptions may be noted, but the bulk of the new industries were established only on the three line-of-rail provinces. Of a total of 532 industrial establishments still in existence in 1969, only eight, or 1.5%, were established elsewhere. Manufacturing employment was likewise concentrated in these few provinces, increasing marginally from 96.7% of the total in 1966 to 97.3% in 1969.

In 1971 the world copper price plummeted to a post-independence low, about 25% less than its 1969 average. Stringent exchange controls and import licences were introduced in 1972 to reduce the resulting balance-of-payments deficits, while the closure of the Rhodesian border in January 1973 further reduced imports. At the same time, the wholesale price index of all domestically used goods rose about 26 points from 1968 to 1972, and another 4.2 points in the first five months after the border closure.

All of these factors affected the manufacturing sector. The total value-added in manufacturing continued to rise by about 10% a year from 1970 to 1972. Perhaps a fourth of this apparent increase was attributable to rising prices. Nevertheless, the continued expansion of the manufacturing sector was one of the brighter features of the economy in this period. Partly due to the stagnation of the Gross Domestic Product, manufacturing value-added increased to about 13.4% of the total GDP, about twice what it had been at independence. This somewhat offset the dramatic decline of mining's contribution, caused primarily by the fall of the world copper price, from over 40% of GDP in 1969 to about 24% in 1972. Yet examination of the limited data now available suggests that the pattern of industrial growth changed but little during this later period.

In short, what appears on the surface to be a success story of rapid expansion of the manufacturing sector in Zambia, turns out to contain seriously disturbing aspects. It is true that the share of GDP added by Zambia's manufacturing sector almost doubled in the few short, relatively prosperous years after independence. By 1972, it had actually reached the target of 13% projected by the *Second National Development Plan* for 1976. But closer examination of the reality behind these apparent success indicators suggests that the manufacturing sector had contributed very little to restructuring Zambia's inherited dual economy.

The Explanation: Dependence on Existing 'Market Forces'
It is not enough simply to show that the manufacturing sector failed to spread productivity to all sectors of the economy, as anticipated by Zambia's planners. Rather it is crucial to explain this failure so that new policies may be devised to change the role of this critical sector in the future.

The explanation appears to lie in two fundamental aspects of the planning and implementation processes. First, the planners by adopting an import-substitution policy, permitted inherited 'market forces' to shape decisions as to which manufacturing industries should be established, where, and how. This policy was reinforced, secondly, by the role of the inherited sets of institutions which, directly or indirectly, tended to ensure that existing 'market forces' did in fact govern the actual investment decisions made.

The Inadequacies of an 'Import-Substitution' Policy
Both the first and second national development plans explicitly adopted a policy of expanding social and economic infrastructure, and encouraging the establishment of import-substitution industries. Even in theory, however, this approach appears more likely to aggravate rather than restructure the dualistic features of an economy like that of Zambia.[12] Here, as in other Third-World countries, the lop-sided structure of the economy is reflected in the distortion of the existing market for imports. Thus the composition of consumer imports is almost entirely shaped by the demands for luxury items of the 10% of the population which accumulates over half, and perhaps as much as three-fourths, of Zambia's national income in the form of high salaries, profits, interest, and rent. The remaining 90% of the inhabitants either earn little more than bare subsistence wages,[13] or produce a major share of their needs on semi-subsistence farms. They buy a distinctly limited range of goods, most of which are already produced in Zambia: foodstuffs, mainly mealie-meal, constitute over half the purchases of low-income wage earners; in addition, cloth, paraffin, matches, soap, salt, maybe a little sugar, coffee, and tea are also bought. Those who obtain a little additional cash may purchase a bicycle or a radio. Not a few buy beer and cigarettes, thus providing the basic demand for the expanding beverages and tobacco industries which dominate Zambia's manufacturing sector.[14]

To build industries to produce goods previously imported primarily to supply demands of the elite in Zambia is to perpetuate an economy geared to their needs. It is almost inevitable that the technologies of such industries will be relatively capital-intensive, and reliant on imports of parts and materials.

The production of refrigerators, automobiles, air conditioners, radios, television sets, and so on, is technologically complex. It requires a level of industrial development which cannot be achieved in Zambia for years to come. For a long time, 'manufacturing industries' producing such items are likely to consist primarily of last-stage assembly and processing of imported parts and materials. This inevitably reduces the potential 'spread' effects.

The argument that industry should satisfy the demands of consumers, giving them the full range of choice to which their *kwachas* entitle them, may hinder the expansion of local production in two ways. First, the import of items considered by high-income groups to be 'superior' may directly reduce the market available for what is produced domestically. Secondly, the import of several different 'brands' or 'makes' of a given item reduces the possibility that the demand for a single product will expand sufficiently to achieve the necessary economies of scale in the local production of standardised materials and parts.[15]

In the context of such a distorted market, attempts to construct manufacturing projects to substitute local for imported products will actually tend to aggravate the inherited dualistic pattern. This may be illustrated by two examples chosen from the list of such projects incorporated in the *Second National Development Plan:* the new car assembly plant in Livingstone, and the expansion of the Kafue Textiles plant to produce rayon and cotton-polyester materials.

The car assembly plant has already been built by the Italian firm, Fiat; the Government of Zambia provided 70% of the capital. Its annual output of 5,000 vehicles is clearly designed to meet the expanding domestic demand of high-income groups for private cars, and indeed is barely 1,000 less than the total number of passenger vehicles newly registered in 1971. In reality, the few hundred workers employed in the plant do little more than assemble a kit imported from Italy. Essentially, when in full operation, the plant's main achievement is to guarantee that Fiat, by providing 30% of the investmet, will have a near-monopoly of the limited Zambian market.

This is not to argue that, if the production of private cars should be high on the priority list of Zambian manufacturers, Fiat is the wrong vehicle to introduce. Its small size and relatively low cost make it preferable to many other possible alternatives. In fact, it can only be hoped that, as the Livingstone plant achieves full production, the Government will prohibit the import of competing models so that it can operate at full capacity, and that an increasing share of the parts may be locally produced.[16]

But several questions would appear to require consideration. First, should Zambia, at this stage in its development, use scarce government investment funds to produce private cars for the few people with high incomes? Or should it give priority to the production of simple tools and equipment — for example, animal-drawn ploughs, maize-grinding machines, bore-hole drills — to increase rural productivity and levels of living? Or, alternatively, should the Government invest in the more rapid expansion of lorries and buses, to provide cheap transport for low-income rural dwellers and the goods they produce and buy?

Secondly, the extent to which specific plans have been made for 'backward' linkages with the rest of the economy remains unclear; but the Zambian market appears too small for some of the linkages to be viable for a considerable length of time to come.

Thirdly, should Zambia, given its limited existing market, embark on this project alone? Would it not be more sensible to combine with, say, neighbouring Tanzania (also with plans for a Fiat factory) to establish one project for both countries which could take advantage of the much larger economies of scale? A higher regional output would facilitate the establishment of associated plants to produce the necessary parts and equipment, reducing imports from the Italian factories, and increasing local employment and value-added.

The second example, the doubling of the Kafue Textiles annual capacity from 12 million metres of cotton fabrics to 25 million metres of cotton, polyester and rayon fabrics, presents a different set of issues. The most critical question is whether Zambia should at this stage in its development expand the production of synthetic textiles at all. This will of necessity require the import of new machinery and equipment, for the plant is now primarily designed to weave and spin cotton fabrics. In addition, it will require the continuing import of rayon and polyester materials for processing. Zambia itself will not, for a long time, have the technological capacity to produce these materials. They require advanced chemical industries with large economies of scale, which cannot be established in Zambia's currently limited market. The extra capital equipment and machinery, as well as the continued import of intermediate materials, will constitute a serious burden for the balance of trade. Add to this the high cost of skilled manpower required to manage the project and operate the new machinery, as well as the profits of the participating foreign partner, and the balance-of-payments strain is likely to be considerable.

On the one hand, most of the consumers of these relatively expensive textiles are likely to come from the tiny high-income group which tends to insist on 'quality' regardless of cost. The average Zambian, who can seldom afford more than one or two shirts and dresses, is much more likely to accept 'lower quality' cotton cloths if the price can be kept down.

On the other hand, the importation of parts and materials for these 'higher quality' goods will limit the possible 'spread' effects which could be generated by the production of more cloth using Zambian cotton. The fact is that the local farmers can and do produce cotton. There have been some recent difficulties in maintaining the level of output in the Eastern Region, one of the main cotton growing areas. Research indicates, however, that the problem is related to marketing difficulties and the relatively high price of maize compared to cotton.[17] The expenditure of much smaller sums than are required for purchasing new machinery and equipment to enable the Kafue plant to process the imported materials might go far in remedying these problems. Small lorries — especially if they could be built locally — would aid the upcountry collection of agricultural produce, and a more rational pricing policy would make cotton relatively more profitable to the small farmers. Such measures could ensure that the expanded demand for cotton would increase the possible impact of existing investments in the Kafue plant by spreading productive employment opportunities through the expanded output of local raw materials.

If the Government is to encourage cotton production and processing in Zambia it may be necessary to prohibit the import of competitive materials. This would, it is true, sharply reduce 'consumer choice', but since only 10% or less of the population really have any choice as to materials purchased, it does not seem to be too great a sacrifice to make.

These examples are introduced here to illustrate how the adoption of the catch-all phrase 'import-substitution', given a distorted market like that of Zambia, may foster the establishment of manufacturing projects producing goods primarily to meet the demands of a small high-income group associated with the narrow export enclave. They do not produce items which might help to increase the productivity or better the standards of living of the 90% of the population living at bare subsistence levels. They cannot contribute much employment or local value-added, for they rely primarily on the importation of sophisticated parts and materials which cannot, for a long time, be produced in such a narrow local market.

The Reinforcing Impact of Implementation Machinery
The role played by the sets of institutions shaping critical investment decisions affecting manufacturing tends to reinforce the impact of an import-substitution policy in fostering the distorted growth of the manufacturing sector in Zambia. A peculiar combination of ministries, manned by civil servants, and linked with 'autonomous' parastatal organisations, facilitates the operation of existing 'market forces' within the pattern of inherited dualism, rather than contributing to decisions to alter it. These forces are further strengthened by the commercial banks and foreign trade interests, still more remote from the realm of direct government influence.

The term 'market forces' does not have the same meaning in Zambia as in traditional western theory, which assumes the existence of many competing private firms seeking to maximise their profits. The privately owned manufacturing projects established in Zambia are far from competitive in this orthodox sense. On the one hand, the local market is so narrow that a few large firms, taking advantage of even the minimum economies of scale, can supply most of its demands in any given field. On the other hand, many of the larger firms with the capital and know-how to invest in manufacturing are associated with multi-national corporations, and their profit-maximising decisions are based on consideration of their world-wide assets and marketing networks, rather than on local needs.[18]

In Zambia, as elsewhere in anglophone Africa, 'ministries' have been substituted for the 'departments' of the colonial governments, but their functions have remained much the same. Each ministry deals essentially with one or another aspect of administration and infrastructure: transport and power, public works, trade and commerce, education, health, and so on. This approach rests on the assumption that the local economy lacks capital for investment in productive sectors; hence, its primary task is to create an 'hospitable investment climate' to attract foreign investment, particularly for the manufacturing sector.

It is not true, however, that Zambia lacks investible surpluses. The reality is that this country, with the highest income per capita in sub-Saharan independent Africa, probably produces investible surpluses which total some K500 million to K600 million every year.[18] This is more than double the total 1972 assets of the Industrial Development Corporation (Indeco), the Government's primary instrument for participating in the manufacturing sector. But the necessary institutional changes have not been made to ensure that these surpluses are directed to the appropriate expansion of productive sectors, in order to reduce dependence on copper exports and increase employment throughout the whole economy.

In the first place, an increasing portion of the after-tax surpluses in the private sector was removed from the country — even after the economic reforms of 1968 and 1969 — largely in the way of profits, interest, dividends, compensation for government acquisition of shares in industries, and salaries for expatriates. Together these totalled almost K200 million in 1971 — another K47 million was subsequently said to be lost on account of 'net errors and omissions' — and were provisionally reported to total K167 million in 1972. The 'invisible' losses during these two years alone exceeded Indeco's total 1972 assets by nearly 40%. They add up to about a third of Zambia's investible surpluses, far more than foreign interests have invested in the country as a whole, including the mines, in any one year since independence.

Secondly, traditional civil service attitudes and institutional arrangements have tended to hinder the investment of tax revenues in directly productive activities. Although the Government since independence has succeeded in capturing a significant portion of the investible surpluses produced in the country in the form of tax revenues, it has invested little in manufacturing. In the peak post-independence tax year of 1970, the Government actually obtained tax revenue totalling some K432 million — over a third of the GDP, or about K108 per capita. In the 1970s, with the fall in the world copper price and the change in tax base on the mining companies, the Government's total revenue dropped to a little over K300 million, about a fourth of the GDP. Even during 1971-2, Zambia's tax revenue was K75 per capita, considerably more than triple that of her East African neighbours.[20]

The *Second National Development Plan* projected that only about 8% of the total public investment would go to manufacturing, and that the contribution of private investors would be four times as great.[21] But the experience of the 1960s suggests that, because they seek to maximise profits in the context of existing markets, they are unlikely to make the investments required to expand the manufacturing sector in desirable directions.

The Government of Zambia today, it is true, spends far more on social, as

107

well as economic, infrastructure than did the former colonial administration. This is partly a response to the post-independence political demands of Zambian citizens, but also fits in with the perception and training of civil servants as to their role. The failure to expand the productive sectors outside of the mines, on the other hand, leaves the national economy precariously dependent on world copper sales. This danger was sharply illustrated during 1971-2, when the fall in the price of copper led to a one-third drop in government revenues, and a cutback in both current and capital expenditure for social and economic infrastructure.

Ministerial intervention in the area of manufacturing, however, remains restricted, primarily, to indirect measures, like licensing, quotas, tax holidays, and specific infrastructural projects perceived as incentives for stimulating desirable growth patterns, or inhibiting those contrary to enunciated goals. Even here, the division of responsibility among the ministries creates the possibility of conflicts and contradictory policies. A perusal of the list of activities of various ministries at the back of the *Second National Development Plan* illustrates this.[22]

The Ministry of Development Planning and National Guidance is responsible for overall planning, although no machinery is provided to enforce any decisions which it might take. The Ministry of Trade and Industry is responsible for Indeco, the Government's holding company for dealing with industry, and for the establishment of an import-export agency which may be expected to influence the purchase of machinery, equipment, and supplies for the manufacturing sector, as well as finished goods which may compete with its output. The Ministry of Power, Transport, and Works is responsible for providing important infrastructural facilities which may crucially determine whether and what kinds of manufacturing projects may be established in various parts of the country. The Ministry of Rural Development is expected to establish 'intensive development zones', which presumably will include rural industries, as well as agricultural plans to stimulate the production and marketing of essential raw materials, etcetera, so that the final picture is not really very different from the 'departmental shopping lists' that characterised colonial plans.[23]

But these ministerial activities appear to be inadequately co-ordinated, and are sometimes even in conflict with each other. At the planning level, this is illustrated by the fact that the *Second National Development Plan* reports on page 96 that an Indeco subsidiary is to establish eight units to machine-form and burn 160 million bricks, while on page 244 it asserts that Indeco's Steelbuild Division has on hand studies for two large-scale mechanised factories to produce 160 million bricks!

Conflicting policies and measures are even more likely to arise at the implementation stage. The Ministry of Finance, for example, is responsible for expanding tax revenues to meet the Government's growing budget requirements, and in recent years has been seeking ways of increasing tax revenue from the mines, which produce over half the investible surpluses available in the economy. The Ministry of Mines, on the other hand, has been seeking to reduce taxes on mines to induce foreign investors to expand their investments and increase copper exports. Without entering here into the complex question of 'who is right',[24] it is self-evident that the two Ministries appear to be working in opposite directions.

There is a wealth of literature to suggest that, everywhere in the world, bureaucracies are designed to look after the machine, not to change it.[25] In Zambia, as in other former colonies, the inherited system was designed to provide infrastructure, leaving the productive sectors, particularly manufacturing, to take care of themselves. This apparently remains the basic function of the ministries today, and simply to append new policies and programmes onto the old structure appears unlikely to ensure that they will change their role.

In line with the philosophy that productive activity is best governed by 'commercial criteria', like those employed by private investors, the parastatals which hold the Government's shares in various productive sectors of the economy have remained, even after the 1968-9 economic reforms, several times removed from cabinet supervision. The overall government-created Zambia Industrial and Mining Corporation (Zimco) consists of several sub-holding companies. Of these, Indeco has been designed as the Government's main instrument for the development of industrial manufacturing.[26] Since the Mulungushi reforms, Indeco's role has been significantly enlarged, yet still seems to have relatively little impact on altering the national pattern of manufacturing growth, and this leads one to ask whether it is organisationally adequate for its task.

Indeco is a lineal descendent of the Northern Rhodesia Industrial Loans Board, established in 1951, and reorganised in 1960 as the Northern Rhodesia Industrial Development Corporation. In its new form, it functioned much like the development corporations set up in other British colonies to stimulate private investment in industry.[27] It was later renamed the Industrial Corporation of Zambia, Ltd., and commenced participating with foreign firms in establishing new large-scale industries to help 'ensure the efficient and profitable operation of such ventures'.[28]

Its role in the economy was greatly enlarged as a result of the 1968-9 economic reforms. In 1968, Indeco's net group assets totalled about K35.5 million. By 1972 these had multiplied over six times to K233 million,[29] and its productive divisions employed about 45% of all manufacturing workers. The total profits of Indeco subsidiaries had multiplied almost ten times, from K283,000 on a turnover of K1,863,000 in 1968 to K27,086,000 on a turnover of K286,002,000 in 1972. Its own share of profits had jumped from K340,000 to K7,083,000 in the same period, while the Government's tax revenue from its subsidiaries totalled another K11,714,000. Indeco's foreign partners received K8,269,000 as their share of after-tax profits, most of which they remitted to their home countries, along with the compensation they received for the Government's acquisition of shares.

Indeco has continued to operate essentially as an autonomous parastatal primarily to facilitate investments initiated by its foreign partners.[30] Its board of directors is composed of government ministers and members of the business community. It is expected to make decisions much like a private firm, primarily concerned with the economic viability of the projects it undertakes. Accepting import-substitution as a main goal, its directors appear to take the existing market as 'given'. The *Second National Development Plan* explicitly declared that Indeco's role should be to accumulate profits from projects established within the framework of the existing high-income urban market, in order to invest in industries designed to contribute more effectively to spreading productive activities to other sectors of the economy. The Chairman of the Board of Directors, A. J. Soko, has recently re-emphasised, however, that Indeco has mounted a 'sustained drive towards import-substitution'.[32]

The organisation of Indeco, furthermore, appears likely to reinforce, rather than diminish, the tendency to shape decisions about manufacturing ventures in accordance with the dictates of prevailing 'market forces'. It is sub-divided into eight divisions, each holding several of the nearly 50 productive companies in which the Government, together with foreign investors, has shares. Each subsidiary is operated in accordance with a separate agreement reached — generally after extensive negotiations — with the foreign partners. They have minority representation on the board of the company in accord with their shareholdings, but more importantly they provide the day-to-day management. In the words of a leading European commercial analysis: 'a large number of Western investors in Africa consider joint ventures attractive, or at least the surest way to gain acceptance by the host country . . . local participation will ensure that managerial control lies with the foreign investor and at the same time satisfy many of the requirements of "national interest".'[33]

Indeco has been given autonomy in dealing with foreign investors and financial interests. The Chairman has argued that this 'demonstrates the spirit of self-reliance'. But it also creates an environment in which the subsidiary managements may make decisions relating to individual projects without considering the imperatives of any kind of overall strategy concerning the need to restructure the economy.

Examination of the details of Indeco's operating divisions suggests that, for the most part, they tend to follow the pattern of already established manufacturing industries — see Table 2. Only five divisions are actually engaged in productive activities, and even here some subsidiaries are still more involved in the import and distribution of parts and materials than in local production. They tend to concentrate on producing or importing items demanded by higher income line-of-rail customers, or for the mines and associated activities. Only Rucom Holdings, the smallest of the eight divisions in terms of assets, is explicitly designated to invest in projects away from the line-of-rail. All Indeco projects seem on the average to be considerably more capital intensive than the average of the nation's manufacturing firms. The Breweries is the largest division, in terms of both employment and profits returning to Indeco itself.

Three divisions are not engaged in any form of productive activity. Indeco Trading clearly has a vital role to play in ensuring increased government control and direction of imports as well as regulating prices. Presumably its goal is to hold down the prices of necessities to consumers, as well as to facilitate the spread of specialisation and exchange throughout the economy. Unless there are clearly defined criteria delineating Indeco's role, however, it is conceivable that the attainment of this goal may on occasion conflict with its policy of establishing profitable projects.

The second of the two largest non-productive divisions, Indeco Real Estate, appears to provide a means of using Indeco funds to subsidise housing for higher income Zimco employees. Its total assets are almost double those of Rucom Holdings, and continually operates at a loss. The inclusion of this division in Indeco hardly seems justifiable, given the necessity of redirecting every *kwacha* of Zambia's investible surpluses to projects designed to increase productive employment opportunities in all sectors of the economy.

In short, Indeco does not as yet appear aptly designed to play a decisive role in altering the increasingly distorted manufacturing sector so that it may contribute more effectively to spreading productive employment opportunities to all sectors of the Zambian economy. Its stated policy of import-substitution appears to have perpetuated, rather than altered, the undesirable post-independence trend of manufacturing growth. Indeco's organisation as a system of autonomous parastatal holding companies, inserted in layers between the Government and the foreign managers of individual subsidiaries, seems unlikely to facilitate efforts to introduce socially-oriented criteria for the expansion of old and the establishment of new projects. Analysis of the available information relating to Indeco's operating subsidiaries appears to substantiate this conclusion.

Other Institutions Influencing Manufacturing Development

Import and internal wholesale institutions help determine the kinds of goods brought in to support and develop the manufacturing sector, as well as those which may compete with local output. The banks play a major role in determining the availability of credit for the day to day operations of specific projects. While it is not possible here to examine these institutions in depth, it is necessary to touch on certain aspects as they have tended to foster the distorted growth of the manufacturing sector.

Zambia's inherited trading institutions functioned primarily to provide a market among the high-income consumers along the line-of-rail for the manufactured goods produced in the expanding manufacturing sectors of first Britain, and later Rhodesia and South Africa. Upon attaining independence, Zambia sought to break its trade links with Southern Africa, both for political reasons and as a precondition of national economic development. It was also essential to increase imports of capital machinery and equipment for the Zambian manufacturing sector, while reducing imports of luxury consumer goods.

Table 2
Indeco Divisional Statistics, 1972[1]

K000

Productive Divisions	*Turn-over*	*Profit (loss) before tax*	*Profit (loss) after tax*	*Net Profit (loss)*	*Net assets*	*Net em-ploy-ees*	*Profits (% of assets before tax)*	*Profits (% of assets after tax)*	*Value of assets per em-ployee*
Breweries	70,395	8,015	5,786	2,829	31,441	4,924	25.5	18.4	6,300
Chemicals	77,646	8,789	5,437	2,611	94,802	3,640	9.2	5.7	2,600
Industrial Holdings	32,323	1,304	275	–(179)	13,873	2,841	9.4	1.9	4,800
Steelbuild Holdings	19,026	3,658	1,883	1,073	37,780	2,910	9.6	5.1	18,000
Rucom Holdings	27,464	2,885	989	268	12,578	3,557	22.9	7.8	3,500
Indeco Trading	60,989	2,379	1,078	589	14,288	3,555	16.7	7.5	4,000
Indeco Real Estate	804	–(273)	–(310)	–(310)	21,751	283	–	–	7,600
Other	355	289	194	182	–(3,320)	226	–	–	–
Total	286,000	27,046	15,332	7,063	223,193	21,917	12.1	6.1	10,000

Source: Indeco, *Annual Report, 1973,* p. 40. The figures in parentheses indicate loss.

To attain these objectives, the Government took major steps to reorganise its import and internal wholesale trading mechanism. The urgency of breaking trade relations with the South was increased by Rhodesia's unilateral declaration of independence, and by Zambia's efforts to implement the UN boycott as rapidly as possible. The construction of the Tanzama Pipeline, the Tazara Railway, and the Great North Road in co-operation with Tanzania were all explicitly designed to provide alternative routes to the sea through a friendly independent neighbour. The Government also introduced import licensing. As part of the 1968-9 economic reforms, it took over a majority of the shares of the major importing companies, Consumer Buying Corporation (CBC, a subsidiary of the British firm Booker McConnell), ZOK (a South African firm), Mwaiseni, and the National Drug Corporation. The National Import and Export Corporation was then established on the foundation laid by the Zambia National Distribution Corporation, initially set up to handle goods imported from China.[34]

The Government's share of ownership in the big importing houses was lodged, as already noted, in the Indeco Trading Division. Initially, the foreign partners provided the management of the firms in which they still held the minority of shares. The Trading Division's turnover of about K61 million in 1972 equalled about two-thirds of the value of all imported consumer goods, but less than 20% of Zambia's total imports. The rest of the capital goods, machinery, parts, and materials imported were handled by separate parastatals, government agencies, and private firms. Overall state control was only exercised through foreign-exchange regulations and licences.

After the 1973 border closure, all importing through Indeco Trading was turned over to the Export-Import Corporation under the management of Bookers, the British parent company of CBC. The Government purchased ZOK outright. Imported goods were distributed by the Corporation, through various Indeco subsidiaries and private retailers, in accord with their projected requirements based on past experience.

These measures were particularly effective in reducing trade with Rhodesia. While overall imports multiplied 2.5 times from K156 million in 1964 to K403 million in 1972, Rhodesia's reported share dropped from over a third at the time of independence to less than 3%.[35] By March 1973, soon after the border closure, and with the expanded output of the Kafue hydro-electric project, reported imports from Rhodesia dropped to 1.5% of Zambia's total imports.

In relation to South Africa, the Government's measures became effective more slowly. Here the absolute value of Zambia's imports more than doubled from 1964 to 1968, exceeding the overall rate of expansion of imports into the economy. South Africa's share declined after the 1968-9 economic reforms, however, from 23% to 15% in 1972, although in absolute terms remaining about double what it had been in 1964. The 1973 border closure reduced South Africa's share of Zambia's total imports to slightly over 9% by March of that year.

The Government appears to have been considerably less successful in achieving the second objective of reducing entry of consumables as compared to capital equipment and machinery.[36] The import of goods for fixed capital formation in the manufacturing sector expanded at about the same rate as all imports, so that its share of the total from 1966 to 1970 remained between 5 and 7%, falling to 5.3% in the latter year. The import of materials and parts for manufacturing kept pace with the overall expansion of imports — an aspect of the growing dependence of this sector on intermediate goods — but increased only marginally, from 14 to 16% of the total. Imports of consumer goods, on the other hand, declined only marginally, from approximately 28% in 1966 to 26% of the total much larger import bill of 1970. Foodstuffs actually increased from 3.6 to 7.7 per cent of the total.

The tightening of exchange controls and import licensing restrictions during 1971-2 — to reduce the balance-of-payments deficits as the world copper price fell — was designed, in part to change the composition of imports more significantly. The main shift over the next two years was an increase in the proportion of machinery and transport equipment from 38.5 to 42.9%, and an absolute decline in value of imported mineral fuels and oils, as well as a fall in their share of total imports from 11.7 to 7.5%.[37] Presumably this latter was primarily accounted for by the Tanzama Pipeline. At the same time, items continued to be imported which could have been produced by local firms. It is hard to obtain precise data on this, but illustrations may be cited — thus the Indeco subsidiary, Kafue Textiles, reportedly suffered losses because of the import of cotton piece goods.

The available evidence suggests that the importing agencies have not yet given sufficient attention to altering the composition of imports to support the kinds of manufacturing industries which might spread productive employment opportunities throughout the economy. This may reflect the lack of an explicit industrial strategy in the context of which specific projects could be designated for support by all government agencies. Or it may reflect the fact that, throughout the period under consideration, the managements of the importing agencies, typically provided by the foreign partners, were more concerned with purchasing materials and supplies from their own associated concerns in other parts of the world. Whatever the reason, unless imports are explicitly designed to strengthen, rather than to compete with, domestic enterprises, it seems hardly likely that a more appropriate manufacturing sector will emerge.

In Zambia, as in other former colonies, the banking system was initially established to facilitate the expansion of the foreign-dominated export-import trade and associated activities.[38] After independence, the continued operation of the major commercial banks along traditional lines almost inevitably fostered the lop-sided expansion of the manufacturing sector shaped by the existing 'market forces'.

Three big foreign-owned banks, Barclays, Standard, and National Grindlays, remained the primary source of credit for manufacturing projects in Zambia.[37] Standard and Barclays, together, have some 51 branches located primarily along the line-of-rail, with a few in some of the larger towns in the other provinces. These banks have been locally incorporated in Zambia since 1971, but are still directed by managers and boards of directors in the context of the parent banks' overall interests. The banks in which the Zambian Government participates are far smaller. The wholly state-owned National Commercial Bank, established after the economic reforms to 'promote the average Zambian entrepreneur by offering him lending policies not readily available in the past',[40] has opened five branches in the main line-of-rail towns, and the Commercial Bank of Zambia, with some state participation, has also moved in the same direction.

There has been no general shortage of credit for manufacturing since independence. The expansion of credit granted by the commercial banks to manufacturing has actually exceeded that sector's growth, multiplying more than six times from 1964 to 1971, and continuing to expand during this decade. But the criteria for loans — in accord with commercial banking practices everywhere — are dependent on the bank managers' assessment of the profitability of individual projects and the security offered, rather than their potential contribution to the spread of productive employment opportunities throughout the economy.[41] In Zambia, as elsewhere, these credit policies reinforce the tendencies of manufacturing firms to conform to the existing market.

The Government's attempts to influence the credit policies of the banks have been restricted to indirect, negative sanctions exercised through the Central Bank,[42] except in the case of the two relatively small banks in which it participates directly. In 1969, and again in 1972, the Central Bank attempted to reduce the amount of credit provided by the banks as part of an effort to reduce inflationary pressures. In the latter year, it also tried to reduce the balance-of-payments deficits resulting from the continual expansion of imports in the face of declining export earnings. These efforts to restrict the quantity of credit tended primarily to reduce employment and to affect smaller business adversely.[43] Larger firms, especially those with foreign links, have better credit relations with the big commercial banks, as well as overseas sources of funds. This may have been a factor contributing to the trend towards the reduction in the number of smaller, more labour-intensive manufacturing firms which has characterised Zambian industry in recent years.

The Central Bank's efforts to reduce imports through exchange controls in the 1970s were also hampered by the fact that the commercial banks helped the big firms to obtain overseas credit for imports. As a result, customs data indicate that actual imports exceeded those for which foreign exchange had been licensed by over 20% in 1971 and 1972.[44] These unauthorised imports cost the country over K80 million a year in foreign exchange.

In other words, the post-independence policies of the commercial banks have tended to foster the shaping of the manufacturing sector by the existing 'market forces'. The indirect methods of control available to the Central Bank appear to have been inadequate to alter this effect, and may actually have aggravated the consequences.

The Explanation Summarised

The explanation here suggested for the lop-sided growth of manufacturing in Zambia since independence is not intended to be exhaustive.[45] It aims primarily to present available evidence which shows that the adoption of an import-substitution policy, backed by inherited sets of institutions concerned with the economy, fosters the shaping of decisions affecting manufacturing expansion by the existing 'market forces'.

Zambia's experience tends to substantiate a growing body of theoretical analysis drawn from other Third-World countries as to the consequences of an import-substitution policy. Efforts to substitute local production to meet the demands of a limited high-income group are likely, in the early stages, to foster the production of a few of the technologically less sophisticated items — beer, foodstuffs, and textiles — for which the internal market may be broadened, in part by putting many of the smaller local firms out of business. Continued import-substitution is likely to become increasingly characterised by the establishment of large foreign firms for last-stage processing and assembly of imported parts and materials, producing a range of consumer durables which are technologically complex and require economies of scale not likely to be realised in the relatively small Zambian market for many years. In other words, the Government's efforts to stimulate the expansion of import-substitution manufacturing projects may be expected to perpetuate and even aggravate the externally-dependent dualistic economy. The relevant institutions which shape the manufacturing sector appear to function in accordance with assumptions and criteria which inevitably contribute to this outcome.

In short, the explanation for the failure of Zambia's manufacturing industry to contribute significantly to the spread of productive employment opportunities into all sectors of the economy appears related to the fact that the Government — both in terms of policy and control exercised over the machinery of implementation — has tended to leave the decisions affecting manufacturing to be shaped by the inherited distorted market pattern dominated by foreign private firms.[46]

Towards a Long-term Industrial Strategy

If the reasons indicated above for the distorted growth of Zambia's manufacturing industry are valid, it follows that a new strategy must be designed to embrace two fundamental aspects. First, the proposals should be carefully worked out in the context of a long-term perspective plan for those specific manufacturing projects which will contribute explicitly to restructuring Zambia's economy. Secondly, the strategy must be concerned with the necessary institutional changes required to facilitate the implementation of such a far-sighted plan.

A 20-year Perspective Plan for Manufacturing Industry

To alter the pattern of manufacturing in Zambia, it is necessary to state explicitly the new set of criteria which must guide the formulation of plans to be implemented over a time span of, say, 20 years. The above explanation of the past performance of the manufacturing sector in Zambia suggests that the following criteria should form the core of this perspective plan.[47]

(1) The output of new projects should contribute explicitly to expanding productive employment opportunities, and the gradual improvement in the standard of life of the 90% of the population who now vegetate at subsistence levels.

(2) Employment creation should be carefully considered in determining whether the technology used in specific projects ought to be labour- or capital-intensive. Given the fairly wide range of possible technologies available, the choice should tend towards the one using more labour and less capital, wherever this is consistent with the other criteria here enumerated.

(3) The location of each project should be considered in terms of the possibility of establishing poles of growth and essential linkages in each province and district in the national economy. Obviously, some projects must be located near sources of raw materials, while others may require to be close to existing markets and external economies to be viable. Over the longer time perspective, projects should be located to *shift* the pattern of markets and external economies to the advantage of the less-developed rural areas.

A 20-year perspective plan should be conceived as establishing the appropriate kinds of manufacturing industries in a series of interlinked stages. These may be incorporated into successive five-year plans, each sufficiently long to permit the creation of essential projects required to implement its major goals. Each stage should be designed to overcome various constraints and to open up specific possibilities upon which the next stage may be built. The objective of the stages, taken as a whole, would be to reduce dependence on the export of copper, and to achieve a more national integrated economy, capable of providing increased productive employment in all provinces.

For example, the first stage of the perspective plan in Zambia could be directed to producing simple, essential farm inputs and basic consumer necessities to raise the levels of living in rural areas, as well as for lower-income groups in the cities. Animal-drawn ploughs, wheelbarrows, axes, and shovels would help semi-subsistence farmers to increase their output for sale. These tools should be relatively inexpensive and easy to use, so that small farmers could afford to buy them and could operate them efficiently. Attention should also be directed to providing adequate seeds, fertilisers, and irrigation facilities.

Simultaneously, small processing plants should be established in the rural areas to buy the farmers' increased output and process it for sale. These might include: simple fruit and vegetable processing projects, perhaps with re-usable containers produced by the Kapiri-Mposhi glass factory; small-scale rice mills in the several potential growing areas; cheap grain-milling machines in each village; meat processing plants; and so on. Wherever possible, new projects in the local areas should be fairly labour-intensive, and 'meshed' with crop-growing and harvesting seasons so as to increase rural employment opportunities and incomes. They would provide the market needed for expanded agricultural output in each province, while substituting local production for many items now imported. By increasing the incomes of farmers, they would simultaneously broaden internal markets for the growing output of the expanded manufacturing sector.

Not all manufacturing projects established in this first stage should be small. A large vertically-integrated factory like Kafue Textiles, for example, can provide an expanding market for domestically-produced and locally-ginned cotton, as long as competitive imports are prohibitied and appropriate measures are taken to stimulate local cotton production. Even for such large plants, however, significantly different degrees of capital- versus labour-intensive technologies exist.[48] Wherever possible, it would seem preferable to use the less capital-intensive technology to conserve scarce capital while increasing the impact on employment.

Once a larger integrated project has been established to produce a basic material like cloth, smaller industries can be encouraged in every province to produce wearing apparel to meet expanding local demand. The same holds true for a range of industries. A careful study of particular projects should determine which might best be enlarged, thereby functioning as poles of growth which may set off a chain reaction throughout a wide area. Once these are identified, the linkages must be planned to ensure that potential spread effects do in fact take place.

In the first stage, projects should also be built to produce essential transport equipment and machinery to facilitate the spread of internal markets and production of raw materials as domestic output and incomes increase. Again, some of these could be fairly small projects located in regions — for example, building carts and wheelbarrows. Larger projects could produce lorry and bus bodies to expand transport facilities for passengers and goods over longer distances. The West African 'mammy lorry' might serve as a prototype: the bodies are locally made of wood, while the wheel-base and engines are imported. If these could be standardised through the import of a strictly limited number of types, it should be possible in a later stage of the long-term plan to produce domestically all the parts and equipment, even eventually the engines. Repair shops and garages could be established in the rural areas, as Rucom Industries has begun to do, to ensure that transport and farm equipment is kept in running order.

Manufacturing projects should be established in each province to produce construction materials to build schools, hospitals, small factories, and improve local housing. The local production and use of timber, bricks, and tiles should be encouraged. Improved tools and equipment should be provided so that small local establishments can produce low-cost wooden furniture.

The first stage of the plan, in sum, would be directed to linking new manufacturing establishments to specific improvements in the productivity and levels of living of the low-income population. No new large-scale project would be established on the Copper Belt, or along the line-of-rail, until every possibility of setting up smaller units in several regions to produce an equivalent output had been thoroughly explored. The need to spread employment opportunities and utilise local raw materials would become primary criteria for the evaluation of any proposed industry.

This is not to say that there would be no room for larger-scale projects requiring considerable machinery and equipment. It is self-evident that the mines must continue to use modern, relatively capital-intensive techniques to enable them to compete on the world market. Their role will continue to be to provide foreign exchange for capital equipment for the range of other industries which will be planned throughout the economy. At the same time, the local production of supplies and materials required by the mines should be encouraged by cutting off imports of competitive products wherever long-run economic feasibility can be established. Some of these projects, too, may need to be relatively capital-intensive — for example, the chemicals plant producing explosives for the mines, as well as the petroleum refinery at Ndola. Factories set up to process copper into finished products are also likely to be relatively capital-intensive, in order to benefit from the economies of scale. Zamefa, for example, produces wire and cables on a large scale. Expansion of its output to meet domestic needs, as well as for sale in other countries, should contribute significantly to foreign-exchange savings as well as earnings. The output of such plants should be systematically examined within the context of the long-term perspective plan to determine how they can best contribute essential inputs to expanding other sectors of the economy as well as the mines.

In later stages of the perspective plan, greater emphasis should be placed on somewhat more technologically complex manufacturing industries.[49] As productive employment and incomes rise, the market for a wider range of manufactured goods may be expected to expand. The parts and materials for increasingly complex farm and transport machinery and equipment may be produced in Zambian factories. An expansion of hydro-electricity should facilitate the use of machinery and equipment in every rural area, thus creating a demand for more sophisticated power-driven tools in many industries.

The specific ingredients of each stage of the perspective plan should be carefully evaluated in light of the progress made previously. Ongoing research and increasing involvement of local people are essential in order to discover and utilise all the possibilities in each province and indeed every village. Rapid expansion of educational facilities is essential to provide technical skills, as well as to foster the spread of manufacturing projects to stimulate national and local development. Manpower planning must accompany the decisions to develop the manufacturing sectors in order to expedite the replacement of foreign high-level manpower by Zambian personnel at every level.

The details of the long-term perspective plan and its stage-by-stage development cannot be blueprinted here. It will require a careful study of the available resources of each province and district. This will necessitate the appointment of personnel on a national, provincial, and district level to bring together existing information, and to begin work immediately on further research as the foundation of such a perspective plan. What can be emphasised, in view of Zambia's post-independence experience — as well as those of many other less developed nations — is that without such a perspective plan the pattern of manufacturing industry created is likely to continue to perpetuate and aggravate the external dependence and lopsided growth of Zambia's inherited dual economy.

The Need for Institutional Changes
It has been suggested that the entire state machinery is not capable of implementing any kind of alternative pattern of manufacturing expansion. This inadequacy relates to the inherited ministerial structure: the para-

statals holding the Government's shares of ownership in industry, the export-import and internal trade institutions, and the banking system. A crucial aspect of any long-term industrial strategy designed to alter the existing pattern of growth, therefore, must be directed to restructuring the institutions and working rules which have in the past contributed to the distorted manufacturing sector.

Essentially, the existing institutions foster the domination of decisions relating to manufacturing growth by 'market forces', despite the Government's acquisition of 51% of the shares of an important segment of the larger industrial firms. In Zambia, the crucial decisions are, in reality, shaped by the pressures of the large multi-national corporations seeking to take advantage of the country's small but high-income market. Any effort to devise an industrial strategy to restructure the Zambian economy must seek to alter these institutions, and their working rules, to ensure that investment decisions are increasingly influenced by those who would eventually benefit, particularly the lower-paid wage earners and rural dwellers. This implies that, wherever possible, participation by those who stand to gain should be built into the new institutional arrangements.[50] Presumably this places a political responsibility on UNIP, the trade unions, and various other organisations of the people. While this political aspect is crucial to altering the role of the inherited sets of institutions, the aim of this article is not to examine how this may be achieved. Rather, it seeks only to indicate changes in the implementation machinery itself which seem essential, if the proposed 20-year perspective plan is to stand any chance of being realised.

First, there appears to be a need to change the ministerial system, both in respect of its perceived role in fostering productive activities, and its overlapping, and even conflicting activities in execution.

As a basis for formulating and implementing a long-term perspective plan, primary responsibility must be lodged with a sufficiently centralised agency to ensure that a cohesive, integrated scheme is devised. The cabinet and parliament should approve this overall plan, and each of its successive stages, so that these have behind them the force of law. At the same time, a built-in system must be created to achieve on-going evaluation and two-way channels of communication between the planning authorities and all those affected, in order to correct mistakes in the original plan and take advantage of the new opportunities that may emerge. Furthermore, since the Government, through its tax powers, has been able to capture a significant share of the investible surpluses produced in the economy, it must itself take a more direct financial responsibility for investment in the productive sectors, notably manufacturing.

Secondly, the role and method of operation of parastatals responsible for manufacturing industries must be integrated into the overall system of plan creation and implementation. To leave the parastatal managements — mainly provided by foreign firms — to operate autonomously, several times removed from the centre of governmental decision-making, contributes to the probability that they will continue to make critical investment decisions which may contradict the Government's stated goals. Careful re-evaluation of the techniques of management and control should be directed to ensuring that the day-to-day decisions of parastatals are implemented in accordance with the requirements of the long-term perspective plan. In this connection, the ways and means of increasing workers' participation in management decisions should be considered.

Thirdly, the institutions governing import and internal wholesale trade need to be re-examined to ensure that they contribute to the long-term strategy proposed. Tariffs, exchange controls, and licences appear to have been rather indirect and inadequate means of changing the composition of imports to support the appropriate kinds of domestic manufacturing growth. Leaving critical decisions of what imports to order — and from what sources — in the hands of the foreign private partners of the trading agencies appears unlikely to facilitate a rapid shift in the import pattern. As quickly as the domestic manpower constraint permits, it ought to be possible to ensure that these decisions are more thoroughly considered within the framework of carefully devised criteria.

The financial system is the final major area of institutional change suggested by the explanation of the causes of Zambia's distorted manufacturing sector. What appears to be required is the creation of a sufficiently centralised authority to formulate and implement a national programme which would effectively channel the investible surpluses already produced into the long-term perspective plan and its successive stages. The financial plan should include the following features:

1. Formulation of an incomes policy which would explicitly guide decisions affecting all incomes, taxes, and prices. This policy should govern not only wages and salaries, but profits, interest, and rent as well. It should aim to ensure a steady improvement in the real levels of living of the lower-income groups in rural and urban areas, while capturing and directing a major share of the inordinately high incomes of less than 10% of the population to essential productive activities.

2. Co-ordination of the collection and use of a significant share of tax revenues, as well as profits accumulated in the parastatal sector and long-term savings institutions, for the purpose of financing the planned expansion of the productive sectors.

3. Control of commercial banks to direct domestic credit, as well as any funds which might be borrowed externally on favourable terms, in order to implement specified projects in the context of the long-term perspective plan.

A system of co-ordinated institutions for formulating and carrying out these physical and financial plans to restructure the Zambian economy cannot be created overnight. Nor will any system designed for this purpose ever be 'perfect'. What is essential immediately is that priority be given to the creation of such a system which can start now to formulate and begin to implement the stages of an effective perspective plan.

Summary and Conclusions

An analysis of the available data indicated that Zambia's post-independence manufacturing industrial growth, while apparently exceptionally rapid, has not contributed much to restructuring the economy. If anything, it has tended to perpetuate and even aggravate the inherited dualism. The explanation for this distortion appears to lie in the adoption of an import-substitution policy, backed by an implicit assumption that the choice of projects is best left to existing 'market forces' dominated by a narrow high-income group and giant multi-national corporations; and the failure to make the essential institutional changes required to ensure that a major share of the rather large investible surpluses produced in the country itself are directed towards the implementation of a more appropriate pattern of manufacturing industry growth.

If the above explanation is valid, it argues strongly for the necessity of formulating a long-term perspective plan explicitly elaborating the stage-by-stage development of manufacturing industries to spread productive employment opportunities into the rural areas, altering the inherited distorted income and market patterns. At the same time, it suggests a fundamental change in the role of various ministries, parastatals, and financial agencies which must assume responsibility for implementing such an approach.

In short, only a long-term industrial strategy, linked with institutional changes required to guarantee its implementation, can ensure that the growth of the manufacturing sector will contribute more effectively to increasing productive employment opportunities and improving the real conditions of Zambians in all sectors and provinces.

References

This essay was first published in *The Journal of Modern African Studies*, 12, 4 (1974).

1. See Ministry of Development Planning and National Guidance, *Second National Development Plan, January 1972-December 1976* (Lusaka, 1971), p. 93; and, for example, R. B. Sutcliffe, *Industry and Underdevelopment* (London, 1971), p. 103.
2. O. Kreye, 'The Myth of Development Decades', in *Die Dritte Welt* (Meisenheim), II, 3, 1973.
3. The 'line-of-rail' is the term commonly used in Zambia to refer to the agricultural and industrial developments, established in the colonial era, that stretch along the railway from the Copper Belt in the North to Livingstone in the South. Africans were removed from about 20 miles on both sides of the railway to make way for settler farmers. Cf. W. J. Barber, *The Economy of British Central Africa: a case study of economic development in a dualistic society* (Stanford, 1961).
4. A number of recent studies substantiate this point in considerable detail, notably L. van Horn, 'The Agricultural History of Barotseland', History Seminar No. 14, and C. P. Luchembe, 'Rural Stagnation: a case of the Lamba-Lima of Ndola Rural District', History Seminar No. 17;

University of Zambia, Lusaka, 1974.

5. Source: calculated from *Monthly Digest of Statistics* (Lusaka), I.X., 7 July 1973, Table 54. There was some change in the system of national accounts in 1970 so the 1965 figures are not entirely comparable.

6. All statistics relating to the Zambian economy — unless otherwise cited — are in, or calculated from, the *Monthly Digest of Statistics*, July 1973.

7. H. B. Chenery, 'Patterns of Industrial Growth', in *American Economic Review* (September 1960), p. 646.

8. Value-added here refers to the gross value of the output of domestic manufacturers, minus the value of imported inputs, and the data in this section are from the *Census of Industrial Production* (Lusaka, 1966 and 1970). The beverages and tobacco industries produced about a third of the value-added in Ghana, where total manufacturing value was about the same proportion of GDP as in Zambia, and about 15% of value-added in Kenya, where manufacturing produced about 13% of the GDP. Cf. Ann Seidman, *Comparative Development Strategies in East Africa* (Nairobi, 1972), p. 23.

9. These are discussed in more detail by Michael Faber, 'The Development of the Manufacturing Sector', in Charles Elliott (ed.), *Constraints on the Economic Development of Zambia* (Nairobi, 1971), pp. 301-7.

10. The actual increase in real terms was probably considerably less, for official data indicate that prices of manufactured goods had risen about 40% between 1966 and December 1972.

11. The evidence to be found supporting this analysis appears in the *Census of Production* (Lusaka, 1965 and 1970); *Monthly Digest of Statistics*, July 1973, pp. 20 and 54; *External Trade Statistics* (Lusaka), 1970; and *Second National Development Plan*, especially p. 172.

12. Extensive evidence has been gathered in Latin America, where the import substitution process was initiated in the Great Depression of the 1930s. Cf. U.N.E.C.L.A., *The Process of Industrial Development in Latin America* (Santiago), p. 29; J. M. Katz and E. Gallo, 'The Industrialization of Argentina', in C. Veliz (ed.), *Latin America and the Caribbean. A Handbook* (New York, 1968), p. 602; A. G. Frank, 'Economic Dependence, Social Structure and Underdevelopment in Latin America', 1969 typescript; S. Marario, 'Protectionism and Industrialization in Latin America', in *Economic Bulletin for Latin America* (March 1964); N. H. Leff and A. D. Netto, 'Import Substitution, Foreign Investment and International Disequilibrium in Brazil', in *Journal of Development Studies* (April 1966); A. O. Hirschman, 'The Political Economy of Import Substituting Industrialization in Latin America', in *Quarterly Journal of Economics* (February 1968); and C. Furtado, 'Industrialization and Inflation', in *International Economic Papers*, 12, (1967).

This experience has also been repeated in other countries. Cf. Seidman, *Comparative Development Strategies in East Africa*, especially ch. VI; R. Soligo and J. J. Stern, 'Tariff Protection, Import Substitution and Investment Efficiency', in *Pakistan Development Review* (Summer 1965); C. F. Diaz-Alejandro, 'On the Import Intensity of Import Substitution', in *Kyklos* (1965); H. G. Johnson, 'Tariffs and

Economic Development: some theoretical issues', in *Journal of Development Studies* (October 1954); and J. H. Power, 'Import Substitution as an Industrialization Strategy', in *Philippine Economic Journal* (Spring 1967).
The effect of the distorted distribution of income on import-substitution has been explicitly discussed by J. L. Lacroix, 'Le Concept d'import substitution dans la theorie du developpement economique', in *Cahiers economiques et sociaux* (June 1965), p. 174; and by Sutcliffe, *Industry and Under-development*, pp. 267-8.

13. The distribution of income in Zambia has been analysed by Ann Seidman, 'The "Have-Have Not" Gap in Zambia — or, What Happens to the Investible Surpluses Produced in Zambia?', University of Zambia, Lusaka, 1973.

14. See *Consumer Price Index — Low Income Group. New Series, 1969 base* (Lusaka), for a budget survey by the Central Statistical Office of 2,600 low-income households in the main line-of-rail cities in Zambia which shows that the families of workers earning the average wage that year could not expect to get through the month without borrowing. The average rise in wages since that period has essentially been cancelled out by rising prices.

15. An international business research publication, *Prospects for Business in Developing Africa* (Geneva, 1970), emphasises in discussing market strategies on p. 39 that 'many companies that want a piece of the long-term action are now establishing African "beachheads".' This danger is aggravated to the extent that foreign managers of importing firms seek to maintain the Zambian market for their overseas affiliates' produce.

16. See Sutcliffe, *Industry and Underdevelopment*, p. 227, for the worst horror story of the import-substitution automobile 'manufacturing' industry is probably that of Chile where, by 1967, 19 firms had been established to assemble parts and materials to 'produce' annually 16,400 vehicles, although the economies of scale of integrated production dictated a minimum output of at least 100,000 vehicles! None of the firms could operate at capacity, the possibilities of backward linkages were thwarted, and the impact of the 'industry' in restructuring the economy to reduce its dependence on copper exports was nil.

17. S. Geza and third-year Economics Students: oral report of research into causes of the decline of cotton output in Eastern Province, University of Zambia, Lusaka, 1972.

18. A recent study of the 80 most successful businessmen in Lusaka showed that most were in retail trade and real estate. Almost none were engaged in manufacturing activities, other than simple repair shops, because of their lack of technical background as well as the larger amounts of capital necessary to establish modern industries. A. A. Beveridge, 'Converts to Capitalism: the emergence of African entrepreneurs in Lusaka, Zambia', Ph.D. dissertation, New Haven, 1973.

19 Seidman, 'The "Have-Have Not" Gap in Zambia', p. 11.

20. Seidman, *Comparative Development Strategies in East Africa*, p. 263.

21. This would constitute about 21% of all private investment, while about 52% was expected to be in the mines. *Second National Development Plan*, p. 43.

22. *Ibid.*, pp. 197-304.

23. Reginald H. Green, 'Four African Development Plans: Ghana, Kenya, Nigeria, and Tanzania', in *The Journal of Modern African Studies, 3*, 2, (August 1965), pp. 249-79.

24. Cf. Ann Seidman, 'Alternative Development Strategies in Zambia', Department of Economics, University of Zambia, Lusaka, 1973.

25. Cf. Bernard B. Schaffer, 'The Deadlock in Development Administration' in Colin Leys (ed.), *Politics and Change in Developing Countries: studies in the theory and practice of development* (Cambridge, 1969), passim.

26. The information relating to Indeco, unless otherwise cited, is from its *Annual Report, 1973* (Ndola, 1973). Zimco's holdings include: Mindeco, which until recently held the Government's shares in the copper mines, although these are now the direct task of the Ministry of Mines, apparently leaving Mindeco responsible only for the development of small mines; Findeco, responsible for the Government's financial holdings; the National Hotels Corporation, which looks after most of the Government's tourist facilities; and the National Transport Corporation, which handles the Government's transport interests.

27. E. g. see Ann Seidman, *Planning for Development: problems and possibilities in sub-Saharan Africa* (New York, forthcoming); also Y. Kyesimira, 'The Public Sector and Development in East Africa', Makerere Institute of Social Research Papers, January 1968; Gold Coast, *Government Proposals in Regard to Future Constitution and Control of Statutory Boards and Corporations in the Gold Coast*, Part 1 (Accra, 1956), especially p. 5; and Arthur D. Little, Inc., *Tanganyika Industrial Development. A Preliminary Study of Bases for the Expansion of Industrial Processing Activities* (Washington, U.S. Agency for International Development, 1961).

28. Indeco, *Annual Report, 1973*, p. 10.

29. It might be noted that, even before the reforms, Indeco's assets were as large as those of Tanzania's National Development Corporation *after* the implementation of the Arusha Declaration; George Kahama, 'The National Development Corporation and the Industrialization Process in Tanzania', Public Lecture, UNIDO Seminar, 26 January 1969. By 1973, the assets of Indeco were about six times the size of those held by Tanzania's NDC.

30. *Second National Development Plan*, p. 194.

31. *Ibid.*, p. 195.

32. Indeco, *Annual Report, 1973*, p. 4.

33. *Prospects for Business in Developing Africa*, p. 55.

34. To enable the People's Republic of China to acquire the necessary Zambian currency to finance the local costs of building the Tazara Railway, the Government agreed to facilitate the sale of Chinese goods. From Zambia's point of view, this merely meant the replacement of certain imports from another source, thereby enabling China to make a long-term loan for the railway which included the local costs of labour

and materials.
35. Most of the imports from Rhodesia in 1972 were in the form of hydro-electric power from the Kariba project, which had deliberately been constructed, before independence, on the Rhodesian side of the border.
36. Data relating to composition of imports, unless otherwise indicated, are from the Central Statistical Office, *External Trade Statistics* (Lusaka), 1966-70 series.
37. *Bank of Zambia. Report and Statement of Accounts for the Year Ended December 31st, 1972* (Lusaka, 1972), p. 39.
38. Cf. Seidman, *Planning for Development*, ch. 18; see also W. T. Newlyn and D. C. Rowan, *Money and Banking in British Colonial Africa* (Oxford, 1954).
39. It was announced that the Government would acquire 51% of the shares of the banks as part of the 1968-9 economic reforms, but apparently the negotiations for implementation broke down, and they remain entirely foreign privately owned.
40. *Zambia Daily Mail* (Lusaka), 23 October 1973.
41. Cf. C. R. M. Harvey, 'Financial Constraints on Zambian Development', in Elliott, *op. cit.*, pp. 136 ff.
42. *Ibid.*, pp. 125 and 133-5.
43. Cf. Mark Bostock and Charles Harvey (eds.) *Economic Independence and Zambian Copper — a Case Study of Foreign Investment* (New York, 1971).
44. Bank of Zambia, *Report . . . Year ended December 31st, 1972*, p. 36.
45. One issue that requires further research is the extent to which the new Zambian top civil servants and parastatal managers, who receive salaries 27 to 50 times that of the minimum wage earners, consciously or unconsciously identify their own interests with those of the narrow high-income group which receives the bulk of the national income in Zambia itself, as well as the multi-national corporations which seek to capture the existing market for manufactured goods.
46. This explanation might well be strengthened by a thorough examination of the evidence concerning the extent to which the emergent class of Zambians — who have since independence assumed control of the civil service and the parastatals — may in fact be pursuing policies of the type outlined above in its own perceived self-interest. This hypothesis is well formulated by Brian van Arkadie, 'Development of the State Sector and Economic Independence', in Dharam P. Ghai (ed.), *Economic Independence in Africa* (Nairobi, 1973), especially pp. 108-12. Some of the theoretical aspects are further analysed in the same book by John S. Saul, 'The Political Aspects of Economic Independence', pp. 123-50.
47. The possibilities of such an approach are discussed more fully by Seidman, *Planning for Development*, chs. 6 and 7.
48. Summary data relating to two textile mills in Tanzania with the same output, but very different labour-capital ratios, are provided by the National Development Corporation, *Third Annual Report, 1968* (Dar es Salaam, 1968), p. 55.
49. It goes without saying that such possibilities would be greatly en-

hanced by co-ordinated planning and implementation of industrial development with neighbouring countries, but there is inadequate space here to discuss these. Cf. Reginald H. Green and Ann Seidman, *Unity or Poverty? The Economics of Pan-Africanism* (Harmondsworth, 1968), passim. Green also discusses the necessity for further research to realise these possibilities in 'Economic Independence and Economic Co-operation', in Ghai, *op. cit.*, pp. 45-87.

50. This argument is more fully developed by Seidman, *Planning for Development*, chs. 3 and 4, and is increasingly emphasised by other academics: e. g. F. Holmquist, 'Implementing Rural Development Projects', in Goran Hyden et al. *Development Administration: the Kenyan experience* (Nairobi, 1970), p. 228, as well as in *T.A.N.U. Guidelines, 1971* (Dar es Salaam, 1971), p. 9. In Zambia, participation is considered a fundamental tenet of Humanism; cf. Kenneth Kaunda, *Times of Zambia* (Lusaka), 13 November 1973. The problem is to create the necessary institutional machinery and working rules so that the broad masses of the working people, the peasantry, and the unemployed, are increasingly involved in decision-making to ensure that the Zambian economy is, in fact, restructured in their interests.

Study Questions

1. Has increased productivity in the import-substitution industry been geared to the basic needs of the Zambian population?
2. In what ways has the import-substitution industry succeeded (or failed) in stimulating other sectors of the Zambian economy?
3. What are some institutional obstacles inhibiting a rational import-substitution policy?
4. Has lack of capital been a factor in restricting the growth of an import-substitution industry?
5. If you were the Minister of Industry, what factors would influence your plans for a long-range industrialization policy for Zambia?

8. Werner Biermann

The Development of Underdevelopment: The Historic Perspective

To understand the socio-economic difficulties facing contemporary Zambia one has to situate them in a historical context.[1] Despite rather low standards of production and trade, the pre-colonial African tribes and village communities living in the region were rarely confronted by problems of famine, unemployment and poverty. The roots of these phenomena, which are a basic element in any neo-colonial society, must be seen in the context of characteristic socio-economic processes. These include military occupation and the implantation of economic structures designed to supply imperial capitalism with cheap labour and cheap raw materials. The great economic and financial asset of present day Zambia, copper, has also been the persistent engine of underdevelopment.[2]

This paper deals with two closely related aspects: (1) the analytical dimension, which includes the definition of underdevelopment, and (2) the concrete dimension, that is, the mechanisms of underdevelopment with reference to the colonial past of Zambia.

The Meaning of Underdevelopment

In general terms, underdevelopment defines the socio-political and socio-economic situation of any society which is no longer structurally able to achieve the self-determination of its political superstructure and its economic basis. The causes of this lie in the external influences which are superimposed upon distorted traditional structures. The external force is defined as colonialism or imperialism.[3]

Although colonialism cannot be solely related to the emergence of the capitalist mode of production, it is nevertheless the dialectical linkage between the internal emergence of capitalism and its outward orientation that constitutes the new form. If we look at the historical development of Europe, South America, the Mediterranean, or India, we see the process at work. The Roman Empire established its sphere of influence by colonizing large parts of Spain, France, Greece, Turkey and North Africa. The Aztec and Inca empires had their colonies as well. The medieval Mediterranean region was dominated by the Arabs (Sicily, Malta, Spain) who occupied and subdued independent states. India, on the eve of British conquest, was confronted by an invasion of the Moguls. But the impact of these conquests was less intensive and far-reaching than the waves of colonialism and imperialism by the emergent capitalist European nation states.

Whereas the 'classical colonialism' referred by Schumpeter[4] was based on the control of long-distance trade relations,[5] capitalist colonialism led to the total deformation of the conquered societies. Capitalism as a mode of production was based on the total reorientation of a society towards commodity production. Labour became a commodity, while in feudal and Asiatic economies labour was strictly based on personal relationships — the serf was obliged to work for a feudal landlord who not only chose the serf's wife but also used their children as labourers. In the capitalist mode, the means of production and the organisation of production were dictated by the market.[6]

In the capitalist mode class stratification took on a new dimension: production of commodities was primarily for the benefit of a numerically small class of bourgeois who controlled the means of production and the market, through their monopoly on capital which became the determining factor of economic life. Commodity production became the new orientation of society. Those who controlled the economic base became the ruling power. The emergence of capitalism in Europe was accompanied by bourgeois revolutions and the overthrow of the old feudal order.[7] Capitalism was highly competitive in its early stages in Europe and the state had to modify the broad divergencies between capital and labour. Over a hundred year period of struggle Parliamentary democracy emerged as the form of bourgeois rule.[8]

The genesis of English capitalism clearly indicates that external expansion served as an economic accelerator to intensify and hasten internal capitalist expansion.[9] The new character of expansionism that emerged in the latter part of the 19th century, that is, colonialism under capitalism, was inseperable from the internal production process in Britain. The more developed the internal productive processes, the more powerful the state and the military apparatus became, and the easier it was to move on to new conquests abroad.[10]

As capitalist development progressed over more than a century, the early forms of colonialism reflected this process. Mercantile capitalism had acted mainly to control and subordinate the external sphere of commerce and distribution. Only when industrial capitalism in the metropoles had been achieved did colonialism change its character. It was then that the production relations, the productive forces, and the political superstructure of the colonized societies were destroyed or deformed for the benefit of colonizing capitalism. These societies ceased to exist as autonomous self-determining entities and became integrated parts of capitalism which had by now established itself on a world scale. This process, which is defined as imperialism, unilaterally linked the colonialized societies with the highly industrialized societies.

On a socio-economic level, the expansion of capitalism created a system consisting of a few dominant countries, known as the metropoles, and the colonies, the periphery.[11] This system perpetuates itself economically by overaccumulation on the one side and underdevelopment on the other. The peripheral countries are forced to offer their natural wealth and their social potential (wage labour) for the benefit of the metropoles, whereas they receive little in return.

Underdevelopment is therefore characterised as:

1. the distortion of political and economic autonomy,
2. the imposition of capitalist structures which are not indigenous to these societies,
3. the orientation of the production processes to the economic needs of the metropolitan country,
4. the indigenous economy is not reproduced, its surplus is transferred abroad, leaving the colony impoverished,
5. the metropolitan economy overaccumulates, that is, the profits generated are larger than can be expected with the existing means of production,
6. the transfer of value from the periphery accounts for the increase of value in the metropole.[12]

With this basic presentation of the mechanisms of underdevelopment we can now analyse the same process in the context of Zambia's colonial past.

Underdevelopment in Action: Northern Rhodesia

The driving force behind the conquest of the uncolonised South African hinterland was British finance capital.[13] Having already monopolised the Witwatersrand gold and diamond fields, the goal of capital was to bring the prospective mineral bearing territories of Southern and Northern Rhodesia under control. This move coincided with an economic crisis in the South African mining industry. The new conquest had two aims: to expand the sphere of influence of British capital and simultaneously prevent rival capitalist interests from penetrating this region, and to overcome the South African crisis by broadening the field of accumulation. The rush for the hinterland was organised by the British South Africa Company (BSAC), representing Anglo-South African mining interests and British finance capital.[14] Whereas the ambitions of capital with respect to Southern Rhodesia were partially fulfilled, the territory north of the Zambezi proved to be an economic failure. Neither gold deposits nor other minerals were discovered. The BSAC found itself in possession of a colony which offered no economic advantage.

In contrast to the brutal colonial conquests elsewhere, Northern Rhodesia was taken over by means of treaties signed by various chiefs. Even the Bemba, whose economic system of slave trading and tribute raiding was greatly affected by the colonial intruders, were integrated into the new system relatively easily.[15] At this time the copper deposits were not yet exploited,[16] because the neighbouring Katangese mines were less expensive to operate and the processing of Zambian sulphide ores demanded a technology which was only perfected twenty years later. Furthermore, world demand for copper was low and easily met from North and Latin American sources.

The BSAC had close economic links with the Katangese copper mines and used these and other sources to generate income.[17] A railway system was established linking Katanga with Southern Rhodesia and South Africa from which the tariffs produced valuable income. The ever increasing demand for labour for the Katangan mines was satisfied by Northern Rhodesian migrants who by 1930 constituted more than 50% of the total labour force.[18] Hut and poll taxes were introduced, the classical method for partially integrating subsistence-oriented economies into capitalist commodity production. The peasants were either forced to sell a portion of their surplus on the market to pay their taxes to the colonial administration, or they were forced to seek employment for wages. This latter process happened where there was no market for their output as was frequently the case in the underdeveloped colonial capitalism of Northern Rhodesia. By these means the BSAC was able to satisfy two aims. It was able to meet the labour needs of the Katangan mines, and to cover the costs of administering an otherwise unprofitable colony. Up to 1923, the last year of BSAC rule, hut taxes alone accounted for more than two-thirds of colonial income in Northern Rhodesia.

If the initial returns to the colonial administrators were meagre, it was the same for the settlers.[19] Most of the settlers in the region were poor Boers trying to escape capitalist competition by moving north. They often by-passed Northern Rhodesia because of her poor soil and because the markets for agricultural produce were small. There was also little infrastructure. The internal market for settler farming was made up by the needs of officials, the mining prospectors and the labour force. The latter worked for the Broken Hill lead mine, the only one in operation, and the railways. These farmers also had to face the competition from the more efficient, price-cutting farmers of Southern Rhodesia who controlled the markets set up by the flourishing mining industries in their region. So most of the Northern Rhodesian settlers left agriculture and either engaged in transportation for their livelihood or left the colony altogether. Hence Northern Rhodesia never became a settler colony despite the low price of land. The administration tried to help by driving Africans into the reserves in the least fertile areas away from the line of rails.[20] Shortly after the First World War British colonial officials claimed that Northern Rhodesia was the poorest and least developed of the whole Empire.

This situation changed dramatically in the mid-1920s when the mining economy was finally established. It is therefore correct to date the beginning of the process of underdevelopment to 1925. From this time on, extractive industries exerted a tremendous effect on social transformation. The results still prevail, accounting for the socio-economic conditions of modern Zambia.[21] The creation of mining industry affected both the base and superstructure. This is why the approach of dualist theory is misleading both in methodology and in its neglect of the tripartite linkages between the world market, the mining industry and the subsistence sector. Dualism, which postulates coexisting – but unrelated – modern and traditional sectors cannot explain the basic aspects of the system. It cannot illuminate why the traditional sector is underdeveloped nor why the modern sector is unable to attain stable, self-generated growth despite high productivity and capital efficiency.[22] Dualism neglects the historical aspects of colonial development and is merely an ideology advocating foreign capital inputs as the only means of overcoming underdevelopment.[23] The creation of large-scale mining industries had severe effects on the colonial economy. The existing socio-economic structures were transformed into an outpost for the interests of international mining capital. The reasons for the emergence of a Northern Rhodesian copper industry are to be found in the development patterns of European and North American industrial accumulation.[24]

The First World War gave the basic impetus for new technological demands. The automobile and electrical industries led and shaped economic growth in the following decades. Their demand for raw materials, especially copper, was tremendous. Formerly, copper had been a strategic mineral used for military purposes, but now it became part of the industrial production and consumption nexus. This meant that additional mineral deposits had to be discovered and exploited. As the largest producer and consumer, the United States gained monopolistic control of the world copper market, and US monopolies developed a strategy to maintain this position. This explains why US capital secured 45% of the Copperbelt's production. Britain had felt her dependence on US supplies during the First World War, and therefore tried to achieve self-sufficiency in copper. Lacking large-scale funds necessary for starting mining operations, the British mining companies had to be supported by British finance capital which was subsidized by government. Roan Selection Trust (RST), the representative of US monopolies, and Anglo-American Corporation (AAC), the vehicle for British imperial ambitions, brought the Copperbelt under their control.[25]

The impact of these companies on the colonial economy was enormous. More than 90% of exports were and still are accounted for by copper. This means that long range planning has not been possible because of price fluctuations on the world market and that the Zambian economy is now confronted by unstable, perverted growth whose determining factors are outside national control. The two companies were the largest taxpayers in the country and the administration relied almost entirely on these revenues which gave the companies a hold on official policy. This explains why the companies were given a free hand in the way they exploited labour. Acting as monopolists in the labour market, RST and AAC dictated the wage rates offered, as well as the employment rate and in fact the very system of wage labour as a whole.

Due to the geological formation in Zambia, mining was mainly carried out underground. This means that the use of machinery was limited and the industry depended on the use of manpower. The skills required of mine labour were very limited so mining capital could employ untrained labour. Mining capital was motivated solely by the desire to extract surplus value and was not concerned about the social conditions of the labour force, nor the sources of new labour supplies. The perpetuation of high surplus value and the maintenance of a steady labour force were the main objectives of mining capital in the country. These aspects cannot be explained by the concept of dualism for the following reason. Suppose that the two economic sectors (capital and labour) were clearly separated from each other so that an equilibrium between wage rates and labour supply were to evolve. As long as the wage rates offered remained extremely low, the supply would be minimal. But this is not what happened in Northern Rhodesia. Wage rates were low, but there was abundant labour.

When the autonomy of the subsistence economy was broken, the peasantry had to enter the market. The subsistence surplus was exchanged for the commodities of capitalist production. This exchange was unequal because the penetration of merchant capital destroyed traditional trading partners such as local traders and craftsmen. Peasants were thus forced to rely on capitalist market exchange in order to guarantee their own reproduction and survival. This relationship, which was initiated with the aid of force, required the peasantry in the subsistence economy to comply with the system of wage labour in order to maintain their *status quo* and to pay taxes.

The peasant economy was thus structurally eroded and underdeveloped. It was integrated into the capitalist system without the possibility of resistance.[26] The patterns of underdevelopment are thus easily discerned; the peasantry offered its surplus in which more socially necessary labour time was incorporated than in the commodities received. Thus a permanent drain of value was begun. The peasantry responded by increasing the amount of surplus offered, thereby reducing the portion available for the reproduction of life. To ameliorate this situation, peasants entered into wage labour. But the mining companies dictated that the wage rates and the relief for the peasants from this source was very limited. The companies were working in collaboration with the state power to maintain this state of affairs. They were thus able to extract super-profits and achieve superaccumulation which was redirected to the benefit of the metropolitan economy.

The roots of underdevelopment in Zambia are therefore embedded in the establishment of mining monopolies which regarded the colony as a source of accumulation and raw material. This was the source of the process of underdevelopment and dependency.

Several aspects of capitalist development need to be emphasized. The process of 'super surplus value' extortion was only possible because of the outward orientation of the capitalist sector which had no concern for the problem of value realization. At the same time the reproduction costs of wage labour were covered by capitalism. After organizing wage labour, mining capital succeeded in erecting a double mechanism of super-exploitation. Wage rates were minimized by the monopoly power of mining capital as the sole employer of labour, and the reproduction of the labour force was guaranteed by the non-capitalist, that is, peasant sector.

A typical worker was employed for a contract period of one and a half years. Thereafter he was urged to return to his village. It was the village economy which provided his long-term reproduction costs including security in old age. His family normally remained in the village and was cared for there. This is in marked contrast with conditions in highly industrialized countries where the whole family is dependent on the wage alone.

A process of industrialization never began in the colony even though profit rates were high. This was because mining capital erected a colonial monopoly and carefully screened any new capital coming into the country. Only those factions of capital which saw their sphere of value generation guaranteed in the metropolitan countries had an interest in investing in the colony. It was mainly capital which wanted to lower capital costs in the metrpolitan industries (mineral resources in the case of constant capital, and food in the case of variable capital) which penetrated the colonies. (This pattern of uneven industrial development continues even now. Although modern technology has been established in the periphery, the very latest technology — software — is concentrated exclusively in the industrial core countries). The outward orientation of the capitalist enclave allowed super surplus value extortion. If new capital had taken wage labour as a field of realization, the colonial economic structure would have collapsed.

Conclusion

The colonial economic structure was oriented towards maximizing the profit of the capital that was directly engaged, in order to fulfil the strategic target of metropolitan capitalism which was to lower the capital input in the industrial plants of the metropole. This meant that with the same amount of capital, more industries could be established or that with a relatively small amount of capital, a plant could be established which might otherwise have demanded much greater capital.

The subjugation of the indigenous people was a precondition for the success of the imposed colonial economic structure. The object was to force the indigenous population to offer their labour and their surplus production for the benefit of the colonial capitalist sector.

Although capitalism did not extend beyond the enclave stage, its impact on the indigenous society was enormous. The entire socio-economic structures were transformed and distorted for the exclusive benefit of metropolitan capital. Underdevelopment, therefore means the distortion of once autonomous economic and political relations, and the implantation of a capitalist sector which, as an outpost of international capitalism, extorts raw materials (minerals) and human resources (labour) for the benefit of the colonizing power. Zambia was forced to undergo the process of underdevelopment because of its mineral wealth.

References

I wish to thank the German Research Foundation (DFG) for the financial support to do research work at the National Archives of Zambia in Lusaka. This article is a summary of part 1 of my book *Zambia: Abhangigkeit und Unterentwicklung*, Bonn 1979.
1. These are mainly concentrated on two levels: (1) the structural gap

between town and country, and (2) the incapability of the capitalist sector to achieve a self-gearing growth independent from international capital.

2. This will say that Zambia occupies a strategic place in the accumulation processes of international capital which relies heavily on her raw materials. As the raw material industries were historically established for the sake of international capital which even today informally controls the world market Zambia's colonial heritage was the reliance on copper production and on the cooperation with international capital.

3. Colonialism can historically be defined as early phase of capital expansion which due to the low standard of production forces was closely linked with direct occupation. Whereas imperialism means both direct occupation and informal control (neo-colonialism).

4. J. Schumpeter, 'Zur Soziologie des Imperialismus', *Archiv Fur Sozialwissenschaft und Sozialpolitik*, 46 (1919).

5. In economic terms, this means that the political superstructure of the colonized society was eroded in one strategic aspect — the military domination — whereas the organization of the production processes remained largely intact.

6. Emergent capitalism was therefore simultaneously accompanied by driving free peasants from their land in order to deprive them of their means of production and to force them into wage labour conditions of the newly established manufacturers. This pattern applies to all capitalist societies, be it the colonial or the colonizing society.

7. For example, cf. the English 'Glorious Revolution' and a century later the French Revolution.

8. This aspect needs a deeper discussion in respect of the adoption of Western political models in post-colonial African states.

9. Cf. E. Mandel, *Marxist Economic Theory*, 2 vols (New York, 1969).

10. For example, the history of the 'Scramble for Africa'.

11. These terms indicate that capitalism as a world-wide system is structurally based on uneven development. That means that successful revolution, for example, in the periphery must at first overcome the burden of capitalist deformation.

12. W. Biermann, 'The relevance of the Latin American debate on "Dependencia" ', (Paper presented in April 1979 at University of Zambia).

13. T. Gregory, *Ernst Oppenheimer and the Economic Development of Southern Africa*, (Cape Town, 1962).

14. R. E. Baldwin, *Economic Development and Export Growth: A Study of Northern Rhodesia, 1910-1960* (Berkeley, 1966).

15. L. H. Gann, *A History of Northern Rhodesia* (London, 1964).

16. The deposits were known since 1905. See J. Bancroft, *Mining in Northern Rhodesia* (London, 1961).

17. Particularly Tanganyika Concessions which was associated with French and Belgian finance.

18. H. Heisler, *Urbanization and the Government of Migration: the interrelationship of urban and rural life in Zambia* (London, 1974).

19. See L. H. Gann, *The Birth of a Plural Society* (Manchester, 1958).

20. See, for example, R. H. Bates, *Patterns of Uneven Development*

causes and consequences in Zambia (Denver, 1974).

21. Northern Rhodesia and post-colonial Zambia depend on copper production: copper forms more than 90% of the total export volume; copper industries' share at the GNP amounts to an average 50%; copper industries are the greatest taxpayers and the greatest labour employers. In the case of crisis, as in 1930 and 1974, the economy suffered from a tremendous setback with a GNP declining by more than 10% p.a.

22. See the calculations of Baldwin, *op. cit.*

23. Defining the traditional sector as low productive, the economic take-off can only start if massive capital inputs take place. These inputs can only come from abroad due to the low level of internal accumulation for industrialization.

24. See L. H. Gann, 'The Northern Rhodesian Copper Industry and the World of Copper', *Rhodes-Livingstone Journal*, 8 (1955).

25. See Gregory *op. cit.*

26. As their social values were extorted and as no alternative trade partner was existent the peasants had to rely on the capitalist market relation. Furthermore they could not return to autarky because their economy was an open one.

Study Questions

1. What are the historical roots of underdevelopment?
2. In which way do colonial societies differ structurally from the colonizing metropoles?
3. Which are the elements of underdevelopment?
4. How did underdevelopment start in Northern Rhodesia (Zambia)?
5. Which periodization can be discerned?
6. Discuss the mechanisms of superaccumulation and superexploitation in the concrete Northern Rhodesian context.

9. Robert Klepper

Zambian Agricultural Structure and Performance

Agriculture in Zambia has not fulfilled its potential. The basic structure of the economy remains heavily biased toward the production and export of minerals as it was in the colonial period. The nation imports large quantities of foodstuffs and relies heavily on a relatively small number of commercial and emergent farmers for its domestic agricultural output.[1] Zambia has become one of the most urbanized economies in Africa as people continue to desert the countryside for the greater economic opportunities in urban areas.[2] This essay attempts to elucidate the basic structural causes of this continuing imbalance in the economy and the limitations of government policies that have attempted to change it.

The development, or underdevelopment, of the rural sector in Zambia fits neatly into the framework of dependency theory. Colonial Zambia was developed as an export enclave; agriculture was secondary to the concerns of mining. Labour was drawn from the rural sector to work on the mines, and the rural sector served as a reserve to which this labour returned at the end of mining contracts or in old age. A settler class of European farmers was established to provide food for the mines and for the urban sector that grew around mining activity. The resulting development was extremely uneven. A rich export enclave was supported at the time of independence by about 1,200 expatriate farmers and a few thousand African farmers who produced for this market. Rural areas experienced considerable emigration of working-age adults which reduced the ability of the population in those areas to produce surpluses or even to meet subsistence needs. The highly skewed income distribution in the economy generated demands for imported luxury goods.

A fundamental barrier to agricultural development in the post-colonial period has been the continued dominance of the mining economy. Soon after independence the new government announced development goals that would have restructured the economy had they been achieved.[3] The economy was to be diversified into manufacturing and improved agricultural production. Income differentials were to be reduced between rural and urban areas. Industry was to be located in rural areas and comprehensive rural development was envisioned. Now, fifteen years after independence, Zambia still has a mono-economy.[4] Gross Domestic Product (GDP) and agricultural output have grown, but agriculture as a share of GDP has remained nearly constant.[5] Agricultural exports have grown a little in monetary terms, but when the effects of inflation are considered the real value of agricultural exports is no higher now than at independence, and agricultural exports are still dwarfed by the exports of minerals.[6] No survey has been conducted that would allow a calculation of recent income distribution, but data for 1972/73 show no substantial improvement in the first years of Independence, and there is no reason to believe that the situation is any different today.[7] Labour has continued to migrate from rural to urban areas, and if this flow has slackened recently, it is a consequence of the economic crisis of Zambia in the mid and late 1970s, which has raised unemployment rates in urban areas and caused real incomes to fall.[8] Rural areas are still labour reserves for the urban economy. Development within agriculture itself has been very uneven between regions and between households within regions.

There have been government initiatives in agriculture, but they have consisted mostly of provision of infrastructure and services. These are necessary for rural development, and they have been helpful for selected farmers, but for reasons elaborated below the majority of Zambia's peasant farmers are unable to utilize government services effectively.

The Colonial Period

To understand the problems of Zambian agriculture it is necessary to have some understanding of the colonial past.[9] The whole colonial effort was launched by the granting of a charter to the British South Africa Company on the expectation of discovering and exploiting minerals. It was almost forty years before these expectations were realized with the discovery of copper sulfide ores in the Copperbelt in the mid-1920s. Mining boomed in the period before the Great Depression in the 1930s and again in World War II and thereafter.

Twenty years after the discovery of copper the underdevelopment of rural areas in Zambia was well advanced. Colonial agricultural policy was twisted to the service of mining. European farmers were settled in Central, Southern and Eastern Provinces, in the areas of good soils and easy access to markets. In the process African farmers in these areas were resettled, frequently on poorer soils and in areas with more difficult access to markets. Hut and poll taxes were levied to drive African labour into mining and the urban sector. African farmers away from the line of rail and the transportation routes in Eastern Province had no means of delivering output to markets even if they could produce a surplus, and large numbers migrated to the mines and urban areas in search of employment. In the period of the Great Depression when demand for foodstuffs for the mines plummeted, the reduced market was largely reserved for European farmers, and for more than ten years in the 1930s and 1940s the colonial government paid African farmers less than Europeans for the same crops. Virtually no extension services were available to African farmers. Those few who adopted more advanced technology did so by imitating European methods, and these farmers were largely confined to the line of rail and Eastern Province. Colonial development plans after World War II concentrated on infrastructure for the mining economy. The few agricultural programmes initiated specifically for Africans reached a very small fraction of all African farmers, and they were motivated mainly by concerns for deteriorating soil quality and erosion, not production levels and farm income. Government provided no formal training programmes for African farmers or agriculturalists. In short, colonial economic policy viewed Africans and the rural areas as sources of cheap labour for the mines and urban sector. Agricultural policy reinforced this goal, and its primary objective was the provision of cheap food for the mines.

Zambia's export enclave economy created enormous problems for agricultural development in the newly independent country. Most marketed agricultural output was produced by slightly more than one thousand European farmers, half of whom left in the first five years of the post-colonial period. African farmers who produced a surplus for the market, and who were in the cash economy, were concentrated in Central, Southern and Eastern Provinces. Other areas of Zambia without access to agricultural markets and with virtually no agricultural services suffered severe emigration to urban areas. The underdeveloped rural areas of Zambia suffered shortages of labour, they had virtually no fixed or working capital for agriculture, and agricultural technology and skills were limited to traditional subsistence methods. The outlying provinces of Northern, Luapula, Northwestern and Western are also areas of poor soils and the traditional crops in these regions are cassava, sorghum and finger millet which have limited markets in the urban economy. In summary, the colonial policy created conditions of severe resource constraints for hundreds of thousands of Zambia's peasant households reducing their viability as subsistence units with little or no potential of producing a surplus for the market.

Post-colonial Government Policy

In the last two decades Zambia has had a few successes in its agricultural economy. In most years the country has been largely self-sufficient in maize. The government established a successful sugar plantation in cooperation with a multinational firm that made the nation self-sufficient in sugar by the mid-1970s. The poultry industry has grown substantially; much of this has been under the tutelage of foreign firms.[10] But the areas in which the nation falls short of its goals of self-sufficiency and the expansion of agricultural exports are far larger in number. The production of wheat, cotton, oilseeds, milk, tea, coffee and rice are all less than the levels necessary to meet national demand.[11] There would still be large imports of beef if the government had not stopped beef imports in the mid-1970s. Agricultural exports, primarily tobacco and maize, have remained virtually unchanged in the post-colonial period, and no significant new exports have been developed. Nor has the government succeeded or made progress in reducing income differentials between urban and rural areas and between the more developed and the less developed rural areas.

Like other Third World countries Zambia has had problems of shortages of skilled labour and managers.[12] It has had to grapple with the problems of introducing new technology. Its natural resources for agriculture are not distributed equally throughout the country.[13] Like other exporters of primary commodities Zambia has faced a world in which the prices of its imports have risen relative to the prices of its exports.[14] But it also had the advantage in the immediate post-colonial period of sizeable surpluses from copper production.[15] The poor performance of the rural sector cannot be entirely blamed on lack of resources, relative prices, technology and lack of skilled manpower. A basic reason lies in the continued dominance of the mining economy.

The mining economy and urban sector that surrounds it have received most of the investment, much of the expenditure on infrastructure, most of the talented management and skilled personnel.[16] It has been uppermost in the concerns of Zambia's civil servants, businessmen and political leaders and has received most of the attention of foreign investors. Civil servants avoid living and working in rural areas if possible because they earn more in urban employment.[17] Even graduates of Zambia's School of Agriculture would prefer to work in urban areas. The Zambian government has failed to break the economic dependency and the dominance of the mining economy and has failed to build a vigorous, thriving agriculture. The remainder of this essay provides an outline of the major directions in government agricultural policy and seeks to explain why government policy has had so little success.

There are three major contradictions or conflicts that run through most agricultural policy choices in Zambia. The first is the conflict between urban pressures and rural pressures. On balance urban interests overwhelm rural interests. The second is the choice that arises between concentrating government efforts and programmes on commercial and emergent farmers or on peasant farmers. Government policy favours farmers who are already better off. And, finally, there is the conflict between pursuing a capitalist or a socialist approach to agricultural development. Zambia has adopted the capitalist road in agriculture.

Shortly after independence the government made an ill-fated attempt to end the nation's reliance on the relatively small number of European commercial farmers and emergent African farmers who produce most of the marketed agricultural output, and set out to expand agricultural output on a broader base. A programme of producer cooperatives was initiated in 1965 which was to be a vehicle for bringing hundreds of thousands of peasant households into the cash economy producing marketable surpluses that would restructure Zambian agriculture and provide a surplus beyond the nation's requirements for export. The resulting increased incomes in the peasant economy would narrow income differentials and provide one of the prerequisites for further rural development. Rural development in turn would act to hold people in rural areas and stem emigration to the cities.

This policy evolved at the same time as President Kaunda was beginning to expound the nation's ideology of Humanism — one variant of the range of populist approaches to development which are frequently termed African

Socialism.

Producer cooperatives failed and the failure had far reaching consequences for agricultural policy in Zambia. Government rhetoric still refers to the peasant agricultural sector and to agricultural policy as 'Humanist' and 'socialist', but in reality peasant agriculture is firmly organized along capitalist lines and government policy toward peasant farmers is essentially one of providing infrastructure and services. As I shall argue in more detail below, this approach offers little hope of rapidly improving agricultural technology among peasant farmers, bringing them firmly into the cash economy and narrowing income differentials. The capitalist approach might have effectively spurred output from commercial and emergent farmers if it had been properly executed. But there is abundant evidence that inadequate price incentives, uncertain supplies of agricultural requisites and poorly conceived and executed government production schemes reduced this potential to a mediocre performance.

Any ten people could register as a cooperative and become eligible for government loans. Cooperatives could be formed in a wide range of enterprises including building, fishing and marketing, but most of those registered were agricultural producer cooperatives. Once registered, agricultural cooperatives were eligible for seasonal loans for requisites, medium term loans for capital improvements and farm equipment, and stumping subsidies for clearing land.

By 1969 producer cooperatives had failed in large numbers and were unable to repay the sizeable loans that were made to them. The reasons for this failure are analyzed in a dissertation by Stephen Quick.[18] He argues convincingly that the government provided far too much money in loans and subsidies to most cooperatives. They were incapable of utilizing the capital productively, tended to treat the money as income rather than investment funds, and were unable to repay. The inability of cooperatives to use the capital to increase output also related to the low level of farming ability and general managerial ability of members of most producer cooperatives. The programme seriously misjudged the capabilities of the peasant farmers to run rather sophisticated agricultural enterprises. Furthermore, the producer cooperatives were premised on the assumption that the traditional village was a kind of natural cooperative unit which could be transformed into a modern communal production unit with the addition of modern agricultural technology. Quick's analysis challenges this assumption as does the work of other social scientists for other African countries.[19] The government failed to organize and train cadres to work in rural areas and bring to the peasantry ideological training as a complement to putting fertilizers, tractors, and ploughs in their hands.

With the failure of most producer cooperatives, the Zambian government revised its agricultural policy toward small farmers. Policy is now oriented toward the individual household through the provision of services.[20] There have been no further attempts to build cooperative or communal production units, although marketing and service cooperatives are still encouraged by the government.

The organization of peasant agriculture is more accurately characterized as capitalist or pre-capitalist than socialist. The interaction between peasant families, and between peasant families and state institutions is capitalist in nature. The state owns all agricultural land which is alienated to peasant families under traditional tenure, but once in control of a piece of land a peasant family usually has perpetual rights to the land and any improvements on it so long as they continue to farm it. All other means of production are privately owned. The reinvestment of profits or surplus is entirely a private matter. The relationship between the peasant household and the state credit and marketing agencies is typical of lending and marketing arrangements in other developing countries, where agriculture is organized along capitalist lines. The intervention of the state through planning, if indeed the state intervenes at all, is limited to the provision of a well, a school, a clinic or a feeder road — the provision of infrastructure — and it has nothing to do with the organization of production or production decisions.

The current policy toward peasant households is twofold. Most important is the provision of marketing, credit, extension, health and education services. The second component is the initiation of various settlement schemes. Neither approach is adequate for rapid and comprehensive rural development. While government services are a necessary condition for the transformation of peasant agriculture, government services alone are insufficient for the many peasant households facing constraints so severe that they are unable to qualify for or are unable to take advantage of the services offered.

Credit through the Agricultural Finance Company (AFC) might offer the greatest hope of overcoming the constraints faced by poor peasants. Credit could be used to provide draught power, hire labour and purchase modern inputs, but farm credit does little to aid the poorer peasants. The AFC uses a package system that specifies certain levels of various purchased inputs according to the crop and the area planted with that crop. This package system is not designed for the needs of peasant farmers. The smallest areas for which the AFC will make loans are frequently larger than the total area cultivated by a typical peasant household. The package makes no allowance for the poorer soils which many peasants cultivate and does not provide for hiring labour until relatively large areas are under cultivation. No loans are made for cassava, finger millet and sorghum which are major crops for peasants.[20] Fewer than 5% of all peasant households receive loans from AFC.

The frequently poor quality of government marketing services discourages peasant production of surplus for sale. Marketing in the outlying provinces of Zambia is now superior to that of the colonial period, but there are continual and well-founded complaints about marketing services. The depots are too far apart in some areas; agricultural requisites are frequently late for planting, fertilizing or insect control; supplies may be inadequate; the wrong materials may be stocked; and the quantities in which requisites are sold are sometimes too large for the areas that many small farmers cultivate. The marketing agencies are frequently late in buying the farmer's output; purchases are not made in units of less than 90 kg for most crops; the farmer is not paid in cash but by cheque; and he frequently must wait months for payment. Any one of the above-mentioned problems may be sufficient to deter a poor peasant farmer from marketing output or marketing as much as he would if marketing services were better. And, of course, no amount of marketing services will help the peasant farmer who is unable to produce a surplus for sale.

Extension services are now provided while there were practically none in the colonial period, but the extension effort has faults. The government has provided a network of agricultural camps staffed with extension agents that spans the country. The average number of farmers per extension worker is lower than in many African countries, but the training and ability of extension workers is not the best. And extension is plagued by a shortage of transportation which reduces the number of farmers who can be reached by each extension worker.[21] Farmer Training Centres and Farm Institutes have been initiated to bring farmers into residential training programmes which concentrate training and reduce transportation problems. But evaluations of the extension service have shown that it is biased toward farmers who are already better off, frequently uses methods of instruction poorly suited to farmers who are illiterate, and tends to ignore women who do much of the agricultural work in Zambia.[22]

Aside from services, the government has initiated a range of production schemes administered by various parastatals. The typical formula is to resettle selected farmers on state land, provide services and infrastructure such as water, roads, extension, credit, marketing, tractor hire and general project management. In the context of general rural development two points are important. First, the better farmers are selected for the schemes. Once again farmers who are already better off have greater opportunity. Second, and more important, the government's production schemes benefit a very small fraction of Zambia's farmers, and the overall effort is too small relative to the total Zambian agricultural output to have much influence on imports and exports.

The failure of producer cooperatives in the early years after independence and the subsequent adoption of a policy of services to individual peasant households defeated the hopes of rapid, widespread agricultural development in Zambia. The government has continued to rely heavily on the relatively small number of European commercial farmers as well as African emergent farmers producing substantial surpluses for the market.[23]

Government policy measures have fallen far short of the steps that would have brought forth the greatest rate of growth of marketed output from these farmers and stimulated Zambia's agricultural exports. A major problem has been government pricing policy which has provided inadequate incentives for commercial and emergent farmers. Additional problems have been created by the government's exchange rate policy and the erratic provision of inputs. These problems stem from the dominance of the mining sector in Zambia's economy and the conflicts this generates for government policy.

Independent Zambia inherited from the colonial regime a system that held down food prices for the mining and urban sectors by paying low prices to farmers and by subsidizing the transportation, handling and processing of foodstuffs for urban consumers. This policy was continued in all its essential respects. Pricing policy has been less than generous to farmers over most of the post-colonial period. Producer prices have frequently been set at levels substantially lower than those Zambia paid to import the same agricultural commodities from other countries. And, until recently, government set much higher consumer subsidies than those in the colonial period. In her analysis of Zambian pricing policy, Doris Dodge condemns this for making the achievement of all the nation's goals in agriculture more difficult.[24]

Furthermore, government pricing policy directed agricultural output, particularly from commercial farmers, away from grain, oil seeds and tobacco and toward livestock production. Grain prices.are controlled and the wholesale price of livestock is not. Selling cattle or pigs on the uncontrolled wholesale market has the additional advantage of allowing farmers to escape close scrutiny by government officials and thereby hide some farm income from taxes. When these factors are combined with the uncertain availability of agricultural requisites and the now exorbitant cost of farm machinery, commercial farmers have increasingly been motivated to shift their production away from crops and toward livestock production.

Exchange rate policy has had an adverse effect on agricultural exports.[25] Throughout much of the post-colonial period the Zambian government has overvalued its currency making the cost of imports in kwacha artifically low and the export prices of Zambian commodities in foreign currencies artificially high. Zambia was already in a poor position to expand agricultural exports because of the long and expensive transportation routes to the sea and the very limited markets for Zambian agricultural output in neighbouring countries whose economies are also based on agriculture. Exchange rate policy put one more obstacle in the path of expanding agricultural exports. Again, it is the mining and urban sectors that benefit from the cheap imported goods and the opportunity to remit dividends and gratuities that are worth more in foreign currency if the exchange rate is overvalued.

Another obstacle to agricultural progress has been the uncertain provision of agricultural inputs to farmers. Too frequently inputs have arrived late and in insufficient quantities or not at all. Acquiring spare parts for farm machinery became increasingly difficult in the mid and late 1970s when Zambia's economic crisis slowed the flow of imports of essential commodities for months at a time.

The net effect of these impediments to commercial and emergent farmers in Zambia has been to retard the rate of growth of Zambian agricultural output and exports.

Summary
Zambia's agriculture has not fulfilled its promise. After fifteen years of

government declarations of intentions to diversify the economy into agriculture and raise agricultural exports, Zambia's economy remains firmly entrenched in its dependence on minerals and mineral exports. The goal of narrowing income differentials has also been unfulfilled. The distorted and misshapened economy was born in Zambia's colonial past. The colonial government built an export enclave in which agriculture served mining. Government policy in the last two decades has been inadequate to the task of freeing Zambia from this dependency.

The producer cooperative movement of the mid and late 1960s was an initiative that might have started the process of rapid rural development, but it was poorly planned and executed, and there was no political mobilization of the peasantry which would have been a precondition for the success of a socialist rural development policy. Producer cooperatives failed in large numbers and the whole programme was abandoned a few years after it was launched. Government then chose a capitalist rural development policy of providing infrastructure and services to peasant agriculture, but the previous underdevelopment of the Zambian peasantry rendered many peasant households incapable of effectively utilizing government services. And in many instances the services have been biased toward emergent farmers.

The capitalist road Zambia has followed in agricultural policy has had a poor payoff for commercial and emergent farmers. Price incentives have been inadequate and have favoured the mining sector; exchange rate policies have worked against expanding agricultural exports and have favoured the mining sector; and the provision of inputs to agriculture has been uncertain in recent years. All these factors have worked against a more rapid rate of growth of output from commercial and emergent farmers.

Behind these inappropriate policy choices for genuine rural development is the continued dominance of mining. Until Zambia breaks the grip of mining on its economy, progress in rural development is likely to be slow, uncertain and uneven.

References

1. It is now customary to distinguish between three types of farmers in Zambia: commercial farmers who market nearly all of their output, peasant farmers who market less than 50% of their output and emergent farmers who have risen out of the ranks of the peasantry and market more than 50% of their output.
2. Approximately 50% of Zambia's population now lives in urban areas.
3. For development goals, see Central Planning Office, *An Outline of the Transitional Development Plan* (Lusaka, 1965), and Office of National Development and Planning, *First National Development Plan, 1966-1970* (Lusaka, 1966).
4. Government officials readily conceded the unbalanced nature of the Zambian economy, for example, 'Address by Mr. L. C. Sichilongo,

Permanent Secretary, Ministry of Finance to the Economics Club, 28 February 1979,' mimeo.

5. Total agricultural output including production for subsistence rose from an estimated K97.4 million in 1965 to K260.3 million in 1977. If the effects of inflation are removed and output is measured in constant 1965 prices, agricultural output rose from K97.4 million in 1965 to K137 million in 1977. The share of total agricultural output in Gross Domestic Product was 13.7% in 1965 and 13.5% in 1977. There has been virtually no change over the period since Independence. These data are in various issues of Central Statistical Office, *Monthly Digest of Statistics* (Lusaka) or can be calculated from data in this source.

6. By far the most important agricultural exports are tobacco and maize. The value of tobacco and maize exports was K6.8 million in 1965 and K9.3 million in 1977. Since Independence the value of these exports has ranged from a low of close to K3 million to a high of slightly over K12 million. But exports of these two commodities have always been less than 3% of the value of mineral exports in any one year since Independence and were a mere 1.4% of mineral exports in 1977. These data are calculated from various issues of the *Monthly Digest of Statistics*.

7. Jobs and Skills Programme for Africa, Employment Advisory Mission, International Labour Office, *Narrowing the Gaps; Planning for Basic Needs and Productive Employment in Zambia* (Addis Ababa, 1977) Table II-3, p. 292. These income distribution data do not differentiate between urban and rural incomes, but most of the poor in Zambia live in rural areas. The 1969 Turner Report to the Government of Zambia estimated the annual income of mine workers at K1,300, wage earners outside the mining sector at K640 per year and peasant farm income of K145 per year, *Report of the Second National Convention on Rural Development, Incomes, Wages, and Prices in Zambia* (Lusaka, 1970).

8. See Jacob Mwanza's essay on migration in this collection.

9. The material in this section is drawn from a number of sources which include Doris Jansen Dodge, *Agricultural Policy and Performance in Zambia* (Berkeley, 1977); S. N. Makings, 'Agricultural Change in Northern Rhodesia/Zambia: 1945-1965,' *Food Research Institute Studies* 1, 2 (1966); and John A. Hellen, *Rural Economic Development in Zambia, 1890-1964* (Munich, 1968).

10. Data on marketed crop output are available from the Planning Unit, Ministry of Agriculture and Water Resources, 'Summary of crop intake by official marketing organizations in Zambia as from 1964-65 to date,' mimeo, n. d. Marketings of livestock and livestock products are available from the same source, but these data are much less reliable because of the large, unknown fraction that is marketed privately and escapes enumeration by government agencies.

11. Food imports have constituted less than 10% of the total value of Zambian imports in most years since Independence (see the *Monthly Digest of Statistics*), but imports of some individual foods have been large relative to domestic production. For example, in 1975, the most recent year for which detailed import data are published, Zambia

imported 1,120 tons of rice as against 358 tons domestically produced in the 1974/75 marketing season, 12,000 tons of wheat and 444 tons of wheat flour as against virtually no domestic wheat output (marketed wheat output increased to 934 tons in the 1975/76 marketing period), and 435 tons of coffee and coffee products versus 11 tons of domestic production.

12. Richard Jolly, 'The Skilled Manpower Constraint', in Charles Elliott (ed.), *Constraints on the Economic Development of Zambia* (Nairobi, 1971) and Management Development and Advisory Service of the Management Development Unit, 'Final Report of the Zambia Managerial Manpower and Training Needs Survey of the Private and Parastatal Sectors,' (Lusaka, 1977).

13. Jurgen Schultz, *Land Use in Zambia, Part I: The Basically Traditional Land Use Systems and Their Regions* (Munich, 1976).

14. See the index numbers of unit value of imports and exports in the *Monthly Digest of Statistics*. On a base of 1969 = 100, the 1975 import unit value index stood at 213 while the unit value index for exports was 71.

15. Data for central government current revenue and expenditure are in the *Monthly Digest of Statistics*. From 1967 through 1970 government never received less than K150 million in revenue from mining and in 1970 mining revenues were K250 million.

16. In the past much of total government investment in agriculture was channelled through the Ministry of Agriculture. In the whole of the Second National Plan period (1972-76), direct government investment in agriculture was never greater than 5.5% of total government investment and in most years it was less than 5% of the total. Calculated from *Financial Report for the year ending 1972 through 1976* (Lusaka, 1977).

17. For example, school teachers with Form III education earn twice as much as agricultural extension workers with the same education. From an address by Mr. Alexander Chikwanda, Minister of Agriculture to a seminar at the School of Agriculture, University of Zambia, 16 February 1979.

18. Stephen A. Quick, 'Bureaucracy and Rural Socialism: The Zambian Experience' (Stanford University, PhD dissertation, 1975).

19. See S. E. Migot-Adholla, 'Traditional Society and Cooperatives', in Carl Gosta Widstrand (ed.), *Co-operatives and Rural Development in East Africa* (New York, 1970).

20. 'The basis of our farming industry ought to be the *small-to-medium sized* family farm. This is socially the most viable structure; it is economically feasible and it is fully in line with the principles of Humanism . . . Therefore, development officers, e.g. in credit, co-operatives, extension and training, research departments and others in this field, should in the future see it as their main task to promote the family farm.' (emphasis in original) Address by the President K. D. Kaunda at the Opening of a Seminar on Rural Development, held in Lusaka in 23 March 1970, mimeo.

21. N. Mukutu, 'The Department of Agriculture—Extension Services,' (Ministry of Rural Development, mimeo, 1975).

22. David Honeybone and Alan Marter, 'An Evaluation Study of Zambia's Farm Institutes and Farmer Training Centres' (Rural Development Studies Bureau, University of Zambia, 1975).

23. There are no firm estimates of the number of farmers by type in Zambia, but commercial farmers number 1,000 or less, and there are twenty to forty thousand emergent farmers. By way of contrast there are more than 600,000 peasant farm households.

24. D. J. Dodge, *op. cit.*, p. 138.

25. G. L. Scott argues for devaluation in 'Kwacha Devaluation; A Case to Answer', *Enterprise*, 3 (1978).

Study Questions

1. In what ways has the mining industry affected the pattern of agricultural production in Zambia?

2. What methods did the Zambian government introduce to improve agricultural production in the post-colonial period? What were the results of these initiatives?

10. Lionel Cliffe

Labour Migration and Peasant Differentiation: Zambian Experiences

Peasants in Zambia, as elsewhere in Southern Africa, were drawn into the world economy as labour migrants, and even now, when urban employment is more permanent, the rural areas are given over more to the reproduction of labour than to the production of commodities. The resulting general impoverishment has not, however, precluded significant differentiation among the various regional peasantries. Moreover, in these peasantries, where many men are absent, resulting changes in property rights related to kinship and in the division of labour between sexes mean that the position of women within the pattern of class formation must be specially examined. Differentiation and the special position of women have to be taken into account in assessing the political potential in societies whose complexity gives special meaning to the 'worker-peasant alliance'.

Much of the southern half of the African continent is aptly termed 'Africa of the labour reserves'[1]. The terms on which most of the African people of most of the areas of Southern and Central Africa have been integrated into the capitalist world economy have been through labour migration rather than the direct production of commodities. In all the countries immediately to the north of the Zambezi, as well as the well-known examples to the south, not only have large numbers of African men come as *gastarbeiter* in mines, farms and industries installed by whites and run as capitalist production units; but the communities from which these migrants come have become geared to the production and reproduction of this special form of exported labour power.

This phenomenon of labour migration has, of course, received a great deal of scholarly attention for at least a generation. In Zambia with which this paper is chiefly concerned, this theme was the chief focus of a considerable body of research, from the late 1930s until Independence in 1964. Intensive case studies were made of both the rural areas denuded by the labour exodus, and the townships that received them. But the subject deserves renewed consideration as the momentous crisis facing the region, and its central magnet South Africa, looms closer. Any assessment of the social forces at work in Southern Africa to transform the structure of 'labour reserves' must in fact come to terms with the whole 'set' of social relationships embracing 'temporary proletarian' and 'partial peasant' status. In particular, this paper will seek to relate patterns of labour migration to the different peasantries which spawn them, and in so doing will raise three basic issues.

The first concern will be to scotch the implicitly accepted notion that because such patterns of labour migration as have developed in Southern Africa have produced, and in fact required, a particularly virulent and backward form of underdevelopment in the 'reserves', then any tendency toward differentiation among the peasantry is swamped by the general impoverishment. Rather, we shall show that although the source areas are not primarily producing commodities (other than labour power) nevertheless the cash nexus, entering by the back door, does set in train a process of class formation in those areas.

A second matter, that is of considerable relevance in the present crisis, concerns our conceptualisation in class terms of people who do not fit snugly into either the 'worker' or 'peasant' pigeonhole. Answers to the questions of where they should be situated, what their 'consciousness' amounts to, and their revolutionary potential have been offered for many years. Indeed, in a work only recently accessible to an English audience, Kautsky recognised that such migrants had dual characteristics and might even play a dual and apparently contradictory role: 'while they constitute a backward element in the towns, often acting as strikebreakers, or impeding unionisation, they are tremendous agents of progress in their own villages . . . It is often these elements who become agitators and instigators of class discontent and class hatred in their home villages.'[2]

One recent study of this issue in relation to Zambia comes to an opposite conclusion to that above, similar though it is to that of Cabral who stressed the significance of such young migrants for the struggle in Guinea-Bissau. Palmberg[3] sees these 'worker peasants' as 'simultaneously participants in two different modes of production' but argues that their role will only be progressive in so far as they exhibit an emerging class consciousness *as workers.* In this she is taking issue with an earlier formulation that in Africa the lower strata of (temporary) workers were best considered as part of the peasantry, while the more permanently urbanised, but much better paid workers, were not a proletariat proper but more of a labour aristocracy.[4] That this debate is not solely of academic significance has been borne out by recent events in South Africa. Were the actions of Zulu migrant labourers, the most downtrodden workers in the Republic, in attacking students and other demonstrators in Soweto proof of Kautsky's thesis or the result of false consciousness? Even if a final answer is not offered here, an exploration of how migrants fit into the whole complex of social relationships of production might illuminate the problem. Specifically, we will argue that the issue of consciousness and the migrant's political role cannot be understood without situating the migrant in a certain class position within the particular peasant social formation to which he still has some attachment.

An examination of the problematic of 'worker-peasant' in conditions of labour migration brings us to a final issue. The question of whether the migrant wears the worker or peasant hat is in some sense wrongly posed. The migrating male may well be a participant in two modes of production, but so (on different terms) are the other members of the family. (Indeed the set of relationships known as 'family' is in flux as it is at the heart of the articulation between the two modes.) In a sense, the man is a 'worker' and the woman is the peasant in this kind of situation. Our analysis must therefore explore the dynamics of those relationships of production subsumed under 'kinship', in particular questions of inheritance, marriage and the sexual division of labour. But these dimensions have to be related to the other dimensions of differentiation. In other words, the patterns of peasant differentiation that must be looked for in labour source areas are not simply the inequalities and antagonisms that might exist between different peasant *families* considered as units. A more complex survey of the changing relationships of production, especially as they affect woman and her labour, is required. This in turn means that the 'woman question' is absolutely central to the discussion of political consciousness and action.

The Nature of Labour Migration Systems

The origins of labour migration in Southern and Central Africa were to be found in the need for labour power as capitalist farms, mines and industries were set up by settlers. There was nothing unique about their installation, but the means of guaranteeing the supply of labour power became characteristic of the region. The extraction of the necessary labour power for the newly imposed units of production of course necessitated some penetration of the existing pre-capitalist social formations and their subservience to the demands of capitalist production. But the institutionalisation of labour migration and the efforts to perpetuate what had previously been regarded as a transitional phenomenon had an evolving logic for the capitalists. The responsibility for providing for the long-term reproduction of the labour force — the social security, retirement provisions, the bringing up of the next generation and meeting the subsistence needs of the workers' families — did not fall on the employer nor on the settler state, but was borne by domestic production. The continuation of this pattern typically required further conditions. It required mechanisms, political and/or economic (the poll tax was the favourite), to force certain members of the family to enter the cash economy but at the same time had to limit possibilities for acquiring cash through independent commodity production. In Rhodesia, as Arrighi[5] has shown, this was accomplished only after African producers had started in on a process of simple commodity production. More generally, it required the penetration of the pre-capitalist social formations to make them accept their role but it also had to maintain elements of pre-existing relationships in order to preserve their ability to reproduce the labour force. One concomitant was therefore varying measures to slow down the proletarianisation of the labour force.

Here, of course, seeking to dampen down urbanisation and proletarianisation and partially to maintain the pre-capitalist relationships set in train other contradictions. In different ways and to differing degrees permanent urbanisation and proletarianisation have occurred and the indigenous modes of production have not been able to continue, in their maimed form, to provide the subsistence of families and other costs of reproduction.

Labour Migration in Zambia

There are some reports of Africans travelling to the Cape and elsewhere in South Africa from what is now Zambia long before colonial rule was established there. But certainly once it was installed at the turn of the century, the British South African Company (the administrators) sought to turn the area into a labour pool for their own mines in Southern Rhodesia and the Rand. For a generation or more that is how the territory remained – nothing more than a reservoir for exported labour mainly outside its frontiers. 'Traditional' routes were established. From Barotseland, the kingdom astride the Zambezi flood plain in the west, labour was recruited for the South African mines – and the Witwatersrand Native Labour Association (WENELA) had recruiting agents in that province until 1965. Southern Rhodesia recruited initially from the Southern Province, until possibilities of peasant production for the market offered alternatives to some of the Tonga-speaking people from that area from the 1930s on. Since then the western and eastern areas of Zambia have contributed an increasing share. The legacy of the earlier pattern can still be traced, however, for a survey in the late 1960s showed that 33% of migrations of the existing population of one southern district had been to Rhodesia. Prior to its Unilateral Declaration of Independence (UDI), when further official recruitment stopped, Rhodesia was hosting almost 50,000 workers from Zambia. From the northern end of the country, a regular flow of labourers went to Tanganyika to the gold mines and sisal plantations and even more to the Congo. In fact, the Union Miniere de Haut-Katanga obtained over half of its labour force in the early 1920s from across its border, mainly from the relatively densely populated valley of the Luapula in Northern Rhodesia.[6]

These paths changed significantly with the opening of the Zambian copper mines in the late 1920s. The flow of labour turned inward and Zambia became an importer of labour. The Copperbelt also tended to specialise in its recruitment and the two north-eastern provinces (mainly Bemba-speaking) have tended to supply almost half the miners, with up to a quarter coming from outside the country (mainly from Malawi and Tanzania). By 1930 there were already 30,000 African mineworkers. The total slumped disastrously during the Great Depression but then climbed back to this figure during the Second World War and now numbers over 60,000. With the establishment of 'Labour Camps' for the mineworkers in the 1930s and later of mine townships (and a new capital at Lusaka), there also grew a demand for maize and other basic foodstuffs (as well as ancillary services). This was mainly met through European immigration. In particular a small number of large-scale commercial farmers, never more than a thousand, produced on a sufficiently large-scale to meet most of the internal food requirements and in turn required a labour force (again partly drawn from outside), that numbered 34,000 at Independence (and has remained more or less steady since).

These farms grew up along the 'Line of Rail' a fertile crescent of land stretching between the two wings of the lop-sided butterfly that is Zambia on the map, from Livingstone the entrepot from Southern Rhodesia through Lusaka to the Copperbelt. This narrow strip which had only 5% of the population at the turn of the century now has over 40%. It is also responsible for over 90% of the centralised deliveries of milk and cattle, and of maize, the major cash crop. The outlying areas, where almost all of the African population was originally found, have almost no mining activities; they have none of the manufacturing industries that have grown up; and apart from the Eastern Province with some groundnut, tobacco and cotton production, have almost no saleable agricultural surplus. These Provinces are classic examples of the most debilitating underdevelopment.

They did have the one export, labour power, however. A generation ago it was said of these 'hungry manless areas' that they 'bought clothes with hunger'.[7] But increasingly since then they have turned to *purchasing* food, and almost all these Provinces are net purchasers of maize. In these areas, there is 'ample evidence that the subsistence diet is less adequate than it used to be. . . [and] much hard-won money is spent in rural areas on basic foodstuffs'.[8]

But their impoverishment is not inherent or simply due to natural infertility. Their being starved of investment and missing out on cash crop production reflect the logic of the labour supply needs of the capitalist production sectors. The terms of this subservience to the capitalist mode of production precluded a general transition to commodity production. However, as we shall see, the processes whereby these regions and their own modes of production took on their underdeveloped, labour supply character were not without their own dialectic. Just as Arrighi[9] documented in Rhodesia, the first response of some parts of Zambia to the capitalist economy was a rapid expansion of commodity production. This sale of agricultural surplus was tolerated in earlier colonial days as long as it was compatible with the required labour supply. Indeed, in the interests of maintaining the viability of the 'reserves' and making possible the repatriation of workers, mining capital and the colonial state would be prepared to see some commercial advancement in the peasant areas. It was the growing influence of the European commercial farmers in the colonial state in promoting a coherent transport network, a marketing network and price structure, and adequate agricultural services — all geared to meet their needs first — that finally put paid to commodity production possibilities in many peasant areas. And at that stage state intervention in various forms reversed earlier trends. The Tonga-speaking cash crop farmers of the Southern Province and the few other pockets of peasant production also served by the railway, plus the Eastern Province, remained the partial exceptions to this rule.

Just as the circumstances governing different peasant areas' chances for commodity production changed over time, so too did the forms of employment and urbanisation. In an initial colonial period, a whole paraphernalia of measures, reminiscent of those still in operation in South Africa, were used to limit the presence of Africans in the towns and mines to those who were employed and for the periods when they were employed. The mines at first did not provide married quarters, marriages could not be contracted except in reserves; there was a pass system; property in the towns could not be owned by Africans. Workers were, indeed, typically migrants and were registered as taxpayers back home. After the Second World War there were moves, especially from the mining companies, to stabilise at least part of the labour force. African townships were built in the Copperbelt, with family housing, school provision and other social facilities. So instead of so much circulation there was a tendency of many Zambians to stay in jobs and remain in urban residence longer. Nevertheless, early in this period, Epstein reports that the population of one Copperbelt town had a 'heavy loading of working age population in both sexes' and that amongst the underground workers labour turnover was still pronounced. The provision of housing and even the right to residence was still legally restricted to those in jobs. More unrestricted movement to towns had to await the changed political circumstances of Independence. Since then the flood to town has been at a rate which makes Zambia's urban population about the highest in black Africa. Even so, migrants to urban areas without paid employment and without provided or purchased housing, were tolerated only as 'squatters' living in settlements that had come into existence without official sanction, without titles to property and without the provision of services by the authorities. It is estimated that 40% of the population of the capital live in such 'squatter' areas and it is only in the 1970s that they have been officially recognised and have qualified for some services. The indications are that the urban population is much more settled. Labour turnover is now very low — and lowest of all in the mines, where the mechanisation of under-ground extraction of ores in the 1960s has removed the need for what was formerly the largest group of unskilled workers, the 'lashers', who shovelled out the ore and waste. And officials assume that part of the rapid post-1964 urbanisation was of womenfolk joining their men.

The rural social structure is of course the obverse of these changing patterns in the labour force and the urban population as a whole. Already by the 1940s the rate of migration was on an enormous scale. Richards estimated that 70% of taxable males were away from the Bemba area. As the workers were at that stage regarded officially as members of the rural community from which they came, the tax registers offer a good yardstick of who was away. Throughout most of the country figures show that often a half of all able-bodied males were away from their home areas at any one time. One (official) estimate, among many cited in the literature, suggests that 45% of all adult male taxpayers who were fit were working for wages within the country; another 20% were similarly employed in other territories, and of the minority who were in their home districts perhaps ten per cent of the total were 'engaged in production of economic crops'.[10] Just prior to Independence, in the early 1960s, the figures were still presented in the same manner and the proportion of absent taxpayers varied between Provinces from 43% in Southern to 62% in Northern.

The consequences of this history of labour migration can be seen in the present make-up of the population, as illustrated by Table 1 (figures taken from the last Census).

The population of the capital shows a dearth of old people and also a marked preponderance of male adults. Conversely, the two rural districts

Table 1
Percentage of Populations by Age and Sex

Age group	Total Zambia Male	Female	Lusaka Urban Male	Female	Zambezi District Male	Female	Chinsali District Male	Female
0-14 years	22.8%	23.0%	21.4%	22.1%	17.4%	17.0%	25.2%	25.0%
15-49 years	20.7%	24.2%	28.9%	23.1%	17.7%	27.3%	16.1%	22.3%
50 & over	5.0%	3.9%	2.1%	1.0%	10.5%	9.5%	5.3%	6.2%
Total	49.0%	51.0%	52.4%	47.5%	45.8%	54.2%	46.9%	53.1%

Source: Jackman, M.E., *Recent Population Movements in Zambia*, Zambian Papers No.8, Lusaka.

have far more older people than is the national average and also far fewer males of working age.[11]

The Effects on Peasant Systems

Research in colonial times had already pointed to what were seen as the debilitating consequences of labour migration. Missionaries, like Davis[12] in his 1930s work, and the many anthropologists associated with the famous Rhodes –Livingstone Institute pointed to the breakdown of family life due to male absences, to 'detribalisation' in the townships, and to the breakdown of 'traditional' society and its values. Their findings suggested that in *some* societies male labour could be spared and this migration did not undermine the traditional system and, indeed, might even lead to 'tribal cohesion.'[13] For the most part, however, they saw a process of social disruption running parallel to the environmental disaster pointed out by the government ecologists. They pointed to a 'degenerative cycle' that could all too easily set in, in environments that generally in Zambia received enough rain but were far from fertile, when the indigenous agricultural systems, that rather ingeniously but precariously maintained the fertility, were upset.

One of a number of innovations associated with 'modern' life could create the imbalance. Allan[14] carried out studies that showed that the process of defining 'African Reserves' twenty years earlier and the consequent resettlement that took place, in order to make for an expected influx of Europeans, had created conditions where the carrying capacity of the indigenous systems in some areas were exceeded. The resulting excessive clearing of bush, much of which would ordinarily lie fallow for long periods to regenerate, would set off a cycle of reduced vegetative cover, deterioration of the soil and breakdown of its structure, and eventual erosion.[15] Similarly disastrous consequences occurred as a result of 'modern' implements such as the plough. Migration was seen as having similar consequences, not as a result of relative land shortage but because the absence of male labour meant that bush clearance did not occur so often and shifting cultivation broke down.

Valuable as this literature is as source material, and however humane the 'concern' expressed, it was written from a conservative perspective. The concern was literally 'reactionary' in the bleak view of the future it expressed, with a faint touch of that paternalism that preferred the 'bush native' to the upstart townee: 'For the more distant future, one can see only a degraded people on a degraded soil, a race of "hangers on" inhabiting the midden of the mines, hawkers of minor produce, vice and the virtue of their women, such as it is.'[16] Objectively their perspective was basically that of the colonial state, charged as it was with managing the contradictions generated by the demands of mining capital which wanted to extract cheap labour power from the reserves but wanted them to remain capable of re-absorbing it.

More recent researchers (like those contributing to the collection by Palmer and Parsons[17]) have seized on similar evidence but put it down as a sign of 'underdevelopment'. They see 'capitalist relationships' as precluded and thus the 'economic system was destroyed not transformed'.[18] And that transformation was precluded under colonialism by the exclusion of these peripheral peasantries from access to the market and from those benefits that made the 'Northern Rhodesian commercial farmer (almost all European) one of the best served in the world in terms of research and extension'.[19]

But this approach, however condemnatory of colonialism, fails to recognise that a process of social transformation was occurring even if it was involuted. As well as environmental impoverishment, and tribal dislocation, and 'underdevelopment' there were also differentiation and class formation, even if at a very low absolute level.

Peasant Differentiation and Class Formation

Even if it was not through extensive commodity production, the indigenous social formations were nevertheless involved in the capitalist system. It was the establishment of a 'cash nexus' in the form chiefly of a hut tax, that forced many men into labour migration and this process in turn brought cash back into the community. As a consequence, many social relationships were transformed and involved cash. Thus in most areas the widely differing system of marriage payments increasingly involved cash transfers. (See reports by Richards on the Bemba and Barnes on the Ngoni.)[20] Likewise, there was a tendency for inheritance and property transfers to be affected by the capitalist law of value. Land transactions were reported in the Tonga areas[21] and even a remote area like Luvale (now Zambezi district) in the extreme west corner but were otherwise not so widespread as land was still plentiful.[22] However, Gluckman suspected that chiefs in many areas, who had charge of land allocation, were not above 'holding land against money that the younger men earned away from home'.[23]

A further transformation was that the mutuality of exchanges of labour, traditionally through kin or village based groups or beer parties, gave way gradually to the hiring of labour. Thus Colson reports that among the plateau Tonga in the 1950s, though there were 'occasional work groups through beer parties', with the development of maize production for the market in the area 'now many Tonga prefer to hire their workers'.[24] In fact, an earlier survey indicated that most 'smallholders' in this area producing for the market hired casual labour, and there were already in 1965 some large farmers with permanent employees.[25] A more recent report[26] shows that the same trends have caught up even with a far less commercialised area in the far western Senanga District, where 'cash payment for hired labour is common today although the traditional system of *lubile* (beer parties) is still practised on a large scale'. He also notes a 'drastic' change in the amount of individual as opposed to communal work.

A similar transformation along capitalist lines occurred in the use of tribute labour which chiefs in most regions continued to enjoy until as late as the 1930s. One way in which this form of appropriation was transformed was by payments. Thus Barnes[27] reports that among the Ngoni, while chiefs had 'little call on people's services', these were compensated for as they were 'probably less valuable than the presents they are given by men away working'. Another pattern was set by certain ambitious chiefs among the Bemba and, seemingly from Richards' generalisations about this experience,[28] elsewhere too. They used tribute labour, and then increasingly used their salaries to pay labourers recruited along traditional lines, to establish themselves as 'successful market gardeners' or as large herders or traders. Similarly when tribute labour had been abolished in Barotseland much earlier (as a measure by the British South Africa Company to increase the outflow of labour), chiefs took to hiring labour to cultivate their own fields.[29]

Livestock were another means whereby pre-existing inequalities were the basis for an accumulation now possible in an era of commodities and the operation (even if only partial) of the capitalist law of value. Thus in Barotseland cattle were theoretically a monopoly of the ruling families and in practice of the dominant Lozi people. In the initial colonial period such elements were best placed to take advantage of the trade in cattle that prospered until settlers came to dominate the national market. Nowadays, over half of cattle-owners in the Province are from that 20% of the population that are Lozi.[30] In the Tonga-speaking areas where commodity production by African farmers had been most advanced, ownership of cattle became crucial in taking advantage of possibilities of agricultural production for the market which was increasingly based on ploughs and oxen. In almost all areas where cattle are not precluded by tsetse, their ownership and use (whether simply for grazing and accumulation or for ploughing) is highly unequal. Among the Lozi, there is 'wide variation in the size of herds' and half of the present owners bought their first beasts.[31] In an agricultural area near the Copperbelt where cattle were newly introduced in the colonial period (and were used for ploughing and therefore were the basis for production of surplus) they were in the hands of only 15% of families.[32] And a more recent farm management survey in one of the Central Province areas reveals that half the farmers had no cattle.[33]

This kind of differentiation is a feature of the articulation of different pre-capitalist modes with the capitalist mode of production, and the particular patterns of class formation owe much to the differentiation present in the indigenous modes. The tendency to ignore these emerging capitalist-influenced relationships is paralleled by, and perhaps a result of a similar playing down of indigenous class or strata differences. Thus a distinguished anthropologist can contradictorily assert that: 'in an egalitarian *(sic)* society like that of Ndembu (a people of Zambia's north-west) slaves were not markedly exploited'; and on the next page further contradicts himself by telling us that 'slaves had to work in the gardens of their owners . . . even after they were married'.[34] (And the institution of slavery persisted until the 1930s at least!) In a similar vein, Gluckman, though recognising that Lozi society had 'broad class divisions' — royalty, aristocracy, freemen and subject peoples — becomes an apologist by asserting that the exploitation that occurred did not lead to any personal accumulation, but was redistributed as bounty.[35] Moreover, he gives an explicit clue to the subjectivity which leads many western observers to ignore both past and contemporary class divisions in rural Africa, when he states that '... serf and master lived at approximately the same standard . . . It is impossible for an outsider to detect those of servile origin.' Yet, the fact that both serf and master enjoy a level of material culture that to a western intellectual seems primitive should not blind us to the *antagonistic relationship* between them.

The significance of understanding emerging class divisions in terms of relationships and not living standards is illustrated by a more contemporary case detailed in the literature. Bates spells out how remoteness from the market, compounded by the inadequacy of agricultural service bureaucracies, consigned a village in Luapula Province, with better contact with Zaire than to the rest of Zambia, to continued underdevelopment; and how, in particular, a small group of farmers seeking to produce for the market, using mechanisation (hired) and other modern techniques, were in fact getting virtually nothing for their efforts and were as poor as the rest.[36] But Bates does not, in stressing the poverty-stricken state of these farmers, omit to tell us that they physically and socially distanced themselves from other villages, that they got prior access to government credit (even though it did them no good), and that some funds have been used for hiring some of their neighbours. It is crucial, in analysing the more peripheral areas of labour supply in a country like Zambia, to look beyond the general underdevelopment and material impoverishment in order to identify the antagonistic relationships that do exist even if confined to a low absolute level.

Many contemporary rural studies do not, however, look at differentiation in terms of relationships of production. If data are not simply aggregated or averaged, they are merely presented in terms of *stratification*. A generation ago, Allan[37] in his pioneering work distinguished between:

'subsistence cultivators'		10 bags of maize or less
'small holders'	defined as those	11-100 bags
and 'farmers.	who sold	over 100 bags

He showed that 85% of a Tonga survey population were in the first category and only 0.4% in the third. A German team used the *method* of cultivation to distinguish between the 50% hoe cultivators, the 30% 'two ox-cultivators', and the 20% using ploughs with more than two oxen in the nearby Gwembe district.[38] The Agricultural Census of 1970 differentiates on the basis of land cultivated and of some 750,000 households in what was termed the 'Traditional' sector (only 40% of whom had sold any produce in the last season), 75% cultivated less than 4.5 acres (50% less than 2.5 acres) and only 3% cultivated more than 30 acres. In the 'Commercial' sector (consisting of 645 African and 433 non-African proprietors, and employing 20,000 workers) on the other hand, 70% of the land area was farmed in units of over 5,000 acres. Other official discussions nowadays use an amalgam of these criteria to distinguish between some 50,000 'emergent farmers' situated between the mass of 'subsistence farmers' and the 'commercials'.

In trying to assess the emerging class structure behind these statistics of inequality, and its dynamics, it is useful to refer briefly to the role of the state. In the colonial period state power was used in a multitude of ways to guarantee labour supply. And even when the mechanisms of an established cash economy were sufficient to maintain the flow, and mining interests were promoting a 'stabilisation' of both the labour force and the peasantry, the influence of European commercial farmers skewed the availability of agricultural resources and the marketing services to their own benefit and, very secondarily, toward some of their African neighbours situated along the line of rail. With Independence there were pressures to diversify the benefits, although government policy has always had to be ready to make short-term concessions to commercial farmers to ensure immediate food supplies. As more Africans have joined this select band, a few of whom carry political weight, the tendency for commercial farmers to enjoy credit, fertiliser subsidies and other advantages has persisted. But two other initiatives have been applied in an effort to promote agricultural production in African peasant areas. A whole succession of state-sponsored 'Schemes' have been initiated over the years. Producer co-operatives — launched by giving subsidies to groups who cleared land — sprang up in the late 1960s, only to fade after a couple of years. 'Settlement Schemes' were a variation tried later and the current version is a policy of 'Rural Reconstruction', a paramilitary exercise taking youngsters off into camps to clear bush. In profit and loss terms most of these planned schemes did not pay and many have ceased to exist but they do provide some legacy of a form of agrarian production in which grouped, supervised producers use state (and even private) capital to produce for the market. The returns to the State agencies are such that the schemes are more a form of subsidisation to selected settlers rather than a form of surplus extraction. But Siddle has made the observation that given their capital- and management-intensive nature these 'Single focus schemes' can have but an isolated impact on the peasantry as a whole.[39] Settlers, however, are often privileged to begin with, as well as in the state resources they subsequently receive. Thus a practice whereby settlers were recruited 'on the basis of wealth' and kept their larger than average plots outside the scheme and used hired labour to carry out the work on their scheme plot is by no means unique.[40] Another survey suggests that such rich peasant and capitalist farmer elements are in the forefront of current moves to make some of the settlement rumps into 'multipurpose co-operatives' that will control local marketing.[41]

Similar differential impact results from the other type of government programmes in the post-Independence period. These consist of an array of extension, credit, supply and marketing services made available in the peasant areas.
The overall tendency in these programmes is to concentrate the buying posts,
the seed and other supplies and credit on maize production – a crop often
'not very profitable on small acreages' especially in more distant areas. This
emphasis is strengthened by the practice of agricultural extension, whose
agents limit credit to those who follow 'approved farming practices'. In those
peripheral areas, these approved practices are often equated with maize
growing and with permanent as opposed to shifting agriculture. And so government today is still periodically issuing the same condemnations of, and orders
against, *citemene* (a slash-and-burn system) that were first made in 1906. But
the evidence is that this form of shifting cultivation, although requiring much
fallow, produced yields of the indigenous staples (including the millet for
brewing) from poor soil as high as European grain yields and at the same time
maintained the limited soil fertility.[42] Permanent agriculture is of course
possible in such areas without total degeneration of the soil – but only if
artificial fertilisers are used. This alternative is only available for those who
can afford the cash outlays. For the poorer peasants bans on movement or on
burning condemn them to a cycle of soil degeneration and impoverishment.

Thus to produce for the market at all requires a certain package. Perhaps
the only crop that can be readily sold is maize; saleable maize can only come
from *purchased* hybrid seed, and will require fertiliser and perhaps insecticides
to get adequate yields and preserve fertility. As it is a crop only profitable on
a more extensive scale, ploughs or access to a tractor (through the government's
mechanisation stations, private hire or purchase) are needed and a reasonable
planted area in turn requires hired labour for weeding and harvesting. Access
to credit, and thus some initial security (or political leverage), is thus the key
to all these inputs. Agricultural commodity production is thus subject to the
oversight of government-provided finance capital. It remains limited in scale
but does promote not only the stratification between what are termed
'subsistence' and 'emergent' farmers but inevitably hiring and other antagonistic
relationships between these classes and between them and finance capital. The
patterns of class formation do, as we have indicated, vary. Some preliminary
investigations by students of the University of Zambia can perhaps be used to
typify some of the major areas.

Parts of the Tonga-speaking Southern Province have combined commodity
production with limited labour migration for almost two generations. A small
class of clearly capitalist farmers has emerged, land is scarce and class divisions
have become more polarised. One village here in the Choma district was dominated by one farmer with a tractor and a herd of over 100 cows, cultivating
130 acres of land with a permanent labour force of 16 workers as well as
temporary hired help. Three other farmers were producing regularly for the
market using some temporary labour whereas the other three-quarters of the
dozen farmers were cultivating less than 20 acres usually by plough with
family labour.

The Eastern Province's Nyanja-speaking peoples like the Ngoni and Chewa were removed and confined to reserves and suffer a degree of relative land shortage. The extent of labour migration was limited by both commodity production (of groundnuts and these days cotton) and by local employment opportunities. In Chipata district three out of a dozen villagers were petty capitalists owning shops and bars as well as cultivating commercial crops, two of them had tractors; they had Agricultural Finance Corporation Loans, used fertiliser and employed seasonal labour. The rest were hoe cultivators using their own labour; four cultivated between two and five acres and also worked as labourers in a nearby quarry; another five were poor peasants cultivating less than three acres.

The Northern Province, with a largely Bemba or Bemba-speaking population is generally the least fertile, with agricultural systems formerly based on *citemene* now breaking down, and heavy migration rates. The absolute levels of living were much lower but still differentiation occurred. Thus in Iwaka village in Mbala district, land was not scarce but the means to cultivate were. Eight out of ten farmers used hoes and could not afford to get into commodity production. Two had ploughs, a handful of cattle and chickens but through their ability to use a surplus to brew beer and thereby obtain labour they maintained their surplus and 'dominated' the village economy.

The present Western Province including what was the Bulozi kingdom, had a pre-capitalist social formation that had the most complex internal differentiation. This was transformed as a result of early commodity production (of cattle, fish and grains) and of the abolition of tribute labour. Then since the 1940s this formation has followed a new trajectory with the destruction of the internal market and the breakdown of part of the state-managed agricultural system when the non-availability of tribute labour led to the destruction of flood control canals. Involution set in, the area became a net food importer; those aristocrats and others who had gone into trading as well as commercial farming lost out to state-run marketing monopolies. The royal family and some of the aristocracy maintained a position, but now more and more as a bureaucratic stratum surviving on Government revenues. The halt in the transition to capitalist relations, with the breakdown of commodity production, seems to have stopped attempts by the aristocracy to assert landlord rights,so the peasant still maintains a stake in a complex if not commercially productive rural economy — a reason put forward to explain why Lozi are less wholehearted proletarians.[43] One group of eleven villages in the Senanga District two years ago had maize sales which averaged only half a bag for each of the 723 inhabitants. Among the 384 adults there were only 62 ploughs and only 22 farmers had received agricultural loans in the last four years.[44] Only perhaps ten of these were 'emergent' farmers in the sense of producing regularly for sale. They had ploughs and were used to hiring casual labour. A picture of extreme underdevelopment but also of differentiation.

The Position of Women in Peasant Differentiation
The extent and forms of underdevelopment and the class formation patterns

experienced in different areas can, however, be only properly understood if
the position of women and their labour is brought into the equation. One
simplistic conclusion has been that, deprived of the strongest and most creative
workers all agricultural systems would be condemned to stagnation. Some
studies have in fact pointed to the different fates of particular regions in coping
with labour migration. The breakdown of the Bemba system was attributed to
the marked sexual division of labour that had existed. The consequence of the
male absence was less frequent land clearance and bush cutting and burning, and
thus a greater burden on women forced to eke out a living on soils of declining
fertility.[45] Gluckman also saw a crisis occurring in Lozi agriculture, due in part
to the filling up of irrigation canals, as a result of the absence of males who
performed the work, but also because of the end of tribute labour for the
aristocracy — itself a provision imposed in the interests of seeking greater
migration.[46] On the other hand, Colson suggests that in Tonga society women
were less dependent on their co-partners and needed only occasional help —
and presumably could cope with the male absence better.[47] Likewise, in a
full-length treatment of this subject, Watson points to the successful adaptation of the Mambwe people to labour migration, putting this down to the fact
that village co-operation was more possible and thus the specialised male tasks
(few anyway) could be done collectively by a smaller number of males.[48] In
addition, it was argued that the Mambwe (and other patrilineal peoples like the
Ngoni) could adjust more readily as the male migrants had a fixed, virilocal
village, in which they had land rights, to return to — in contrast to matrilineal
and uxorilocal arrangements like those of the Bemba, where men had less strong
ties to either a village or to a group of male kin who might look after their
interests while they were away.

Gluckman's generalisation in his Introduction to Watson[49] about what the
latter termed 'the mode of subsistence production and its capacity to produce
enough food in the absence of large numbers of men', was that it was a matter
of whether male labour could be redeployed. The Bemba, with a heavy reliance
on a specialist male task, and the Lozi because of the interrelated complexity of
their agricultural system could not make the adjustment. However, it is instructive to explore Watson's own account which reveals features of the changing
situation which do not tally with this thesis that the key is utilisation of male
labour. First, it must be stressed that apart from the co-operation of menfolk
in tree lopping in the woodland part of the Mambwe area, in the co-operating
groups who maintain the system '*women* supply the bulk of the labour'. In
addition, weeding and other important regular tasks are done by the individual
woman — on land 'whose rights are held by men'. In other words, the 'cohesion'
of the system depends not so much on the male labour being spread to be
available to more women, but on more women's labour being available to menfolk whether they are present or not. Moreover, the need for women to obtain
access to land to feed themselves and their families, in a period of migration
increases their dependence in a variety of ways. 'The surplus women left in
the village are . . . attached to some man through marriage or concubinage'.[50]
Watson's survey of eight villages reveals that 28% of all married male residents

were polygynists. Other 'surplus' women included widows and old women dependent on their kin, or the wives and sisters left behind by workers.

The position of these women must, however, be understood in the context of the whole network of social relationships and of emerging antagonisms in those relationships. In Mambwe society certain elements were better placed to acquire women for work, and we are told that chiefs, in particular, had many wives. However, these latter could still rely, in the 1950s, on another vehicle for acquiring the labour of others, as tribute labour, supposedly forbidden, persisted. There was also yet another medium for labour transfer. Women in need, particularly widows, would join work parties, not as part of a reciprocal arrangement but to work for food, given out then or as a share of the harvests. 'Women and indigent persons are expected to earn food in this way *(ukupula)*, but ordinary people *(sic)* with fields of their own regard such work as shameful!'[51]

The underlying picture that seems discernible below the surface of such sexist reports is of a social formation becoming differentiated into 'ordinary people' — middle peasants plus some rich ones who enjoy the benefits of several wives or perhaps tribute-labour and a poor peasant stratum consisting mainly of dependent women. The same institution of *ukupula* is reported from the Luapula Province although Richardson[52] describes this mode of exploitation as 'a kind of charity . . . to spread the labour of men more evenly!' He reports that four out of 26 women in one village relied entirely for their subsistence on such paid labour. While polygamy was not here so common, women without gardens would become more dependent on their female kin who had land — an extension of the 'traditional' social relationships of production, as Richardson sees it, in this matrilineal society, whereby in-laws fed the newly-weds who in turn provided labour service; but an extension in a capitalist direction. Kinship obligations slow down the rate of proletarianisation and are channels for welfare, but also themselves evolve into commodity relations. Perhaps the most widespread example of *ukupula* is contained in earlier reports from the Bemba areas, where Richards[53] reports that it had 'become very common lately as one of the means by which a very large percentage of deserted wives can eke out an existence during the bad times of the year'.

Another differentiating trend observed in both the above cases, and among the Bemba and other peoples that had depended on some version of the *citemene* system, resulted from one adaptive measure to cope with the loss of male labour for land clearance. There was a tendency, especially on the part of women without menfolk, or in conditions of relative land shortage as in parts of Luapula Province, to shift to the cultivation of a more hardy staple, cassava, rather than millet. This latter crop was ordinarily used not only as a food but for brewing. One consequence of not being able to brew beer was that some women could not host work parties and thus were in turn more likely to be consigned to a poor peasant cycle of no *citemene*, and thus declining fertility and no beer etc. Kapferer[54], however, argues that the general change to cassava in fertile, lakeside Bisa villages gave women greater independence from men, and also 'greater economic security when their husbands were away' as they sold some of the cassava. However, he also noted the few beginnings of 'purchasing cassava' by working in a grower's garden or by helping to pound meal in Bisa areas in the North, similar to the *ukupula* noted above. Moreover, though the sale of cassava does bring some women 'enough cash to satisfy immediate requirements', plus some security and independence of the men away, it also makes possible the greater exploitation of that absent male labour through a greater contribution to subsistence by female labour.

A further change induced by labour migration in the set of relationships of production in which the family was embedded also affected the position of women. The various parts of the country all reported trends towards the greater commercialisation of the marriage contract. Customarily there were two major types of arrangements governing the dues to the bride's family. In the south and west and among the Ngoni, there was a *lobola* system like that found in much of Southern Africa: a payment of livestock to the bride's father. The other system, operating among the northern and north-western peoples and those of the east who also traced descent matrilineally, involved the payment of labour service by the groom to his in-laws. The incorporation of both types of social formation in the capitalist system on labour migration terms set off pressures which led to both an inflation of such payments and their increasingly monetary form. Forced into employment, the migrant has to make provision for the subsistence of his family or future family and thereby his own long term security. 'The demand for land rises, not for the purposes of farming but as a means of setting up house', notes Kautsky.[55] In some areas, as we have seen, the actual purchase of land or the paying of deposits to ensure allocation did occur in areas where there was relative scarcity. In areas where land for cultivation was there for the clearing and where rights persisted as long as it was cultivated, the guarantee of such a stake for the future was a wife (or wives). Women's labour was thus at a premium, and in circumstances where the fact of migration obviously tended to undermine the permanence of marriage the search for security in such changing times tended to bid up bridewealth. At the same time the absence of males in wage employment meant that they were no longer able to carry out labour service for in-laws, or build up a herd by their own efforts; but they were provided with a substitute for either mode of payment in the form of cash. Thus, the well-known effect of encroaching capitalist relationships in reducing everything to commodity applied not only to land (partially) and the labour power of the migrant workers, but also to women and their (domestic) labour.

The precise forms of the changing marital and kinship systems and of the debasement of women varied. Thus Richards reports a 'recrystallisation of marriage institutions', a partial substitution of cash payments for labour service, but also that 'the authority of the father was immeasurably increased', which in turn increased matrilineage elders' domination over both female kin and their spouses.[56] This tendency to 'traditionalise' marriage in the later colonial period may have been general and deliberate — a measure both to stabilise the labour supply areas and to reassert the traditional basis of chiefly authority, at a time when these were under challenge from a number of directions, including an 'incipient movement for feminine rights'.[57] The Tonga had a system of bridewealth payment in cattle, some of which were kept in this matrilineal society for a woman's offspring, but women were not allowed to tend the herds. As cattle became more crucial as draft animals, they acquired a cash value — and so did women — and also became even more of a male preserve, and thus the more prosperous male farmers took over the ploughing, the cash crops and hired labour (both male and female).[58] Among the Ngoni, Barnes reports that payments of bridewealth which were in stages and in cattle, now consist of a single payment, to 'legalise ownership', paid in cash.[59]

Political Consequences: The Nature of the 'Worker-Peasant' Alliance

Having spelled out the kinds of differentiation that have occurred, and the place of women within the emerging class structure,[60] we must briefly conclude with some reference to the remaining one of the three issues raised at the outset: the political role of 'workers' and 'peasants'. The first among several general conclusions is that these categories are difficult to define, as they may not be mutually exclusive in the particular circumstances of Zambia and most of Southern Africa. Different individuals may move frequently back and forth between these different roles; members of the same family may be more firmly in one camp, others in the other. Two further political points follow from the nature of the labour migration economy — a system of super-exploitation both of male labour power paid below its value, and of female domestic labour that makes it possible. Richards[61] long ago expressed the essence of this pattern whereby the reproduction of the labourers' families is not met through the cash wage, in remarking that young men, 'though they feel responsible for clothing their wives and children . . . do not feel bound to feed them until later in life'. But these most exploited elements in the capitalist periphery are neither of them well placed to take political action against their exploitation. The menfolk are only partially proletarianised, and may withdraw from working class struggles because they have a stake back home, and may in turn seek solutions to the unequal exchange imposed on their commodity production not by peasant action but by resorting to employment.[62] Women, who are often subjected to dual and intensified exploitation by the broader capitalist system are not in a position to be aware of that larger system. But the second consequence of this structure is the converse and corollary of this appreciation that women are at the base of the exploitive mechanisms: any strategy for confrontation with this system and its overthrow must — of necessity — recognise that women must have a central part in this struggle. (The only known study in the region which starts from this kind of premise is Young's of the 'Shangaan' people, who provided much of the South African mine labour, in Mozambique.)[63]

A differing set of conclusions emerge, however, if we look at the *dynamics* of the labour migration system. As we have attempted to show, the system is both modified as the need for more skilled labour leads to a more settled, urbanised component of the working class, but also subject to strain as the almost inevitable breakdown of the agricultural systems makes this pattern of exploitation less viable. At such periods the threat to food supplies and the unavailability of cash to purchase them, coupled with increased relative urban unemployment because of the flood to the towns to escape the rural crisis, subject the system to conflict at both the 'peasant' and 'worker' ends. In Zambia's political history this occurred during the Depression when there was militant strike action and in the period after the Second World War. The latter was the time that the Mineworkers Union and nationalist pressures in the towns began to emerge. There was also a varied set of tensions in the rural areas. Bates refers, for instance, to the mood of 'insurgency' that occurred in the late 1950s in Luapula, with open opposition taking the form of burning tax books and the formation of small bands of guerillas.[64] Elsewhere there was opposition to compulsory conservation and other agricultural rules designed to avert the agrarian crisis; and in the north to attempts to prohibit the *citemene* system. But it is instructive to note that such 'nationalist' protest politics also had their embryonic class dimension. Epstein notes how there was for the first time a challenge from unskilled, more migrant workers to the leadership of the more permanent, skilled workers.[65] In the rural areas, a parallel can be seen in the 'rebellion against the misuse of power by the chiefs' in Luapula[66] and even in the 'cleavage between the rulers and the mass of commoners' that Gluckman thought was 'just detectable' by the late 1940s in Bulozi.[67]

This crisis was resolved by a number of social and economic reforms that were wrapped up in the major political concession — Independence. A stabilisation of part of the urban labour force began in the 1950s; virtually unrestricted movement to the towns and significant wage increases followed Independence. There were also many pickings for the various levels of national and local political officials, usually already slightly elevated strata — and for the peasantry there were 'promises', and a few token handouts in the form of tractors that quickly broke down, more schools and other services, and some short-run subsidies.

During the 1970s a new crisis in the system has emerged. Wages have been virtually frozen despite the inflation. Movement to the towns has not meant jobs or decent housing and few services have been provided for recent migrants forced to live in squatter areas. The food-producing capabilities of the agricultural system are clearly inadequate and the various, usually coercive schemes for rural development have not increased production significantly in most of the distant provinces. Economic and political rewards have been enjoyed by the national bureaucratic bourgeoisie. And at the local level there has also been a coincidence of political influence with kulak/trader interests.[68] And faced with the consequences of the crisis of international capitalism, it is the 'worker-peasant' class(es) that are having to bear the brunt of the austerity measures. What has been emerging in the last two years are spontaneous and still somewhat incoherent protests by the urban 'marginals' and the organised workers against their condition — *njalayeka* ('we are starving') is the slogan. It remains to be seen whether this renewed class struggle will be contained by patronage politics and by increasingly repressive measures coupled with a welcoming of South Africa's economic embrace, or whether an articulated programme of demands can couple the mounting urban protest with an awakening of an extremely impoverished, increasingly differentiated, and largely female, middle and poor peasantry.

References

This essay first appeared in *The Journal of Peasant Studies*, 5, 3 (April, 1978).

1. S. Amin, *Accumulation on a World Scale*, (New York, 1974).
2. J. Banaji, 'Kautsky on the Agrarian Question', *Economy and Society*, 5, 1 (January, 1976).
3. M. Palmberg, 'The Political Role of the Workers in Tanzania and Zambia. A Discussion of some aspects of the problems of non-capitalist development', Scandinavian Institute of African Affairs, Seminar on Non-Capitalist Development, 1976.
4. G. Arrighi and J.S. Saul, 'Socialism and Economic Development in Tropical Africa', in their *Essays on the Political Economy of Africa*, (New York, 1973). There is a continuing debate about this thesis; see for instance some of the contributions to R. Cohen and R. Sandbrook (eds.), *Towards an African Working Class*, (London, 1976).
5. G. Arrighi, 'Labour Supplies in Historical Perspective: A Study of the Proletarianization of the African Peasantry in Rhodesia', in Arrighi and Saul, *op. cit.*
6. H. Heisler, *Urbanization and the Government of Migration, The Inter-Relation of Urban and Rural Life in Zambia*, (London, 1974).
7. G. Wilson, *An Essay on the Economies of Detribalization in N. Rhodesia*, Rhodes-Livingstone Paper No. 5, Livingstone, 1941.
8. G. Kay, 'Agricultural Progress in Zambia', in M.F. Thomas and G.W. Whittington (eds.), *Environment and Land Use in Africa*, (London,1969).
9. Arrighi, *op. cit.*
10. W. Henderson, 'Northern Rhodesia in the Second World War', University of East Africa Social Science Conference, Nairobi, 1969.
11. The two districts also show some differences in sex-age distribution. Zambezi is typical of the areas to the west of the line of rail which show a higher proportion of old and mature males than the average, Chinsali in Northern Province is typical of the districts to its east in that the figures suggest less of a tendency to come back home in later life.
12. J.M. Davis, *Modern Industry and the African*, (London, 1933).
13. W. Watson, *Tribal Cohesion in a Money Economy: A Study of the Mambwe People of Northern Rhodesia*, (Manchester, 1958).
14. W. Allan, *Studies of African Land Usage in Northern Rhodesia*, Rhodes-Livingstone Institute Paper No. 15, Lusaka, 1949.
15. Kay, *op. cit.*
16. Allan, *op. cit.*
17. R. Palmer and N. Parsons, *The Roots of Rural Poverty*, (London, 1977).
18. Laurel Van Horn, 'The Agricultural History of Barotseland', in Palmer and Parsons, *op. cit.*

19. R. Roberts and C. Elliot, 'Constraints in Agriculture', in C. Elliot (ed.), *Constraints on the Economic Development of Zambia*, (Nairobi, 1971).
20. A. Richards, *Land Labour and Diet in Northern Rhodesia: an economic survey of the Bemba Tribe*, (London, 1939); J.A. Barnes, 'The Fort Jameson Ngoni', in E. Colson and M. Gluckman (eds.), *Seven Tribes of Central Africa*, (Manchester, 1959).
21. E. Colson, 'The Plateau Tonga of Northern Rhodesia', in Colson and Gluckman, *op. cit.*
22. C.M.N. White, *A Preliminary Survey of Luvale Rural Economy*, Rhodes-Livingstone Paper No. 29, Lusaka, 1959.
23. Gluckman in Watson, *op. cit.*
24. Colson, *op. cit.*
25. W. Allan *et al*, *Land Holding and Land Usage among the Plateau Tonga of Mozabuka District*, Rhodes-Livingstone Institute Paper No. 14, Lusaka, 1948.
26. G. Akafekwa, 'Agricultural Development in Senanga District', Development Administration Research Paper, UNZA, 1975.
27. Barnes, *op. cit.*
28. A. Richards, 'The Bemba of N.E. Rhodesia', in Colson and Gluckman, *op. cit.*
29. Van Horn, *op. cit.*
30. J. Lutke-Entrup, *Limitations and Possibilities of Peasant African Cattle Holders in Western Province*, University of Zambia, Institute of African Studies, 1971.
31. Lutke-Entrup, *op. cit.*
32. W. Allan, *Studies of African Land Usage in Northern Rhodesia*, Rhodes-Livingstone Institute Paper No. 15, Lusaka, 1949.
33. J.E. Bessel, R. Roberts, and N. Vanzetti, *Analysis of Pilot Year Data*, Universities of Nottingham and Zambia, Agricultural Pilot Study, 1969.
34. V.W. Turner, *A Study of Ndembu Village Life*, (Manchester, 1954).
35. M. Gluckman, 'The Lozi of Barotseland in Northwest Rhodesia', in Colson and Gluckman, *op. cit.*
36. M. Bates, 'Rural Development in Kasumpa Village, Zambia', *Journal of African Studies*, 2, 3 (1975).
37. Allan, *Studies of African Land Usage in Northern Rhodesia*.
38. H. Brandt *et al*, 'Report on Development Possibilities of Gwembe South Region, Zambia', German Development Institute, Berlin, 1973.
39. D. Siddle, 'Rural Development in Zambia: A Spatial Analysis', *Journal of Modern African Studies*, 8, 2 (1970).
40. A. Mwanza, 'Settlement Schemes in Zambia', Development Administration Paper, University of Zambia, 1974.
41. Bates, *op. cit.*
42. Allan, *Studies of African Land Usage in Northern Rhodesia*.
43. J. Ault, 'Notes on the History of the Western Province', Private communication, Lusaka, 1975.
44. Akafekwa, *op. cit.*
45. Richards, *Land Labour and Diet*.
46. Gluckman, 'The Lozi'.
47. Colson, *op. cit.*
48. Watson, *op. cit.*

49. *Ibid.*
50. *Ibid.*
51. *Ibid.*
52. E.M. Richardson, *Village Structure in the Fort Roseberry District of Northern Rhodesia,* Rhodes-Livingstone Communication No. 13, Lusaka, 1959.
53. Richards, *Land Labour and Diet.*
54. B. Kapferer, *Co-operation, Leadership and Village Structure,* Zambian Papers No. 1, Lusaka, 1967.
55. Banaji, *op. cit.*
56. Richards, 'The Bemba'.
57. I am grateful to Jim Ault for this important piece of information.
58. Colson, *op. cit.*
59. Barnes, *op. cit.*
60. Since the first version of this paper I am grateful to Judy Kingsley whose own researches in Chiundaponde among the Bisa confirm some of the generalisations of this paper: the existence of pre-colonial classes, including a near-slave system of 'pawning'; the emergence of rich peasants hiring labour, some of it female but some male from as far afield as Tanzania; a change to cassava growing partly as it is easier to cultivate by women alone; but the emergence of *some* female kulaks even though the position of women generally became less free.
61. Richards, *Land Labour and Diet.*
62. Ault, *op. cit.*
63. S. Young, 'Fertility and Famine: Women's Agricultural History in Southern Mozambique', in Palmer and Parsons, *op. cit.*
64. Bates, *op. cit.*
65. A.L. Epstein, *Politics in an Urban African Community,* (Manchester, 1958).
66. Bates, *op. cit.*
67. Gluckman, 'The Lozi'.
68. See M. Bratton, 'The Social Context of Political Concentration in Zambia: Ward and Village Committees in Kasama District', Institute of African Studies Paper, University of Zambia, 1976.

Study Questions

1. In what way has labour migration produced class differentiation in the rural areas?
2. Has labour migration affected the status of women in the rural areas? How?

11. Mubanga E. Kashoki

Indigenous Scholarship in African Universities: The Human Factor

This essay addresses itself to the problem of human resources in African universities and allied research institutions in their attempts to lend support of an original kind to Man's eternal quest for truth. At the core of my thesis is the proposition that indigenous scholarship in Africa (i.e., Africa's contribution by its own daughters and sons) will not flourish, or make a special mark on contributions from elsewhere, until major constraints connected with human resources have been overcome. The mobilization, husbanding and exploitation of these resources toward greater and more widespread intellectual originality I do not regard merely as a question of quantity or even quality but of kind. In this respect, my position coincides with that held by Chango Machyo who, after drawing a line between intelligence and intellectualism, argues that 'although the number of African [university] graduates at all levels is relatively impressive, the number of intellectuals is not'.[1] Indeed, indigenous human resources, later to be deployed in universities, research institutes or in institutions where some form of research is undertaken, not only have received or are continuing to receive their formal training in some of the world's most renowned academic institutions but they have also attained very high levels of academic apprenticeship and distinction. But, despite this welcome and encouraging trend, indigenous scholarship, of a kind to be considered truly original, remains sporadic, in relative short supply, and essentially imitative of, or largely patterned after, contributions by Western scholars. The why of this state of affairs is the subject of this essay. In the main I shall attempt to show that the failure, or rather absence, of truly original, indigenous scholarship in Africa is due in part to the very type of education the majority of African scholars have received, and in part to the patterns of resource deployment and allocation in the countries to which they have subsequently returned after training, and also their inner conditioning (what more usually is referred to as 'brain-washing') and therefore attitudinal orientations. Mention will also be made of the rather inhibiting political climate under which very often emergent scholars have to work, particularly if their work involves, as it should, the evolution and promotion of new vistas of thought or new ways of interpreting reality. Stunted scholarship is also a consequence of limited financial resources. More serious (certainly more critical if originality is the measure of the scholarship expected of the African) is an unwillingness (at least a general lack of positive signs thus far) on the part of African scholars to return to their cultural roots and to consider those roots as the first building block on which to base future scholarship. Yet another serious obstacle to the emergence of distinguished, original, African scholarship, worthy of permanent place in the annals of scientific thought, are the tangled webs of scientific distortion by Western scholars, especially in the social sciences and humanities, that await corrective action by the victims of that distortion. As a result of this obstacle the African scholars will remain enmeshed in defensive stances for a number of years to come and the loser during this period will inevitably be positive, assertive scholarship. Indeed much mental energy is currently being expended, in writing as well as in daily conversations, by the average African scholar in a concerted, if self-conscious, effort to eliminate past distortion and pervasive cultural or ethno-centric bias in international scholarship.[2]

Before elaborating upon these sub-themes, however, a few points of clarification are in order. The first of these concerns my use of the broad term 'African universities' in the title of this essay. This is perhaps too ambitious a claim since my experience has really been limited to a relatively small circle of African universities and certainly anything like primary experience has been restricted to only one university, to wit, the University of Zambia. Consequently, much of what I have to say is based at best on second-hand information and in general on personal impressions and broad generalizations. I am therefore well aware of the fact that my approach to start with suffers from one major deficiency: it does not conform to one of the central, hallowed and time-honoured canons of Western scholarship — empirical evidence. I believe, however, that despite this scholarly shortcoming, the issues which I confront will at least serve as a basis for informed debate or in some fundamental sense lead to systematic inquiry into those factors which have inhibited truly original scholarship in Africa, and by implication other non-Western societies.

Secondly, one point in particular needs to be understood at the outset, namely that, for the purposes of this paper, my definition, or rather understanding, of 'anthropology' is much broader and much more general than would be acceptable among professional anthropologists who tend to approach it from a narrow disciplinary perspective. My broad interpretation of the term accords more nearly with its original meaning as the study of Man and his works (and, I would add, his environment). In this broader definition I would include such disciplines as economics and political science which have tended to be excluded from anthropology and to enjoy only the pariah status of 'related'. The advantage of taking a broader view of the term is that it enables one to include a larger number of African scholars in the analysis.

Technicians Versus Inventors and Thinkers

Prior to the intervention of European colonialism in Africa, indigenous education, with minor or insignificant intrusions, if any, from elsewhere, shaped the mentality and outlook on life of the African. European colonialism more than perhaps any other epoch in Africa's history had the immediate and long-term effect of altering this situation. The effect was not only merely one of undermining African sociocultural systems and institutions; its most pernicious effect was to cause the African to look to Western Man for moral, spiritual, technical and intellectual guidance and leadership. Indeed, it has been said that the single most significant accomplishment by Western Man on a global scale has been the creation (or more correctly the re-creation) of non-Western Man in the image of Western Man.

Because I consider that the seeds of the dilemma of African scholarship are to be found here, the first issue which I confront is Western education and its consequences on and implications for non-Western Man, with special reference to the African. I distinguish three dimensions of the problem: (1) the mechanical, uncritical or essentially imitative manner in which Western education has generally been acquired by the African; (2) the preoccupation with employment-oriented (or what I label 'manpower-factory') education in most African countries; and (3) the consequences of Western theories on African thought and African scholarship.

In regard to the first of these dimensions of the problem, Ronald Dore, in his provocative and stimulating discussion of education and qualification, suggests that developing countries and their (Western) educated people are the 'victims of a system of schooling without education'. As he sees it: 'The effect of schooling, the way it alters a man's capacity *and will* to do things, depends not only on what he learns, or the way he learns it, but also on *why* he learns it. That is the basis of the distinction between schooling which is education, and schooling which is only qualification, a mere process of certificating − or "credentialling", as American sociologists have recently started to call it.' He continues: 'In the process of qualification, by contrast, the pupil is concerned not with mastery, but with being certified as having mastered. The knowledge that he gains, he gains not for its own sake and not for constant later use in a real situation − but for the once-and-for-all purpose of reproducing it in an examination. And the learning and reproducing is all just a means to an end − the end of getting a certificate which is a passport to a coveted job, a status, an income. If education is learning to *do* a job, qualification is a matter of learning in order to *get* a job.'[3] And with few exceptions that is about where we stand in Africa. Due to the prevailing systems of education on the continent and the emphases shaping the education imparted to the learners − the future scholars and shapers of thought in Africa − African societies are producing a surfeit of spanner-boys, machinists and mechanics while inventors and original thinkers are conspicuous by their virtual absence. Since, however, I am more narrowly concerned with the African university scholar, a few observations about the African university and its African academic personnel might be instructive.

The African scholar in an African university may be best described by likening him to his counterpart, the African engineer. The African engineer, in spite of the relatively long period of formal apprenticeship in Western training institutions, is not trained in *how* to invent but in how to check, lubricate, service, maintain, repair or re-assemble engines conceived and assembled in Europe and North America. While he may be tutored in how the particular piece of machinery he is dealing with came about, and in the theoretical foundations upon which it is based, and while this way lead him to marvel at the ingenuity and wonder of it all, transferring that ingenuity and the challenges it poses to his own mental creative processes remains either beyond him or none of his concern. After all, at the end of the long, dark tunnel through which the aspiring, African engineer has to grope lies a tantalizing and an assumed well-earned reward: a good, prestigious job, a handsome income, access to a car and a house, and a special niche in one's own community. What more could one want?

In like manner, the African academic, in acquiring the string of degrees which pins on him an almost automatic badge to teach and/or conduct research in a university, undergoes a similar process of what I can only call imitative learning. For the African academic there is to begin with the underlying problem that quite often the mere acquisition of a degree — the event of being credentialled — is thought to be an achievement in itself, sometimes the single most momentous accomplishment in one's life. For not only is the adding of BA, MA or Ph.D. after one's name intended to leave a lasting impression on the reader and to signal to him that the signatory is a person of social distinction, but it is generally accepted to convey to all and sundry that the possessor of those learned titles is a fountain of infinite worldly wisdom. The more important notion of education — certainly the whole basis of formal theoretical training as being nothing more than a prelude to, and a preparation for meeting, the challenges and tests that lie ahead in the crucible of life is lost in the general preoccupation with income generation, social status and personal glory. More serious however is a general failure to sit back and reflect on *how* the string of degrees were acquired, *what* was learned, *how* it was learned, and to what *end* it was learned. The point, for example, that the mere ability to satisfy formal academic requirements (i.e. to pass examinations) does not necessarily equip one to unravel the wonders perplexing Man is appreciated only really by a small number of African scholars, constantly as they have been told while as students that the solution of the world's problems are solely in their hands upon graduation.

The acquiring of degrees for the sake of acquiring degrees, almost as an end in itself, has had the effect of making African scholars by and large content with *past* achievement, rather than being spurred on to greater heights of intellectual curiosity and therefore distinction. Even where they appear to have exerted themselves intellectually — and there is no doubt that some African scholars have distinguished themselves in a variety of fields — the driving force has been less to do with contributing truly original scholarship to the pool of world knowledge than with consideration of higher status and higher income in the university. This is not to say that monetary and related considerations concerned with the self are bad *per se*, nor that only African scholars are preoccupied primarily with their personal advancement and welfare. If this were so the phase 'publish or perish' would not have been invented to apply to the work and self-promoting antics of academics in North American universities. Nor would it be entirely fair to blame self-serving motives solely on the African scholar himself. African universities as institutions carry part of the blame, for it is the African universities as institutions which devise rule and regulations that tie intellectual accomplishment directly to monetary and other material rewards rather than to some other forms of recognition. It is these institutions which flash the red light to the new academic recruit that unless he/she produces, he/she has little chance of promotion.

It must also be clarified that, human nature being what it is, some form of reward or recognition is required if one is to feel any need to exert oneself more than is necessary. Academics dedicated to scholarship for the sheer pleasure of being a scholar are a rare breed anywhere in the world. Therefore I do not discount the need for some form of reward as a necessary part of the package of social incentives required to inspire African scholars to add their names to the world of original scholarship.

Consequently what is decried about what appears to be a primary concern with promotion and social status in African universities is that such a concern can easily and very often does lead to unproductive and counterproductive activities. Because of emphasis, for example, on promotion, the African university quite often has been transformed by its academic staff into little more than an institution of 'Personal Comparative Notes': who got promoted, why he got promoted, why was *I* not promoted, what has he done, what university did he attend, how many degrees does he have, are they good (even legitimate) degrees, was the university he attended a good school, to what school of thought does he belong, it's who you know and not what you know that counts, etc. Intellectualism preoccupied with personal comparative note-taking, rather than with promoting original scholarship, has tended to divert attention away from positive scholarly productivity, from substantive contribution, and from a concern with issues and their illumination to personal, petty jealousies, much expenditure of intellectual energies into negative channels, and to the reduction of the African university into essentially a political arena where personal differences, instead of the larger, more compelling social issues, constitute the focus of intellectual analysis. The distinguishing feature of such an environment is that it produces persons who are experts at smelling intellectual deficiencies in others but never in oneself. It therefore tends to lead to stunted personal intellectual growth. Even in those instances where inquiry remains focused on issues rather than on personalities, quantity and not quality is pursued in a pragmatic bid to secure the much sought after promotion in the shortest time possible. Another outcome of a concern with promotion and material advancement is that the scholarship that results is often *applicative* and generally patterned after notions, models or theories developed elsewhere without much evaluative inquiry into their efficacy, relevance or general applicability.

From outside its walls the African university is invariably under tremendous pressure from governments, which provide it with the operational funds, to play its part — on occasion the major part — in training the manpower required for national development. Particularly in those countries, like

Zambia, which attained independence with an acute shortage of high-level manpower, the African university was seen – indeed conceived – as nothing more than a manpower factory. The emphasis in Africa on universities producing relevant manpower has far-reaching implications for the emergence of African scholars and probably accounts for their neglible numbers thus far.

It will be remembered that during the late 1950s and early 1960s, when most of the countries in Africa and Asia were becoming independent sovereign states and were themselves assuming the responsibility for their own national development, the emphasis very clearly was on modernizing, or catching up with the West. The process could be summed up in one apt phrase – 'closing the gap'. This was the UN's First Development Decade. In the process of closing the gap, investment in the education or training of the nation's human resources, so that they could man the wide range of institutions and services in the country, was identified as the most pressing priority. Thus national governments diverted the greater part of their financial resources toward the provision of *development-oriented* manpower. As Dore puts it succinctly: 'Their concern was with producing, in the shortest time possible, men to meet the demands for *modern* expertise – civil engineers, factory managers, architects, doctors, accountants, teachers. Afritania, they would say, now, in 1963, has twenty Afritanian engineers. There are another twenty-five expatriate engineers and about twenty unfilled vacancies. If industry grows at 12 per cent a year, the present sixty-five 'slots' for engineers will have grown to 253 in twelve years time. And to make sure that we have replaced all expatriates and built a corps of 253 Afritanian engineers by 1975, and to allow for the likelihood that 20 per cent will brain-drain away, we need to build a university department to come 'on stream' in 1967 and to produce thirty-six Afritanian engineers a year.'[4]

Manpower planning is not a bad thing except for the implications that it has for the African university as a centre of scholarship. In the first instance, because of emphasis on manpower and numbers, the African university is turned almost from the beginning essentially into a manpower factory, whose assembly lines are kept constantly busy so that the requisite numbers of lawyers, teachers and engineers can be churned out every year. Under the pressure to produce, the university reduces itself to a mere lecturing institution and not a place marked by creative thinking and distinguished scholarship. In some instances, African universities can in fact best be described as glorified polytechnics.

The African university as a producer of 'relevant' manpower has another, more serious, dimension insofar as promotion of original scholarship is concerned. The problem is not only that the university teaching staff seldom find the time to engage in serious reflection of their own, let alone apply their training and expertise to original research. The problem also extends to the learners that pass through their hands. These, because of orientations, attitudes and practices in the larger society, see knowledge primarily as utilitarian. In consequence, the products of manpower-factory universities are innovators only in the more limited sense of assisting their societies in the formulation and execution of government policy, and not — certainly only rarely — in the more demanding and crucial sense of contributing original or truly creative thought to the fundamental restructuring of one's society.

But perhaps the greatest failure of African universities, particularly of the manpower-factory type, is to produce men and women who are, in the main, equipped intellectually only to *reproduce* concepts, models, theories and solutions to human problems conceived, assembled and packaged in Western settings by Western Man. The result is that Africa is inundated by African university graduates, with a glittering array of university degrees acquired from local and foreign universities, the greater part of whole lives has been spent in rote learning, without the cultivation of the necessary ability to question the underpinnings of the knowledge so acquired.

The African Scholar: Devout Worshipper of Foreign Idols

In his stimulating article 'The Challenge of a Black Scholar', in which he exhorts Black American (read African) scholars to conduct research guided by Black perspectives, Nathan Hare suggests that a scholar, particularly a Black scholar, is more than just 'a man who contributes original ideas, new insights and information to the existing fund of knowledge.' To him, 'on the shoulders of the black scholar falls an enormous task. He must de-colonize his mind so that he may effectively guide other intellectuals and students in their search for liberation'. His challenge to the Black scholar is this: '[He] must look beneath the surface of things and, where necessary and appropriate, take a stand against the bias of white scholarship. He must be biased against white bias, must be an iconoclast, rallying to the call to arms of all the black intelligentsia, to destroy obsolescent norms and values and create new ones to take their place.'[5] However, to be able to do this, the Black scholar, more so the African scholar, would have to proceed from the methodological premise, as Blauner and Wellman do, that 'scientific research does not exist in a vacuum' but that 'its theory and practice reflect the structure and values of society.'[6] I would be even more explicit. I would contend that all scientific inquiry and discovery are firmly rooted in, and consequently spring from, sociocultural bias. Western scholarship and Western scientific discoveries are not matters of pure accident, divorced from the cultures and belief systems in which they were conceived and given tangible expression.

Let us give but one example by way of illustration. Once upon a time Western Man believed that the fiery orb called the sun went round his own planet, the earth. His cultural bias was buttressed by the daily optical illusion of the sun rising in the east at dawn and sinking in the west at the fall of dusk. Even his Holy Bible told him the sun went round the earth. Then came a bold, daring and even rash man — Galileo. Proceeding from the biases and beliefs *current in his society,* he set out to prove a contrary thesis, arguing in effect that all that belief in rising and sinking and Biblical medicine men stopping the sun in mid-air was a lot of bunkum and so much unscientific poppycock. In other words, he stood the original thesis on its head, advanced that the contrary had to be the truth, and in consequence shook the Western world and its epistemology at the time to their very foundations. For which folly and heretical doctrine the rash Galileo brought down upon himself ecclesiastical wrath, culminating in his excommunication and incarceration as payment for contradicting the laws of God. Today, several centuries afterwards, Galileo is sung by Western Man as one of the world's greatest scientific heroes.

The African scholar could tear a leaf from that experience, for, that experience serves to underscore the message that scientific discovery proceeds from the known to the unknown. Consequently, if the African scholar is to contribute anything new to world scholarship or scientific knowledge — particularly if he is to respond to Nathan Hare's injunction to be biased against white bias, to destroy obsolescent alien norms and values in scholarship, and to evolve new ones in their place — he must return to his cultural roots, to his unique experience as an African, to his sociocultural biases, i.e., to his own epistemology. It is in that epistemology — in the legends, myths, folklore, beliefs, customs, superstitions, religion, philosophy, medicine, government, etc. — that he will find the foundations on which to base his concepts, assumptions, hypotheses, models and theories. In that unique cultural experience, I submit, lie the future of a new African-based scholarship, a new perspective, a new epistemology.[7] Panting after Western scholarship will produce eminent African scholars — eminent carbon copies of Western thought. Only more reliance on and a renewed faith in African cultural systems as the basis for the African scholar's explanatory models to me hold out any promise of original African scholarship. Western scholarship is called 'western' precisely because Western biases, not universal biases, initially formed the basis for scientific investigation and resulted inevitably in Western-oriented generalizations. As Joseph Scott has argued: 'Scientific knowledge in the social sciences in this country (i.e., U.S.A.) is mostly a body of facts and generalizations about white experience. More specifically, it is about the white middle-class experience. In the behavioural sciences, for example, the attitude tests have been "validated" on white people. The intelligence tests have been "standardized" on white people. The statistical curves "represent" the response patterns of white people. The theories of society, of government, of economy, of education and of personality are descriptive of white people.'[8]

Or as Robert Serpell has observed: 'Far too much human psychology is based on studies of White Middle-Class Anglo-Saxon Protestant Undergraduates for us to attach much confidence to the claim that the models it generates describe general characteristics of human beings.'[9]

If the thesis advanced here to return to African cultural systems and the epistemology underlying those systems is accepted as a reasonable basis on which to build new concepts, models and theoretical generalizations, then the African scholar of the future will need to draw scholarly inspiration from experiences characteristic of or unique to his own human condition. Instead of the present almost wholesale adoption of the Western intellectual tradition, the future African scholar will need to construct models and theories based on concepts and biases embedded in his own culture. In the area of the now universally polarized male-female relations, for example, the feminist African scholar ought to resist the temptation of jumping uncritically and blindly on the bandwagon conceived, built and driven by Western feminist thinkers. She must, before joining the band-leaders, question from her own perspective and her own sociocultural background the nature of the wood and metal of which the bandwagon is constructed. It is not African scholarship, not even a sign of being 'educated', for one to adopt a cause or *modus vivendi* largely because it is the fashionable thing to do, or because it assists one to create a mystique, a veneer of sophistication and worldliness in the estimation of Western counterparts.

The feminist African scholar should seek to illuminate and explicate the problem by examining critically such concepts as division of labour and (husband-wife) reciprocal obligations which underpin male-female relations in her society. She must demonstrate their (in)adequacies not only in terms of their original philosophical premises but also in terms of their contemporary (ir-)relevance or (in)applicability in largely changed socioeconomic circumstances and human relationships. By applying her African perspectives and by situating her scholarship in her own special set of circumstances, rather than by conforming to fashionable or seemingly 'modern' or 'radical' views espoused by her Western counterparts educated at Radcliffe, Sarah Lawrence or Bryn Mawr, the feminist African scholar stands a better chance of advancing the cause of scholarship and of contributing positively to her own liberation.

On a broader front, liberated African scholarship is defined as that which would consciously aim to break out of the shackles and strictures of Western scholarship where such scholarship seeks merely to perpetuate the hegemony and tyranny of Western intellectual traditions over other systems of perceiving and interpreting reality. Wherever necessary and appropriate, the African scholar would make informed reference to historical antecedents in the African experience itself and would then draw generalized and generalizable lessons or conclusions from those antecedents. An African perspective of cultural pluralism and national integration, for instance, would regard as particularly critical and of special significance to the contemporary situation how political consensus was achieved in the context of Africa's past; how peoples were incorporated, integrated or assimilated into various African political systems; and what rights, obligations and privileges the citizens enjoyed and how these were exercised. Similarly, in the field of law, the African scholar would be concerned with questions of legality and justice as defined by the African context and in the African linguistic idiom.

African cultural systems and African languages are inseparable, and in the search for a new direction in African scholarship the centrality of language must be assumed. The Western intellectual tradition informs us that 'democracy' was invented by the ancient Greeks and was then subsequently inherited by the rest of the world. One way it attempts to convert us to this point of view is by tracing the word itself back to Greek. A new African scholarship would not take such intellectual evangelization lying down without a protest of analytical appraisal. It would seek to discover whether in fact democracy as a political process was invented or practised only by the Greeks. It would also seek to define (or perhaps to redefine) the word itself. To do either of these two things, it would go to the African linguistic idiom and to the political processes evident in African sociocultural systems to see if all things democratic were indeed on long-term loan from the Greeks.

The African scholar, in his quest for a scientific methodology that takes account of his own sociocultural traditions, need not utilize his languages only toward seemingly negative ends. He should not always appear to be engaged in inquiries which seek only to prove Western Man wrong. He can — and ought to — use his languages and other intellecutal resources more postively. The key to positive scholarship is to recognize that it is in African languages that the concepts and terminology, to serve the new African scholarship, are to.be found. It is in African languages that the denotations, connotations and nuances — the wide range of meanings — required to evolve a new vocabulary, a new terminology, a new scientific lexical infrastructure so far lie dormant waiting only to be rediscovered and given a new contemporary polish.

It is said that when Mwalimu Julius Nyerere, the President of Tanzania, first propounded his Tanzanian brand of socialism and gave it the English name of 'African Socialism', no eyebrows were raised in Western (intellectual) circles. However, as soon as this initial error was corrected by replacing the English name with the Swahili label of *ujamaa*, 'African Socialism' at once assumed an entirely new significance and Western Man sat up upright in his intellectual chair and took immediate note. In this respect, the observation is often made that, in contrast, the failure of Kenneth Kaunda's 'Zambian Humanism' to arouse intellectual curiosity on a wide scale can be attributed in large part to the use of a label derived from the Western intellectual idiom. As such, it does not appear to offer anything new.

One has therefore to ask the question: Would greater use, in future, of Swahili, Hausa, Zulu, Lingala and other African languages lead to the evolution of an intellectual tradition that not only yields a significantly new terminology but also presents to the world a new analytical framework, capable of enriching Man's perception of his environment? On the negative side, would the employment of African languages as linguistic tools for investigation force the African scholar to abandon such Western, ethnocentric, terms as non-white, non-Western, Free World, Third World, developing, developed, Bushmen, extended family, shifting cultivation, etc., and such polarized dichotomies as peasant/proletariat/lumpenproletariat/worker/bourgeois class, or left-wing/right-wing/extremist/moderate, all of which are defined from the vantage point or experience of Western Man? The answers to these questions depend on how original the African scholar intends to be.

Three objectives may be registered against the new direction suggested above. One has a familiar ring. It is the one usually advanced by Africans specializing or who are already specialists in the natural sciences. These often argue that a return to one's cultural roots when other human beings are leaving their bootprints on the moon is to advocate a return to the Dark Ages. Others put it even less diplomatically. They bluntly assert that the White man has discovered all there is to discover, so why play games in the name of misguided cultural nationalism. This objection cannot be adequately countered here except perhaps to say that such attitudes probably explain why expensive foreign liquors continue to be imported into Africa when studies of African traditional forms of brewing beer or distilling alcohol could lead to more meaningful import substitution and less expense; and why progress in agriculture is widely measured in terms of surpluses of celery, cauliflower and cabbage rather than in terms of the abundance of pumpkin leaf, bean leaf or ground peas.

The second objection is similar to the first. It is the fear that emphasis on cultural uniqueness could easily take on characteristics of intellectual xenophobia, resulting in intellectual isolationism. The view is that today's world is a tightly intertwined and interdependent international community, and what happens in one place is bound to have an effect elsewhere. To this view is added the corollary that in any case Western scholarship is not entirely ethnocentric. The latter view is of course correct, and there is not in the argument so far the suggestion that the African scholar should eschew all things Western. Nor have I proposed an antagonistic, anti-Western, polaristic scholarship. Rather, what is not clear, if the world is such a small interdependent place, is why only one part of that small world should have a monopoly on the ripple effect. It is for that reason I would go along with Robert Serpell's assertion that 'consciousness of alternatives is a fundamental right' and that without it 'the freedom to fulfil oneself according to the lights of one culture is illusory'.[10]

The third objection argues that it is the European languages, and not African languages that are the languages already developed and equipped to cope with scientific investigation, analysis and terminology. There is therefore no need to waste time with tools that are inadequate for the job. This is a familiar argument and one which, it needs to be said, has applied to all languages, including at one time (when Latin was the language of scholarship) English and French. It is the sort of argument that makes one wonder whether the logic could be extended to suggest that because Zambia, for example, is not at this point as 'developed' as the USA, Zambia should not bother with development but should instead move all its citizens to the USA so that they could enjoy a higher standard of living. The language behind the miraculous success of Akai, Datsun, Sansui and Toyota is Japanese, and the successful explosion of an atom bomb by China is heralded by shouts and hurrahs in Chinese. Only Africa (with the sole exception of Tanzania) believes in the inevitability of European language as a *sine qua non* of development.

Even without these objections, two major obstacles stand between the African scholar and original scholarship. In the first place, as pointed out earlier, as a result of Western intellectual and scholarly distortions African scholars face the prospect of life-time preoccupations with undoing the wrong and harm that's been done. Only at the end of this long process of corrective scholarship can positive, assertive, non-Western-based scholarship begin to emerge. For years to come much 'original' research will be devoted to setting the colonial record straight or to creating a positive image of the Black man. This means that while criticism will abound, creativity — genuine originality — will remain negligible, and the situation is likely to remain so until the conditions for it are removed.

The second obstacle in the path of the African scholar is that, in his search for illustrative clues from the distant past and recent past, he has for aids only an unreliable and imperfect record — oral transmission. Where his Western counterpart may rely for reference on the accuracy and permanence of the written word, the African scholar has to worry about the reliability of the unrecorded human memory. In these circumstances, reconstructing the record alone is bound to be a time-consuming undertaking. Worse still, the only written record that exists, and the one therefore that the African scholar is compelled to consult, was constructed by the target of his intellectual criticism.

Round Pegs in Square Holes

Two factors, a primary concern with monetary rewards and social status and the shortage of suitably qualified manpower, have already been advanced as being among the probable reasons for the relative absence of distinguished scholarship in Africa. These factors have another, slightly different, conse-quence on African scholarship. It is a well-known fact that, in most African countries, highly trained indigenous personnel in a great many cases are not employed in their fields of specialized training but in some capacity totally unrelated to anything they had ever learned at school. Insofar as the uni-versity is concerned, individual preferences for greener pastures have tended to attract potentially promising academics away from the univeristy and research institutions to areas where conditions of service are considered to be personally more satisfying and materially more rewarding. As a result, poten-tial generators of original thought have become renowned managers of routine administration in the public and private sectors.

Shortage of personnel has had serious consequences in the university itself. In the African university, as a modern bureaucratic institution, the jobs carrying the most social prestige and sometimes the most money are those in the administrative category. In 1976, in the University of Zambia, for example, the majority of those who were appointed as deans of schools had only just acquired their Ph.Ds from various universities around the world. The main motive for this, of course, was the unquestionable axiom that, in an indepen-dent country, important decision-making positions should be placed in the hands of the local people. All the same, snowed under with daily routine adminstration, they could not be expected to contribute in any significant manner to the world of scholarship. This has only one probable outcome. The more bright young African scholars are diverted into administrative posts, the less likely Africa is to witness, at least for the immediate future, a sudden burst on the international intellectual scene of distinguished scholars of her own.

The placing of round pegs in square holes is even more critical in the society at large. In addition to being notorious poachers of talent from their universities, African governments quite frequently misallocate the qualified personnel that they themselves have recruited. Africa has seen, for example, the utilization of medical doctors as ambassadors on a continent where such specialists are said to be in critically short supply. Similarly agricultural engineers have been made overseers of ministries dealing with the tourist industry, and university graduates with a general degree in the liberal arts have been put in charge of technical departments. As I have had occasion to remark elsewhere,[11] the channelling of potentially promising scholars by the larger society into administrative, managerial and political positions has had, and is certain to continue to have, the cumulative effect of postponing the involvement of local scholars in much needed national research and creative thinking.

The African Scholar on the Run

A different set of problems affecting the future of distinguished indigenous African scholarship relates to the political, ideological and social climate in which the African scholar has to work on his own continent. Elsewhere in the world scholars have been compelled to emigrate to the United States to escape what they considered to be an oppressive or unfair income tax system, or because facilities important for their work and for creating a propitious environment in which to prosecute original research were either lacking or inadequate. For roughly the same reasons, thousands of African scholars have opted to stay (on) in Western societies (where they were for the most part trained) mainly because they found in those societies research infrastructures more suited to their level of (academic) training than the facilities available in their own country, and also because those socieites offered them levels of remuneration far above those African countries could afford. Reminiscent of the socio-economic behaviour of their counterparts on the African continent itself who shun the university in pursuit of better material rewards in the public and private sectors, African scholars who make Western societies their temporary (and sometimes permanent) bases of operation appear to rationalize their behaviour from the quite pragmatic, if selfish, viewpoint that the grass is more nourishing where the field is greener.

The intellectual brain-drain, so often and widely lamented in Africa, is also — perhaps more so — the function of the continent's current political instability as evidenced by frequent military takeovers. The inhumanity in South Africa, the lingering colonial legacy in Zimbabwe and Namibia, the recent civil war in Nigeria, the Amin military takeover in Uganda and the political and ideological changes in Ethiopia, all have in various ways resulted in the diaspora of African intellectuals, who, fleeing from socially disruptive conditions at home, have sought temporary refuge in calmer political waters, notably in Europe and North America. In some cases, as in Uganda, the exodus of both local and expatriate academic staff has left the African university teetering on the brink of closure. The consequence most particularly to be regretted is the tendency such a situation has to remove African scholars from their cultural environment and to rusticate them to distant, foreign lands where they often operate as intellectual exiles, denied access to firsthand information. Denied an operational base in the continent of their birth, they tend to revert to analyzing conditions at home through largely foreign lenses, patented by and under warranty of Western intellectual conglomerates.

On the continent itself, a slightly different set of circumstances acts to inhibit indigenous intellectual growth. The emergence of homegrown socio-economic ideologies and/or rigid political manifestoes has on occasion acted as a serious brake on the development of indigenous, independent scholarship. Most would agree that truly original or creative thought, being unconventional, is by definition *revolutionary* and tends to run counter to the accepted norms of society. Originality of thought is particularly unwelcome or most unappreciated — certainly greatly resented — when it fundamentally contradicts the prevailing political credo or socio-economic ideology propounded and cherished by those currently at the controls of power. In Africa, because of the general unstable character of the political infrastructure, one typically encounters a insecure political mood among those in power, to whom new radical ways of thought constitute an immediate threat not so much to the development of the country as to their continued tenure in the former colonial Governor-General's mansion. Thus indigenous political analysts are roundly denounced as political opportunists and challenged to come out in the open: social scientists as arm-chair critics who specialize in misleading the 'masses'; and philosophical analysts as counter-revolutionaries and neo-colonialist reactionaries. In such a political climate, cowardly circumspection becomes the better part of valour, and a reluctance to become involved in public issues and social problems is justified to oneself as a sign of maturity in a political jungle where only the least intellectually or analytically obtrusive have the greatest chance of political survival.

Give Us the Tools and We'll Do the Job

Before concluding this brief examination of the factors which appear to have adversely affected the emergence of original thinkers and actors in Africa, a glancing reference will be made to one final constraint — the lack of suitable facilities and the (financial) means necessary to further original research in Africa.

The history of West Africa seldom fails to record the minute but critically important detail that France's legacy to those of her former African colonies which opted to sever completely the metropolitan umbilical cord at the eve of Independence was to deprive them of the few pieces of chalk that she had made available to them during the years they had acknowledged the Gauls to be their ancestors. Even the telephone was yanked out of its socket to make sure that no orders were placed by merely lifting the receiver. As a result the prosecution of such primary and rudimentary forms of development as literacy was made particularly difficult in these countries, to the extent that African children were reduced to tracing Roman characters in the sand.

To stretch the analogy, African scholars in universities and other research institutions have hardly fared any better. The problem is one of scarcity of resources. As colonial dependencies, African countries were not provided with the necessary research infrastructure by the departing colonial power. As 'developing' countries, characterized by acute shortages of developmental resources, few of them are in a position to divert their meagre resources to the establishment or strengthening of research institutions. In the stiff competition for limited material and financial resources among a wide range of development-oriented priorities, research is seldom perceived as a pressing priority. Typically, African countries prefer to go shopping for ready-made Western solutions rather than invest in investigations of their own. One reason could be that local investigations are considered to be time-consuming (and therefore a brake on development) and costly. Others have suggested that this is indicative of an insufficient confidence among policy-makers in the intelligence of their own local experts.[12] Whatever the reason, research institutions in African generally remain poorly-equipped and ill-endowed. Societal incentives also are only of the rudimentary type. Where in the United States, for example, because of its vast human, material and financial resources, research in every conceivable field is given every possible (public and/or private) encouragement. In Africa generally, research is not especially encouraged. For instance, it is not Africa as one of the continents most adversely affected by the current energy crisis but the United States that is presently frantically investigating the possibilities of utilizing solar energy to replace oil at a future date. Solar energy and the technology to go with it, as usual, will be imported into sun-drenched Africa after Western science has provided the leadership.

Partly as the result of limited resources, partly because of adverse political circumstances and also due to lack of faith in Africa's own institutions, only the most tenuous cooperation at the intellectual level exists among African universities and other research institutions. In consequence very little, if any, sharing of ideas takes place among African scholars. In fact, it would be true to say that in general terms they are not as familiar with each other's work as they should be. On the other hand, they are intimately acquainted with works by Western scholars. This has much to do with the assertion made earlier, namely that it is to Western scholarship and not to the insights provided by his own people that the budding as well as the established African scholar looks for intellectual leadership. Note that even where comparable university courses are available in Africa, an African student will pass up a place in an African university in preference for an experience in a Western university. Even African academic staff prefer to spend their study leaves in Western institutions. London, Paris and Boston and not Ibadan, Cairo or Dakar remain the focal points. Only a radical change of attitude, more infusion of funds into research, greater or more committed public support for African-based research, and the building of adequate intellectual and technological infrastructures to support such research, could significantly alter the present trends and lead to the emergence of a wholly new indigenous scholarly tradition in Africa.

References

This paper was first presented at the Burg Wartenstein Symposium No. 78 sponsored by the Werner-Gren Foundation for Anthropological Research, and will appear in the Proceedings.

1. C. Machyo, 'African social scientists are incapable of making socially correct decisions', *The African Review*, 5 (1975), p.274.
2. A work which is representative of things to come is A. Ladner (ed.), *The Death of White Sociology*, (New York, 1973).
3. R. Dore, *The Diploma Disease: Education, Qualification and Development*, (Berkely and Los Angeles, 1976), p.7-8.
4. *Ibid.*, p.2.
5. N. Hare, 'The Challenge of a Black Scholar', in Ladner, *op. cit.*, pp. 67-8, 73-4.
6. R. Blauner and D. Wellman, 'Toward the decolonization of social research', in Ladner, *op. cit.*, p.314.
7. The psychiatric work by Dr. Thomas Adeoye Lambo in Nigeria, in which a conscious attempt is made to blend Western medicine with the African world view and in the process involving the traditional African doctor (note that I eschew the term 'witchdoctor'), points to a new, healthy realization of the relevance and cogency of Africa's contribution to world knowledge.
8. J. Scott, 'Black science and nation-building', in Ladner, *op. cit.*, p.289.
9. R. Serpell, *Culture's Influence on Behaviour*, (London, 1976), p.10.
10. *Ibid.*, p.11.
11. See my 'The Foreign Researcher: Friend or Foe', a paper presented to the Department of Anthropology, University of California, Berkeley, on 1 January 1978, and to appear in *History in Africa: A Journal of Method*.
12. In his address on the occasion of the Second Graduation Ceremony in 1970, the then Vice-Chancellor of the University of Zambia, Professor Lameck K.H. Goma, remarked that 'Specialists are brought in at very great expense to produce in a few days reports that are worth next to nothing. In some cases, the advice that the visiting so-called experts give today may be identical with what the local expert has been saying for years, but has never been listened to.' To underscore the point, he called attention, on another occasion, to the 'insufficient decolonisation of the mind and the consequent uncritical adulation of foreign experts'. (Refer to 'The Role of the University in National Development' in *The Report of the First National Education Conference*, Lusaka: The Government Printer, 1970).

Study Questions

1. Discuss the view that the traditional African cultural environment did not create conditions for analytical or scientific inquiry, and contrast this with the assertion that original scholarship potential among African scholars has been undermined by excessive dependence on Western

leadership.

2. Is it true that African university education is largely imitative of Western models? If so, is it also true that they produce graduates who only *reproduce* Western concepts and solutions?

3. Examine the view that we need to promote original scholarship in Africa based on Africa's sociocultural roots bearing in mind that it is difficult to prescribe a particular period as the best reference point.

4. Are African languages inadequate instruments for modern education and research? If so why is this the case and what could be done about it?

5. Do you agree that outstanding scholarship in Africa has been inhibited by individual capability and the lack of a suitable climate?

6. Is it still too early to make definite statements about the contribution by Africans to original scholarship in the world arena?

7. Do the prevailing political and economic conditions in African countries promote or hinder scientific inquiry? Why?

12. Lyson P. Tembo
The African University and Social Reform

Eric Ashby, the noted English historian of higher education, once put African universities and motor-cars in the same category. He wrote: 'Just as Fiat and Renault cars are common in Dakar, and Austin and Morris are common in Nigeria, so Dakar has a French pattern of University and Nigeria a British pattern.'[1] That African universities have been like multinational corporations – Western exports into Africa – is a fact which is beyond dispute. The University Colleges of Ibadan, Ghana, Makerere and Rhodesia and Nyasaland, established in the late 1940s and 1950s, were more than appendages of the University of London. They were its extensions. Thus, a graduate of any one of these university colleges put, for example, B.A. (London) after his name. Similarly, the Universities of Dakar in Senegal, Loovanium in the Belgian Congo (now Zaire), Fourah Bay College in Sierra Leone were extensions of the Universities of Paris, Louvain and Durham respectively.

Just like motor cars, these and other African universities were assembled, and also serviced, in Europe. The administrators and academic members of staff were appointed in Europe. The curriculum and courses were designed there. The examination questions and answers had to be checked and approved in Europe. In other words the universities or university colleges were not the universities or university colleges *of* say Ghana, Dakar or Makerere. They were universities or university colleges *in* Ghana, Dakar or Makerere.

The universities mentioned above were established during the colonial period. If these universities were to be beneficial to the imperial powers they had to reflect the values and norms of those various powers. The attitude of the colonial rulers in this matter is well expressed by Sir Philip Mitchell, the colonial Governor in Uganda who was mainly responsible for the basis on which Makerere University College was established. In a speech to the Higher College Council he said: '. . . there is only one civilization and one culture which we are fitted to lead the peoples of these countries – our own. We know no other and we cannot dissect the one we know and pick out this piece or that as being good or bad for Africans.'[2] In other words, what was to be taught in the colleges was to be British or European civilization *in toto*.

Ironically, most of the African nationalists who initiated and carried out the fight against colonialism in their countries which led to political

187

independence were products of Western universities. Kwame Nkrumah of Ghana, Hastings Banda of Malawi, Julius Nyerere of Tanzania and Leopold Senghor of Senegal were educated in British, American and French universities. As Ashby states, African nationalism was born, among other places: 'in America and Britain: in the editorial room of the *African Interpreter* published by African students in the United States, at meetings of the West African Students' Union in London, in Paris cafes. Its sources of inspiration were Jefferson and Lincoln, J.A. Hobson and the Fabians. It grew into popular movements in the newspapers and election platforms and goals of West Africa.'[3]

Most of African countries have been politically independent for more than ten years. Some of them, such as Ghana have been independent for more than twenty years. The universities or university colleges which were already in these countries at the time of independence, and those which were established after independence, were expected by political leaders and the people they led to play an important role in the progress of their countries. On his installation as the first Chancellor of the University of Zambia, for example, the President of the Republic had this to say: 'I confess that the realization of this great enterprise fills me with deep emotion. But the creation of the University of Zambia is much more than a matter of sentiment with me. Many of our hopes for the future of our land and its people are wrapped up in this institution. Without it, we cannot hope to become the nation we want to be. The University of Zambia is one of the keys that can open the door of the future and help us to overcome the persisting evils of poverty, ignorance and disease.'[4]

In this essay, I want to discuss the state of the university in Independent Africa and how that state reflects its performance as an agent of social reform. In discussing what universities ought to be doing one has to consider what the universities are doing, or have been doing in the past.

The university is composed of many parts. There is the institution itself, its academic members of staff, its students and of course its graduates. All these parts of the university may affect society in different ways. But it is the way in which the university is conceived which will determine the nature of the relationship that obtains between it and society and the kind of contribution the university will make to social reform and development.

It must be pointed out here that the universities have not always been agents of social change or reform. Traditional, class-based societies made it a point that university education was used for the ruling class. As late as 1939 in France, for example: '. . . only 2 percent of university students came from families where the father was a worker, whereas 16 percent had fathers who were shopkeepers, artisans, or white collar workers, and 35 per cent had fathers who were professionals or at the head of an enterprise.'[5] This kind of policy ensured that the university was only open to those who benefited from, and therefore conformed to, the values and norms of the ruling class. And the curriculum was such that it reflected those values and did not in any way threaten a deviation from those values.

University education in colonial African ensured that the values and norms which the Africans learned were of the ruling European countries. But independent African countries are not European countries and their values and norms ought not to reflect those values of the West. If African universities are going to reflect African values, they will have to re-orient themselves to the African environment. The contention here is that up to now the African university is still a foreign body and that it does not to a large extent reflect the African society. A brief look at the curricula will illustrate what I mean.

Many of the African universities still follow the curricula and patterns of degrees instituted during the colonial days. Now some of the subjects do not need to be changed. I am here in particular thinking of the subjects in the natural sciences, for the laws of physics or chemistry are not determined by, or dependent upon, the social circumstances or the ideological persuasions of any one society. As it has been pointed out elsewhere, '. . . systems of scientific thought are neutral in the sense that they are not a preserve of any one people or society. Communists, capitalists, Fascists, etc. can use them without affecting the nature of their ideologies one way or another.'[6] Thus the study of subjects in the natural sciences should not be ideologised, nor should mathematics be further mystified by being couched in ideological terms.[7]

Now it is possible to be misunderstood here. In saying that the laws of natural sciences as universal, it is not implied that *objects* of scientific investigations are universal. If the universities in Africa are going to be African, then even in the natural sciences, there is a case for changing the curricula to fit the African environment.

The most important areas for making African universities 'African' are in the humanities and the social sciences, for it is the subjects in these areas which go to define the civilization of a people and which therefore distinguish one people from another. The impact of European imperialism was not only in economics but also on the general culture of the African peoples. The major agents of cultural imperialism were educational systems. The individuals who went through these systems up to the university level were in many cases culturally molded into European forms. The ridiculous extent to which African universities were steeped in, say, the English cultural and social traditions is well illustrated by Ashby: 'Each college . . . bore the unmistakable image of its British origin. Some of it was superficial, a social mimicry of the fripperies of British academic life: gowns, high tables, Latin grace read by a scholar, assembly in combination rooms after dinner with port assiduously passed in the proper directions.'[8] Now some of the traditions which African universities assiduously followed were not mere fripperies. In traditional European universities, the core of civilization was contained in the study of Greek and Latin, and in the study of the people who spoke these languages. Since this study was good for Europeans it was of course good for Africans, and the universities in Africa had no choice but concentrate on these studies. Ashby reports that in the 1959-60 academic year in Ghana twelve undergraduates studied *nothing else* but Latin, Greek and Ancient History. This number was in addition to that which studied these subjects in combination with others.[9] Universities in French and Belgian Africa also reflected the importance accorded to these subjects.

It can of course be argued that this was the case only when the African countries were under the yoke of colonialism. It is true, for example, that the University of Zambia has never taught Latin or Greek since it was opened after independence. Similarly the Universities of Dar es Salaam and Nairobi do not teach these subjects. However, the older African universities still seem to think that Latin and Greek are still important. The University of Ibadan has for its motto, the phrase *Recte Sapere Fons* – a Latin phrase where a Yoruba one would perhaps have been more appropriate.

The point which is being raised here is not that the European classics should be entirely banished from African universities. African countries are part of the world community and the importance of international understanding demands that we understand other people through the study of their civilizations. As Goma has put it: '. . . our Universities must guard against the summary exclusion from their activities, of those subjects or academic pursuits which may be thought to have no immediate . . . relevance. Here one thinks for example of cultural studies, history . . . and even classics.'[10] The point, however, is that in the world there is more than European civilization and European peoples. The study of old Chinese philosophy contained in the works of Confucius or of Sanskrit or Arabic is as important as the study of Western culture for the purposes of communicating with peoples of the world. But what is more important is that before we concern ourselves with other people we should understand ourselves by understanding our own culture. The concentration must be on the reinstatement and development of African culture. In this area, African universities have in general lacked initiative.

The most important medium of thought and transmitter of civilization is the people's language. And yet many African universities have neglected the teaching of African languages. Now it is true that, for example, the University of Zambia has a department of African linguistics. The study of the morphology and phonology of African languages is carried out. African historians are using oral literature as sources for their investigations. But then these languages and their literature, which are useful to linguistics and historians, are not studied in the university, perhaps for the reason that we have been thoroughly conditioned to 'linguistic imperialism'.[11] The result of all this is that the African languages become irrelevant to the academic life of the students and graduates. If the policy of non-teaching of African languages is pursued further the logical conclusion will be disastrous. It will mean that to the extent that the universities increase and expand, and therefore to the extent that the number of graduates increases, to that extent will African languages become *less* viable. This will be a distortion of one of the most important functions of the University anywhere in the world – the enrichment of the language of the culture or society in which the university functions.

What is said above concerning the neglect of African languages in the universities applies to many other areas of African life. African belief systems, African philosophy, the place of traditional medicines are hardly considered. Some universities do have African Studies departments in which some of these subjects are studied, but in many cases the courses are haphazard and are tolerated with reluctance.

Furthermore, except for a very small number of African universities there is no serious development of the arts – music, dance, drama or sculpture. In the University of Zambia, for example, the university is a spectator and unconcerned with these developments.[12]

It can be said that African universities have been under enormous pressures from the governments to produce relevant manpower for the economic, social and political development of their countries. This is true, and understandably, so, given the educational and economic circumstances African countries faced at the time of their independence. At the time of Zambia's independence, for example, there were a little more than 100 university graduates in the country. And yet the manpower survey published in 1969 reported that 12,500 university graduates would be needed for professional and administrative jobs, businesses, laboratories and schools during the decade of the 1970s.[13] Yet the universities cannot expect poor governments to pour hard-earned resources into programmes intended for the creation of a few individuals cultured in Greek and Latin, while the vast majority of their fellow citizens are afflicted by disease, hunger and illiteracy.

Unfortunately most universities have not been innovative. The onus of introducing innovative changes has therefore fallen on the shoulders of the politicians – notwithstanding *resistance* from academics. Many of the proposals for change or innovation in the curricula have, if initiated from outside the university, been opposed by members of the university staff on the ground that this constitutes an encroachment of university autonomy or academic freedom as these concepts are understood, say, in the British tradition. Political leaders have however been adamant. As Azikiwe put it: 'We cannot afford to continue to produce . . . an upper class of parasites who shall prey upon a stagnant and sterile class of workers and peasants . . . We must frankly admit that we can no longer afford to flood only the white collar jobs at the expense of the basic occupations and productive vocations . . . particularly in the fields of agriculture, engineering, business administration, education and domestic science.'[14]

Kwame Nkrumah's creation of the Kumasi University of Technology in Ghana was based on thoughts similar to those of Azikiwe's. Thus, the introduction of applied sciences and technology as opposed to only pure sciences and humanities has been due to political leaders whose concern is the improvement of the life of the masses rather than the approbation of elites. They have also been concerned that technology should also go to rural areas to help alleviate poverty. The academics have just awoken to the realities of African problems many years after political leaders saw them. It is only now, in the 1970s, that African academics can say: 'The African University in the 1970s, must . . . reconsider its priorities. It should participate in the planning, organization, curriculum development and superintendence of institutions for training middle manpower. It should also shift emphasis in its degree programmes from the purely academic to the professional and practical.'[15]

From what is said in the above section, the impression should not be conveyed here that it is the politicians who have made the universities neglect the general cultural aspect of African life because of their insistence on man-power development. This would be untrue. The leaders contend implicitly that there can be no healthy development of African culture — language, thought or belief systems — if the bearers of that culture go starving or have their children dead before they are two years old. In today's world national survival depends to a large extent on the efficacious use of technology.[16]

Even with this concern for national development in economic terms political leaders have been instrumental in ensuring that the universities reflect African cultural values. It was Nkrumah, for example who talked about the importance of African *personality;* the creator of Negritude is Senghor and it is Kaunda who initiated the idea of the Institute of Human Relations in the University of Zambia.

What I have done so far is to complain about the non-Africanness of African universities. I have talked about, perhaps in too general a way, the lack of initiative from African universities in trying to make the university truly African. In what follows, an attempt is made to explore some of the ways in which the university in Africa can reflect the African situation and thereby contribute more meaningfully to social reform.

The first difficulty in making African universities 'African' concerns the African members of the academic staff themselves. The older members of the academic staff, or the first generation African academics joined the universities when their countries were still colonies. The universities these academics attended were in the European countries which ruled the African countries, or they attended the university colleges in Africa. The subjects they took were of relevance to the cultures of the countries which were colonial masters in Africa.

When they became members of the academic staff in Africa, they worked under European professors and administrators who put emphasis on the cultures and needs of their own societies. To gain promotions, they had to per-sistently bend back backwards in their attempts to please their superiors by emulating them in their habits and customs. Mutiso has described these people and the situations in which they worked aptly: 'For this group of academics, there was need to become respectable scholars in the eyes of the colonial academic. Hence they did work which was highly conventional, and did not even fundamentally challenge the intellectual reference points of the colonial education system.'[17] When the universities and university colleges in Africa became independent following the political emancipation of their countries, it was quite difficult for these academics to fit into the new situations and to realise the nature of the demands that would be imposed upon them and their institutions. They were too entrenched in the values and traditions of their masters.

Furthermore, political independence brought with it new opportunities and challenges to those Africans who had some education. The first generation academics in the universities suddenly found that their age-mates, classmates and even their students had obtained important jobs either in the political arena as ministers, or in the bureaucracy. This led to frustration. This frustration led some of these academics to ally themselves with influential politicians so that they could get themselves political appointments.

What are the implications of this for the Africanisation of the university in Africa? In the first place, it is clear that the number of African academics was very small even before independence. The arrival of political independence made this number even smaller. This means that in the first years of independence, the impact of local academics on their universities was minimal. It also means that the foreign educational background of the first generation African academics made it difficult for them to criticise the existing situation. A Senegalese evolue, educated in France in the early 1950s illustrates what is being said here: 'The day you make a distinction between higher studies in the Metropole and those you want to set up in Africa, you will never find a single African in the University of Dakar . . . We want to have higher education at home, but we want it to be exactly equal to that of the Metropole. We want a Metropolitan curriculum . . . for we are as French as the French of the Metropole.'[18] The extent to which the older evolues were immersed in the cultures of their colonisers is further illustrated by Fulbert Youlou, a former Head of the French Congo who boasted: 'In expressing myself spontaneously in French, I do not have the feeling of betraying the African culture. I simply provide an incomparable means of rendering it intelligible to the entire world.'[19] Now it can be argued, as it has been, that the Africans in the French colonies were more conditioned to French civilisation than were the Africans colonised by the British to British civilization. This would be to make fine distinctions. The intentions of the British, French or other colonial powers were not that different. From what is said above, it seems very clear that there is not much hope that this generation of African academics is going to do anything significant in transforming the African University.

The Africanisation of the African Universities is also made difficult by the large presence of expatriate members of the academic staff in some universities such as the University of Zambia. These expatriate members of the staff cannot obviously reflect the values of the African society since the cultures they have lived are different from those of the African countries in which they are working mainly on a temporary basis. In most cases, the presence of these expatriates cannot be blamed on them. They are needed for there are very few educated citizens who can take up academic posts in the university. If the universities are going to be truly African however, efforts have to be made to ensure that local personnel are trained to man them. This is now being done by many universities who find themselves in this situation. What is said regarding the presence of the expatriate members of staff should not be taken to mean that African universities should never employ individuals from other countries. The university, African or otherwise, exists in the international world and the exchange of ideas among academics throughout the world enriches the world of learning. The point being made is that it is ridiculous to call a university 'African' or for that matter 'English' if 80% of its transmitters of culture — the teachers — are foreigners.

The hope of making African universities 'African' in as far as the staff is concerned will increasingly lie with the second generation African members of the academic staff. These second generation academics have a number of advantages over the older first generation academics. Many of them completed their higher degrees when their countries were already independent. Thus they grew up in an environment in which they could feel that they were not being ruled by foreigners who looked down upon the values of their societies. Secondly, many of them had their education, at least the first degree, in the universities of their own countries. Thirdly, in most cases these second generation academics did not go to the universities of the same country as did the second generation academics. In the University of Zambia, for example, young Zambian academic members of staff earned their higher degrees in the United States, Tasmania, Yugoslavia, Britain, India and in other countries. The different experiences these young academics have gone through in different cultures are likely to dissipate the influence of any one culture so that in the end the local culture comes out strong. Fourthly, these young academics are likely to be more committed to their careers in the University, as, for many of them,careers in other fields which attracted earlier academic members of staff do not interest them. More importantly, these young academics are critical of the universities in which they operate. One of their representatives writes: '. . . the colonially created University, like the men who manned colonial outposts, was intended to academically colonise the mind of Africa. Its philosophy and premises were European — it was like the entire educational process, created to kill any remnants of Africanity in the student and the continent.'[20] Of course these ambitious young men will not transform the university overnight. They will have to contend with older academics who are now in power — the professors, deans, deputy vice-chancellors and vice-chancellors who are likely to consider the young academics' views as a challenge their entrenched and well-tried ideologies.

The other point which must be borne in mind when considering academic members of staff and the future of the university is that the future members of staff will come from those individuals who are today students. The way these will reflect the culture of their societies will depend upon the way these students are attuned to their societies. At the moment, most African universities are residential. Students live in quarters segregated from the larger society. Furthermore, their standard of living, at public expense, is far above the standard of living of the common man. In the University of Zambia, for example, students live in rooms cleaned by workers employed by the university, they have their sheets washed, meals prepared and dishes washed for them — all at no cost to themselves. The point is that if the students do not freely mix with their fellow citizens in their ordinary lives and if their standard of living is higher they may begin to think of themselves as a special privileged group. This is not likely to make them understand the problems the society is facing and which demand their action. Ideas of 'ivory towerism' are not conducive to attuning the University to social realities, and students who are brought up in an ivory tower are likely to abide in that tower when they become members of staff.

But in talking about students in the University, and with regard to social reform, we must think of students who have graduated. This group is vital for social transformation. It can in fact be said that the general purpose of the University is *not* to produce university teachers, but rather to produce educated individuals who are going to serve society in the society itself. The relationship between the society and students in African Universities has not always been harmonious. The student has on various occasions been accused of being arrogant, ungrateful and elitist in his views and behaviour.

In most African countries in which education is still a privilege and not a right, there is a danger that education will create a demarcation line in the society. There are wider employment opportunities for the educated minority, and the kind of life style which depends on the more favourable economic emoluments for them will markedly differ from that of the majority of people – and the history of privileged people in Africa is not a healthy one. Whites who were economically privileged for being white during the colonial days lived a life far better than that of blacks who were deprived for being black. The blacks obviously envied the life. This was probably worse for the educated black, for if he was as educated as the white, he wanted to be treated like a whiteman. Being treated like a whiteman had connotations of superiority. The great danger in independent African countries is that the educated African might now take over the habits and attitudes of the whiteman and become in his turn supercilious toward the less formally educated. This kind of attitude cuts across what is decent and what is necessary for social transformation. Being educated in a country like Zambia should be viewed as a debt. It is in this context that Ali Mazrui makes sense when he distinguishes an 'elite of leisure' from an 'elite of labour.' An elite of leisure 'minimises social commitment and exertion and is placed in a situation in which it can pursue a life of comfort without worrying about social disapproval'. An elite of labour on the other hand 'finds it necessary to justify its elite status by providing an example of hard work through its own behaviour and performance.'[21]

One other issue which must be considered in making the African University 'African' is in the area of admission policy. The criteria selected for admitting students into the university determines the kinds of graduates that the university is going to produce. Admission criteria also reflects the kind of society in which that university exists. The criteria for admitting students to university in a rigidly class stratified society will be nothing else than the candidates' membership of that particular class. If a society's concerns are largely in technological development, the university will insist on merit as the criterion for admission. In Africa we want technological development which is possible only through education in the universities and other institutions of higher learning. But we also want our universities to be African in cultural terms. However, if African cultural values are going to be developed in the university, their importance must be reflected in admission policies. If African languages are important in African culture, then the passing of an African language must be a condition for students' entering the university. If African social thought is to be taken seriously in the university, then African oral literature and social thought must be given importance as admission requirements. This applies to the arts as well. African sculpture, dance, music and drama must be taught throughout the primary and secondary school systems if these are going to be viable subjects in the university. This obviously means that what the university demands in this area of entrance requirements will affect the entire education system.

It can be argued here that the major function of the university at this stage of African development is the production of relevant high level manpower necessary for economic development. Therefore, as in the case of the University of Zambia, only mathematics and English language should be the necessary entrance requirements without which a student cannot come to the University. I, however, do not see why the university cannot require both mathematics and an African language. The point I am trying to make here is that either we enforce the importance of African culture or else we conclude that what we need for our existence as human beings is only economic development, without the values that have guided our existence on personal, social and aesthetic levels.

The policy of requiring university applicants to take an African language will necessarily affect staff recruitment policies of the universities. In Zambia at any rate, the best speakers and writers of Zambian languages, and the most qualified sculptors and non-University graduates. There is perhaps no one known among Bemba speakers who is more knowledgeable in Bemba culture than the poet/singer, political and social commentator Chitwansombo. Of course he has no university education.[22] If African languages are to be taught effectively in the university, they will have to be taught by this type of people. If the university demands that only graduates with higher degrees teach then it might as well stop thinking of teaching African languages and literature. In these circumstances, the continuation of studying linguistics in the university becomes unnecessary.

Similarly medical students who want to learn something about the traditional medicine so important in rural as well as urban areas, can only effectively do so from the traditional healers, none of whom have obtained higher degrees in this subject obtained at Princeton or Oxford Universities. In this particular case the government is again ahead of the university for, in 1976, the Ministry of Health in Zambia for the first time organised a conference of traditional healers.

Perhaps one of the most insidious neo-colonial ideas which hampers the proper development of the Universities as African insitutions is that of international standards. The first Vice-Chancellor of the University of Zambia defined international standards as: '. . . something that a University sets in relation to one or two criteria. Standards prevailing at other Universities, or the needs of the country . . . Admittedly, enormous differences exist between the minimum levels of intellectual achievement expected by graduates in different Universities of the same country . . . Nevertheless, there is a sense in which it can be said that certain commonly recognised (international) standards exist, particularly in that part of the University world to which this country looks for leadership.'[23] Now to which part of the world does Zambia or any other African country look for leadership. The first Vice-Chancellor of the University of Zambia was from the West and it does not take much painful thinking to realise that that part of the world he was talking about was the Western world. This is an extension of the old colonial idea of special relationships between university colleges in Africa and the mother universities in Britain. This, as has been pointed out, was a way of ensuring that African universities reflected these values – including political ones – which characterized the societies of the colonial rulers.

The word 'international' itself connotes the intrusion of European nationalism into African Universities for the relationship between African universities and European universities is not truly *international* since only African universities are supposed to emulate European university practices and not vice-versa. I have, for example, never seen a Zambian member of the University of Zambia academic staff go to University of London or Oxford to ascertain whether the standards of Oxford or London compare favourably with these of the University of Zambia. Furthermore, when these people lecture about international academic standards they do not refer to those academic practices that may obtain in the Universities of the Soviet Union, China or India. As Fafunwa observes: 'When an American, Englishman or Frenchman mentions high academic standards, he invariably means the academic standards obtaining in his own country.'[24] The tragedy of it all is of course that most African Universities have accepted this neo-colonial trick. The consequences of accepting this idea of international standards are enormous for the development of the African university as an African institution.

The standards of, say, the University of Zambia are checked by members of staff from foreign institutions. But these external examiners can only assess what they know. What this means is that if the African universities continue to depend on academic standards of other universities, they will never be able to introduce those subjects which are not known, or taught, in those external examining universities. Now as far as subjects dealing with African culture are concerned, this becomes a matter of importance. It means that African languages, dances, drama or music will not be seriously introduced in the curricula of African universities since there are no experts from the outside who can externally examine the performance in these subjects. This brings the African universities back to where they started in the colonial days. Furthermore, since overseas universities require university degrees as qualification for teaching in the university, our universities will never be able to employ any professors in African languages and culture since the only experts in these fields do not have university degrees.

This notion of internal standards does not only affect programmes which affect African cultural values. It affects the kinds of programmes the university undertakes for economic national development. Thus African universities do not normally involve themselves in the education of middle-level manpower. They are prepared to *superintend* the institutions which train this level of manpower, but are not prepared to do the teaching or organisation of the courses themselves.[25]

There may be many reasons for the reluctance of the universities undertaking the training of middle-level manpower. But one of the reasons is likely to be that the subjects which are taught in middle-level, manpower-producing colleges have never been taught in, say, British or French universities. Now there may be other reasons, such as lack of finance, personnel or administration expertise, why the African universities do not teach some of these subjects. But one of the wrong and inexcusable reasons for not teaching them is that they are not taught in the universities to which we look for leadership.

What has been said above should not be taken to mean that any contacts between universities or between academics in different universities should be condemned. I am not trying to champion intellectual isolationism. Conferences, correspondence between academics, visiting lectureships or professorships are necessary for the intellectual and cultural enrichment of the universities and the academics working in them. But African academics should be able to enrich their colleagues in other institutions which the knowledge and experience of their own cultures and societies, rather than with the culture in which their colleagues in foreign universities were born and educated. In this way African universities will not only contribute to the development of the cultures of their own societies but also to the development of world culture as a whole.

Furthermore, in attacking the notion and practice of international standards, it is not being suggested that work done in the African Universities should not be of high quality. The university as the highest institution of learning in any country in the world should insist on the diligence and integrity in *any subject area* of learning or study. No matter how able or learned he may be, an external examiner can do nothing to the quality of performance of students or the University if the teachers are indolent or the students are lazy and unmotivated.

Furthermore, some readers may consider my indictment of European universities' influences in African universities as being too sweeping. Ashby could argue that British universities tried to *adapt* African University colleges to the environment in which they were operating. The recommendations of the Asquith Commission can be cited as examples.[26] But the point is that the decision as to what should be adapted to the African situation, especially the decision to *adapt at all*, should not be in the hands of foreigners.

References

1.   Eric Ashby, 'The Functions of African Universities' in *The West African Intellectual Community*, (Ibadan, 1962), p.48.
2.   Quoted in Kagenda Atwoki, 'Makerere University: The Crisis of Identity' in T.M. Yesufu (ed.), *Creating the African University*, (Lagos, 1973), p.92.
3.   Eric Ashby, *African Universities and Western Tradition*, (Oxford, 1964), p.3.
4.   K.D. Kaunda, 'Installation address by the Chancellor, His Excellency

Dr. Kenneth D. Kaunda' in the *University of Zambia: Inauguration Ceremony,* (Lusaka, 1966).

5. Benard E. Brown, 'French Universities and the Challenge of Modernization' in *Western European Education,* 8, 1-2 (1976), p.45.
6. For an elaboration of this argument, see Lyson P. Tembo, *'Ideology and Education: A Philosophical Analysis',* (Ph.D. dissertation, Columbia University, 1966).
7. S. Niana *Negritude and Mathematics,* cited by J. Ki-Zerbo 'Africanisation of Higher Education Curriculum' in Yesufu *op. cit.,* p.23.
8. Eric Ashby, *Universities: British, Indian, African,* (London, 1966), p.234.
9. See Ashby, *African Universities and Western Tradition,* p.38.
10. L.K.H. Goma, 'The African Universities and Human Understanding' in the *University of Zambia: Seventh Graduation Ceremony,* (Lusaka, 1977), p.9.
11. For further discussion of this issue, see example Gilbert Ansrc, 'A case for African Languages' in *Zango,* 3 (1977).
12. See Andreya S. Masiye, *Singing for Freedom,* (Lusaka, 1977).
13. See *Zambian Manpower,* (Lusaka, 1969).
14. N. Azikiwe, in *The University of Nigeria, Prospectus, 1962-1963,* (Nsukka, 1962), p.7.
15. From the summation on the deliberations of the Association of African Universities Conference, reported in Yesufu *op. cit.,* p.43.
16. Brown, *op. cit.,* p.38.
17. G.C.M. Mutiso, 'The Future University: Towards a Multidisciplinary Research and Teaching Approach' in Yesufu, *op. cit.,* pp.151-2;
18. Quoted in Ashby, *Universities : British, Indian, African,* p.368.
19. *Ibid.,* p.373.
20. Wanyandeh Songa, 'Towards a Relevant University in East Africa', in *East Africa Journal,* 8, 2 (1972), p.5.
21. As quoted in Asavia Wandira in *Teacher Education in New Countries* (May, 1970), pp.31-32.
22. Chitwansombo previously worked for paramount Chief Chitimukulu of Bemba. The government recognised his talents and he now performs and sings on occasions where the Head of State speaks.
23. Quoted in Lyson P. Tembo, 'The University of Zambia: An Analysis of Some Major Issues' in Yesufu, *op. cit.,* p.231. Italics added.
24. A. Babs Fafunwa, *New Perspectives in African Education,* (Lagos, 1967), p.115.
25. *Ibid.,* p.14.
26. See Eric Ashby, *British, Indian, African,* particularly the chapter revealingly entitled, 'The Transplantation.'

Study Questions

1. What do you understand by the term 'elite'? Do you think that elites of any sort have a function in our society?
2. It has often been suggested that 'insufficient decolonization of the mind' is one of the major obstacles to national development. How can the university help decolonise the minds of its students?

3.   How in your opinion are African universities and multinational corporations related?
4.   Do you think African languages should be taught in our universities? How would this benefit us?
5.   Systems of scientific thought are neutral, in the sense that they are not a preserve of any one people or society. Communists, capitalists, fascists, etc. can use them without affecting the nature of their ideologies one way or another. Discuss.

13. Bornwell C. Chikulo
Elections in a One-Party Participatory Democracy

Elections in any political system can satisfy various objectives depending on the specific institutional arrangements of the particular polity.[1] In this paper, we posit the view that the Zambian electoral system has been designed to mobilize consensus in the polity. For our purposes, consensus is defined as a general agreement or accord on the basic institutional arrangements — agreement on fundamentals which makes individuals contending for power accept the 'rules of the game.'[2] In other words, the purpose of the electoral procedures and regulations is to bring about a consensus on the official ideology of Humanism and the socio-economic policies and institutional order it entails. Thus in order to ensure that those contesting the elections are sympathetic and supporters of the Party leadership and its policies, the Party has been made the focal institutional instrument for national political interaction — it controls all aspects of the elections such as the nominations of candidates and the campaign management for both primaries and general elections.

This essay also subsumes a number of more specific questions on elections in a one-party participatory democracy. What degree of choice do elections afford the voter? How does the Party exercise control? What benefits does the regime derive from the electoral system? Answers to these questions will be sought primarily in the analysis of the 1973 and 1978 Parliamentary General Elections.

Political Background
Zambia legally became a one-party participatory democracy on 13 December 1972, thereby granting the United National Independence Party (UNIP) monopoly of political power by making it the only legally permitted party in Zambia. To grasp the significance of this development, the establishment of the one-party participatory democracy has to be placed within the context of the general Zambian political malaise.

Zambia attained national independence in 1964 with a dominant UNIP and a weak but viable African National Congress (ANC).[3] The dominant position enjoyed by UNIP is crucial to our understanding of post-independence political developments.[4] The apparent organizational weakness of ANC, had convinced many UNIP leaders that ANC would die a 'natural death'. Despite

considerable pressure from both the rank-and-file and some of UNIP's leaders
to ban ANC and establish a one-party state by legislative action, President
Kaunda insisted on 'voluntarism' – relying on what Rasmussen has termed
'the snowball or bandwagon' strategy.[5] This assumed that UNIP would
'snowball' both in size and power while ANC would simply atrophy and
disappear from the political arena. President Kaunda and his colleagues had
envisaged bringing about the one-party system by consensual techniques. The
emphasis on consensus was explicitly made by President Kaunda to the General
Conference of UNIP in August, 1967, when he restated a number of principles:

1. That we are in favour of a one-party state;
2. That we do not believe in legislating against the opposition;
3. That by being honest to the cause of the common man we would, through
   effective Party and Government organization paralyze and wipe out any
   opposition thereby bringing about the birth of a one-party state;
4. We go further and declare that *even when this comes about we would still
   not legislate against the formation of opposition parties* because we might
   be bottling the feeling of certain *people no matter how few.*[6]

To this end, UNIP relied heavily upon tactics of coercion and positive induce-
ment to convince ANC supporters that their political and economic interest
could be better served through UNIP – hence the slogan: 'It pays to belong
to UNIP.' However, neither blandishment nor other tactics convinced ANC
of the virtues of dissolution. Instead of dying a 'natural death', ANC steadily
gained strength. Successive elections did not enable UNIP to win the necessary
support for its stated goal of establishing a one-party state through the ballot
box.

The main factor responsible for this was factionalism within UNIP itself.
The factional conflict within UNIP reached very serious proportions at the
fateful UNIP General Conference at Mulungushi in August 1967. The factional
conflict was exacerbated by two related factors.[7] The first was the introduction
of free contested elections for the Party's Central Committee posts – a
departure from previous practice whereby the President of the Party presented
a single slate (which had been agreed upon by the outgoing Central Committee)
to the delegates for endorsement. The second factor was the correlation, for
the first time, between the UNIP Central Committee positions and Cabinet
posts. What was now at stake were official government posts. Securing
positions on the Central Committee therefore came to be regarded not only
as a necessary means of obtaining political power but also of influencing the
allocation of economic resources.

Although various groups and individuals had struggled for ascendancy
within UNIP, the hotly contested Mulungushi elections for the Party's Central
Committee in 1967 destroyed the harmony that had prevailed in the early
years after independence. The elections split UNIP into two ethnically-based
factions: the Bemba-speaking leaders who felt relatively unrewarded and
under-represented joined up with the party's weak Tonga-speaking minority
to unseat leading Lozi- and Nyanja-speaking office holders. The factional
infighting within UNIP quickly spread to the provinces, where it was manifested

in the growth of provincial 'movements'. For instance the *Umodzi ku M'mawa* (Unity in the East) grew in Eastern Province, as an expression of the resentment within UNIP at the elimination from top positions of prominent Eastern politicians, notably the ex-Vice-President Reuben Kamanga who was replaced by Simon Kapwepwe. In the Central Province the *Bantu Botatwe Association* was formed by the Ila-Lenje-Tonga group within UNIP with the main objective of removing Kapwepwe from the post of the Vice-President.[8]

The consequences of the factional infighting were far-reaching. It greatly affected the nature of inter-party competition. To begin with, conflict within UNIP gave the United Party (UP), a small party which had been formed in 1966, a position of political significance. As a result of the polarization of sectional forces in the country, UP's strength grew in Western Province and along the line of rail. Its ability to mobilize political support on the Copperbelt led to violent clashes within UNIP which resulted in proscription in 1968. Thereafter, UP leaders directed their followers to join ANC, and a number of their men were elected on the ANC ticket. Thus though ANC was not effective between 1964-68, its effectiveness began to increase substantially between 1968-73. As a result, the UNIP leadership began to see ANC in a new light, as a possible 'visible alternative' to UNIP capable of attracting dissatisfied elements from UNIP — especially when ANC began to fiercely attack the Matero economic reforms of August 1969.

Between 1969 and 1971 President Kaunda endeavoured to minimize the divisive impact of sectional rivalries within UNIP by instituting reforms in the Party organization. For instance, it was proposed that each province have an equal number of votes and elect two members to the Central Committee. It was also recommended that there be no deputy to the Secretary-General of the Party. Accordingly, the Central Committee of May 1971 contained at least two persons from each province. These measures proved controversial and were deeply resented by the Bemba-speaking faction; the institutional basis of their power was pulled from under their feet and led to their downfall within UNIP. The 1967 arrangement whereby the number of votes cast in the elections to the Party Central Committee by each province corresponded to the number of party regions it contained had given the Northern politicians an electoral advantage — i.e., five out of the eleven Central Committee positions. The redistribution of votes within the party cost them this electoral advantage. Their response was the formation of the 'Committee of 24' — whose main objective was to reverse the new measures and defend the dominant position of the Northern politicians within UNIP. Unable to do so, the Northern faction withdrew from UNIP and formed its own party — the United Progressive Party (UPP) — to try and achieve dominance from outside UNIP.[9] UPP attracted disgruntled groups, non-Bemba as well as Bemba, who felt themselves disadvantaged in the competition for limited national resources.

The transformation of one of the factions into an opposition party (UPP) posed a major threat to the survival of UNIP itself. Pressures within UNIP to declare a one-party state mounted.[10] To save the unity of UNIP President Kaunda declared Zambia a One-Party Participatory Democracy on 13

December 1972, outlawing not only ANC but also future initiatives to establish opposition parties. As the then Prime Minister Mr. Chona succinctly put it: 'Zambia had found from bitter experience that the multi-party system encouraged indiscipline as crooks jumped from one party to another spreading dissension by false rumour. They also encouraged tribalism and now scoundrels have no refuge in one-party participatory democracy. We have fixed them, they are now like monkeys having only one tree.'[11] Whereas the introduction of the one-party state in Ghana was aimed at controlling the opposition existing *outside* the ruling party, its purpose in Zambia was to contain opposition *inside* UNIP.[12]

Officially the introduction of the one-party state has been held to be an integral part of the official Zambian ideology of Humanism. The preamble of the new constitution establishes 'a One-Party Participatory Democracy under the Philosophy of Humanism'. The emphasis under the new system has been on 'taking government to the people', on ensuring that representative institutions of government are identified with the people.

The Electoral Framework

The Electoral Act of 1973 and the Election Rules and Regulations[13] have unquestionably strengthened the role of UNIP in the electoral process by assigning it the task of candidate selection (in the primaries), of formulating the election program, and of handling the conduct of the election at all levels. And, since no extra-party groups are allowed an electoral platform, the party machinery emerges as the only focal institutional instrument of national political activity.

The legal qualifications of candidates for the National Assembly are as follows: candidates are required by the constitution to be citizens who have attained the age of 21 years or over, and who are registered voters and members of UNIP. A person may qualify to stand as a candidate if he or she can read, write and understand simple English. Candidates in each of the 125 constituencies have to be supported at the primary stage by not less than nine registered voters in that constituency. Each candidate in the primary election pays an election deposit of 25 kwacha, which is refundable if the candidate obtains more than five per cent of the votes cast. For the final elections each candidate pays a non-refundable fee of 50 kwacha. Two elections are held – the primary and the (final) general elections.

In the primary elections, the voters are part of an electoral college consisting of local party officials. This college is made up of the following persons resident in the constituency for the purpose of parliamentary elections: (a) In each region: the Regional Secretary, the Regional Women's Secretary, Regional Youth Secretary, Publicity Secretary and two Trustees of the Party; (b) in each party constituency, the Chairman, the Vice-Chairman, the Secretary, the Vice-Secretary, the Treasurer, the Vice-Treasurer, the Publicity Secretary; and (c) In each branch: the Chairman, the Vice-Chairman, the Secretary, the Vice-Secretary, the Treasurer, the Vice-Treasurer, the

Publicity Secretary and Vice-Publicity Secretary.[14]

The principal objective of the primary elections is to produce a list of three candidates out of those who present themselves, and no voting occurs at this stage if the three or less stand. In constituencies where only one candidate has come forward he is (subject to the approval by the Central Committee) returned unopposed. Thus the introduction of primary elections has devolved the power of candidate selection and nomination to local level party functionaries. This is a significant departure from past practice (before the introduction of a one-party state) where the selection of candidates was the responsibility of the President and approved by the Central Committee.[15]

Thus the primaries have given the local party organization a central role and influence in political recruitment — the signifiance of which can only be appreciated if we recall Schattschneider's adage that: 'The Nature of nomination procedure determines the nature of the party; he who can make the nomination is owner of the Party.'[16]

To ensure that those contesting the elections are sympathetic to the Party, its leadership and policies, the three candidates with the highest primary votes go forward to the general elections, subject to approval by the Central Committee. Under Article 75 of the Constitution, the Central Committee possesses considerable discretionary powers to disqualify any candidate considered to be 'inimical to the interests of the state (or party)'. Where the Central Committee disqualifies a candidate, the candidate with the next highest number of votes goes forward to contest the election. The vetting stage has been criticized as being incompatible with democracy. Such criticism is not fully justified since all electoral systems have some kind of control mechanism whether they be one-party or multi-party polities. Indeed, in a one-party polity the role of the party cannot be sustained if it abdicates the right to influence political recruitment. In the general elections every registered voter is qualified to cast his vote, and the candidate who obtains the biggest number of votes is declared M.P. for that parliamentary seat, holding office for up to five years.

The Primaries: 1973 and 1978: The 1973 primary elections took place on 1st November with a total of 532 candidates contesting 124 parliamentary seats. (In the 125th constituency [Chitambo, Kabwe] no one had come forward at the close of the nomination day.) Polling took place in only 76 constituencies; no primary elections were held in 48 constituencies since only three or fewer candidates had presented themselves. The 1978 primary elections were held on 19th October with 766 candidates contesting 125 constituencies.[17] Polling took place in only 114 constituencies; no primaries were held in 11 constituencies.[18] Campaign meetings for the primaries were mostly held indoors before an audience of local party functionaries. All candidates were given equal time to speak on a given topic, usually the official ideology of Humanism and national development.

Following the primaries the names of candidates together with the list of votes received were submitted to the Central Committee which is required by law to screen all candidates. As a result of the vetting 26 candidates were disqualified in the 1973 primary elections; they were suspected of being 'pro-UPP'. In the 1978 primary elections 28 candidates were disqualified. Candidates approved by the Central Committee went forward to the general elections.

The practice of choosing among three UNIP-sponsored candidates affords the voter more choice than formerly. Under the previous multi-party system, voter orientation seemed to adhere more strongly to party labels than to individuals. It was said that the 'constituency belonged to the party' not to the M.P. Whereas in the past UNIP's endorsement in most areas assured election, now the credibility or suitability of the individual candidates may be questioned. Personality is important in determining the outcome of elections since the party organization is supposed to remain neutral.

The General Elections: As the focal institutional instrument, the Party controls the election campaigns and the object is to introduce the candidates to the electorate. The Party is also charged with the task of publicizing and conducting campaign meetings. The officials are required to impress on voters that all candidates are equally acceptable to the Party and that it is up to the voters to decide between them.

Officially the Party does not permit individual unsupervised campaigns, and candidates must therefore canvas at public meetings arranged by the Party. The fear is that candidates may attempt to exploit ethnic or other divisive sentiments in a manner destructive to the Party's priorities of stability and unity. The intention is to ensure fair play between candidates and a nationally-oriented discussion of development policies; candidates have to focus on the achievements of UNIP since independence, Humanism, and the Second National Development Plan. UNIP Rules and Regulations state that '. . . the election campaign itself should focus on those issues which concern you and the nation and not on personalities. It must be based on the desire to *bring together* all our communities instead of dividing them; it must be used to *integrate rather than fragment,* to build the nation instead of dividing the people.'[19]

At the same time candidates in the 1978 election were directed to campaign for the presidential candidate. It was common for candidates to urge the electorate to vote for the presidential candidate and assert that they did not want the vote of anyone who was going to vote against the presidential candidate.

Although the campaigns were supposed to provide an opportunity for propagating UNIP policies, on the whole campaign speeches were devoid of any critical discussion of policies. Candidates usually praised the past achievements of UNIP, before proceeding to call for greater effort in the future. In the former ANC-dominated areas, such as the Southern Province, calls for 'reconciliation' and the 'need for national unity' were common.

To indicate the active support of the party leadership and its goals by the candidates, the presidential and parliamentary election campaigns were conducted simultaneously. However, the presidential campaign was perceived by the Party to be the most important of the two; at every campaign meeting the chairman would begin with praises for the presidential candidate.[20] Thus the campaign mainly sought to legitimize party policies and the central leadership.

The party has obviously been charged with a heavy burden under the one-party system since it scrutinizes the arrangements and conduct of election campaigns. However, the extent to which an election campaign serves the consensual mobilization function is dependent upon the nature and amount of information made available to the voters. As Rose has noted: 'A campaign is . . . a 'feedback' mechanism – a means of exchanging information so that the views of office-holders and electors can be mutually adjusted to the advantage of the electorate.'[21]

Unfortunately, the campaigns revealed characteristics which constituted a major constraint on the party's efforts at consensus mobilization in an electoral context.

The first was the circumscription of issues and the concentration of effort on the presidential campaign at the official campaign meetings. The result was a lack of a real discussion of issues and an abundance of praises for the presidential candidate. The circumscription of issues, coupled with poor attendance at meetings, underline the importance of informal campaigns by individuals. It was the informal campaigns which raised the local issues (or grievances) which the electorate wanted to hear. The prevalence of individual private campaigns, in some instances, resulted in particularistic appeals based on ethnicity, provincial or family ties.[22]

It can thus be concluded that the official campaigns did not at all reflect the essence of the election campaigns, Indeed, the official campaign meetings became something of a ritual in which participants discussed abstract notions of development and Humanism, while the real (unofficial) campaigns progressed largely unchecked.

The poll for the 1973 general elections was held on 5 December 1973. There were 112 contested and 13 uncontested constituencies where single candidates were returned unopposed. In 1978, the general elections were held on 12th December, with 121 contested and 4 uncontested constituencies. *The Results:* The salient feature of the 1973 general elections was the sharply reduced level of voter turnout. Of the 1.7 million registered voters in the country only 39.8% cast their votes. However, this does not mean that there were no constituencies with a high poll. The highest polling constituencies were in the rural areas: Samfya South in Luapula Province polled 68.4%, and Chasefu in Eastern Province polled 68.2%. Some provinces also polled higher than the national gross percentage: the highest was Luapula Province with 54%, followed by Eastern Province with 48.8% and the Copperbelt which scored 46.7%. The lowest polls were recorded in Western Province with 22.0%, Southern Province with 29.2% and Central Province with 36.3%. The 1978 general elections, on the other hand, provide a completely different picture. Out of the 1.9 million registered voters, 66.9% cast their votes.

How do we explain the low poll in 1973 and the relatively high poll in 1978? The low turnout in 1973 has been held to be clear evidence of the widespread opposition to the introduction of one-party participatory democracy. It has been generally assumed (but not demonstrated) that the low poll was a protest vote. As *Africa Confidential* stated: '. . . the low turnout of voters for both elections and poll for presidency suggest a declining enthusiasm for the present political establishment.'[23]

The percentage poll of 39.8 was a sharp drop from the impressive polls registered during the more lively sixties. In 1962, for instance, the turnout was 88.2%, in 1964 it was 94.8%, and in 1968 the corresponding figure was 82.47. The low poll of 1973 therefore clearly did not represent strong legitimacy for the one-party system which had been imposed on the public in the aftermath of serious political cleavage within UNIP. But diminishing participation in the elections has been a continuing trend since independence.[24] What is readily apparent is the fact that since 1968 there has been a discernible drop of

Table 1
Voter Turnout in Zambian Parliamentary Elections

Year of Election	*Overall Percentage*
1964	94.8
1968	82.47
1969 (Referendum)	69.63
1971 (Parliamentary By-Elections)	35.35
1973	39.8
1978	68

Source: Elections Office, Lusaka.

42.67% in voter turnout. Voter participation had been on the decline even before the introduction of the one-party system. Thus if we accept the thesis that the low poll reflected opposition to the one-party state, an obvious problem of validation arises. To begin with, we cannot assume that by not turning out to vote, the voters were doing so primarily out of opposition to the one-party system. For it could be equally argued that some of those who turned out to cast their votes also took the opportunity to exercise what might be construed to be a 'protest vote' in several constituencies. Thus protest can not only be confined to abstentions; voters can equally register their disaffection by participating in the elections. This seems to have been the case in Northern Province where punishment was inflicted on the old leadership who had failed to measure up to the expectations of the electorate. This was either because the electorate thought they had been too far removed from events at the grass roots or because the electorate felt that they should have stood by former Vice-President Simon Kapwepwe and UPP. Thus the voters sought new personalities who might be responsive to their needs. As a result eight cabinet ministers and ministers of state lost their seats. All in all fourteen former cabinet ministers and ministers of state lost their seats.

As a measure of opposition to the one-party, voter abstention is not by itself a wholly satisfactory indicator. It is, therefore essential that in seeking to understand the low poll in the 1973 elections we consider the election result not only within the immediate context but against developments which have been taking place since independence. Several factors may have contributed to the low poll.

First, the capacity of the Party to mobilize the masses in support of the candidates. The decline of party organization has resulted in an inability to mobilize voters. This phenomenon is not peculiar to Zambia; it is general in post-independent Africa.[25] Most observers of African politics are agreed that as far as African political parties are concerned, the trend has been towards inanition. As Fanon has aptly put it: 'After a few years, the breakup of the party becomes obvious, any observer, even the most superficial, can notice that the party, today the skeleton of its former self, only serves to immobilize the people.'[26]

The tendency of Party cadres to gravitate towards government positions has been cited as the major factor for the decline of the Party.[27] The UNIP organization became the most important channel of access to positions in the Central Committee, Cabinet, the Civil Service, the diplomatic service and other sectors. For example, recruitment to the National Assembly in by-elections between 1964 and 1968 tended to favour full-time party officials such as regional politicians.[28] In the 1968 general elections, 24 of the 37 new UNIP members of parliament were recruited from the ranks of UNIP officials.[29]

In the rural areas, local-level UNIP activists used their political positions to gain access to positions of influence in the cooperative movement and local government institutions. Politics, therefore, became more a means to wealth and position than an end itself. The Party became an opportunity structure thereby reinforcing the tendency of party officials to put personal gain before tasks of mass mobilization. This tendency, coupled with the inability of UNIP national leaders to resist pressures from their supporters, inevitably transformed UNIP from a mass mobilization party to that of a pressure group vis-a-vis government institutions, extracting from them material rewards.[30] In the end the Party itself became the victim of this process; those remaining have tended to become apathetic and discouraged, while new recruits to office have lacked the commitment and often the ability of their predecessors in the Party. Thus despite the proliferation of registered branches just before the 1973 elections, there was nothing to indicate that there had been any intensive recruitment of members. Most branches only existed on paper.[31]

Second, while the low poll was partly the result of the declining party capability, in some areas it also reflected the fact that UNIP had never been strongly organized. In the North-Western Province, for instance, UNIP had tended to rely heavily on the civil servants to carry out party tasks.[32] It was only in the late sixties that an attempt was made to establish party organization in the province at all. Similarly, in Southern Province, UNIP had always been overshadowed by ANC. And despite the June 1973 Choma Declaration[33] by which ANC leaders accepted the one-party state and agreed to join UNIP, the attitude of local UNIP officials made it difficult for UNIP to take advantage of the old ANC activists and branches. Although the official policy of UNIP was that former ANC members be admitted to UNIP or convert their branches into UNIP, in some cases, local UNIP incumbents resisted the entry of ANC members to UNIP branches and the registration of new branches.[34] This resulted in the formation of UNIP initiated branches with little mass support which were accordingly unable to bring out the voters.

Third, we shall deal with the extent to which the Party succeeded in educating the masses about the importance of elections. In the early sixties electoral mobilization was one of the areas of political activity which the party performed quite effectively. Its local structures were well organized and enthusiastic. By contrast, the 1973 election campaign was badly organized, Relatively few campaign meetings were held and quite a large proportion of meetings were directed at local party leaders rather than the general public. There was an almost total absence of publicity concerning most aspects of the elections so many candidates remained unknown. Whereas in previous elections party officials knew that their task was to ensure the return of their own party candidates now they were required to act as impartial referees. Party youth were not allowed to drum up people to attend campaign meetings and this obviously limited the mobilization potential of the campaign.

The capacity of the party to moblize votes had also been greatly weakened by the serious divisions which resulted from the formation of UPP in 1971; this weakened the local levels of UNIP and reduced its ability to function free of internal suspicion and recrimination. One observer has noted that on the Copperbelt the serious divisions in UNIP which arose from the formation of UPP meant that the Party entered the election without sufficient time to repair its organization and links with the people. It also weakened the party organization by removing some experienced party organizers who had joined UPP.[35] Gertzel has noted that in Western Province there were attempts to exclude former ANC-UP elements.[36]

By contrast, the high turnout in the 1978 General Elections could be explained by the tremendous effort by the party and government organizations to get the electorate out to vote.[37] Members of the Central Committee, cabinet ministers, political secretaries were detailed to rural areas to spearhead and reinforce the campaign.[38] Great efforts were made by the Central Committee to revitalize and strengthen the Party organization at the grassroots level.as reflected in the increased emphasis not only on the formation of party branches but also on the establishment of Party political committees.[39]

Conclusion

Zambia's adoption of the one-party constitution in 1972 can be regarded as an attempt at consensus mobilization — an attempt to create an institutional structure capable of constraining certain types of conflict and competition, which had dominated the affairs of UNIP since 1964 and had affected the stability of the political system. The one-party system and the electoral system it entails is thus primarily a device for *conflict management*. And since the conflict management and national integration imperatives were primary in the establishment of the one-party state, the significance of the elections should be sought in their consensual mobilization role. The new electoral system has been deliberately designed to help achieve national stability and integration. The function of electoral regulations and procedures — and indeed the constitution itself — is to prevent (or at least limit) narrow sectional interests and social cleavage in order to bring about consensus on major national issues as well as political order. In order to ensure maximum national stability and political consensus, there are built-in features in the electoral process which gives the centre a measure of control. The primary elections, the vetting stages and indeed the conduct of the official campaign itself are designed to ensure the suitability of both contestants and issues introduced at campaign meetings. In short, the primary election and vetting stages are mechanisms for ensuring that those finally elected comply with the fundamental principles and goals of the Party.

The electoral system has been designed to mute sectional conflict while at the same time encouraging a significant degree of competition within the single party framework. Thus it is in this context that the study of the integrative aspect of electoral mobilization fills important lacunae in our understanding of the one-party participatory democracy as a system. Indeed in the modern state the electoral process is of great interest precisely because of its importance in the wider political system.

References

1. See, R. Rose and H. Mossawir, 'Voting and Elections: A Functional Analysis,' *Political Studies*, 15, (June, 1967).
2. For an exhaustive discussion of consensus, see: P. H. Patridge, *Consent and Consensus*, (London, 1971); A Etzioni, *The Active Society: A Theory of Social and Political Process*, (New York, 1968); J.W. Prothro and C.W. Grigg, 'Fundamental Principles of Democracy: Bases of Agreement and Disagreement,' *Journal of Politics*, 22 (May, 1960).
3. For a detailed discussion of the structure and policies, see W. Tordoff and I. Scott, 'Political Parties: Structure and Policies', in W. Tordoff (ed.), *Politics in Zambia*, (Manchester, 1974), pp.107-154.
4. In this context, the dominant party model is very appropriate for our understanding of the developments in Zambia, see A. Arian and S.H. Barnes, 'The Dominant Party System: A Neglected Model of Democratic Stability,' *The Journal of Politics*, 36 (August, 1974), pp.592-614.
5. See T. Rasmussen, 'Political Competition and One-Party Dominance in Zambia,' *The Journal of Modern African Studies*, 7 (October, 1969), p.407.

6. See the Proceedings of the Annual General Conference of UNIP, held at Mulungushi, 14-20th August, 1967, (Z.I.S., Lusaka, 1967), pp.10-11 (emphasis added).
7. See R.V. Molteno, 'Cleavage and Conflict in Zambian Politics: A Study of Sectionalism,' in *Politics in Zambia, op. cit.,* p.68; F. Soremakun, 'The Challenge of Nation-building: Neo-Humanism and Politics in Zambia 1967-1969,' *Africa Quarterly,* 12 (October-December, 1972), p.173; R. Hall, *The High Price of Principles: Kaunda and the White South,* (London, 1969), pp.197-199.
8. *Times of Zambia,* 8 June 1968; *Times of Zambia,* 26 August 1969.
9. R.H. Bates, *Rural Responses to Industrialization: A Study of Village Zambia,* (New Haven, 1976), p.238.
10. Gertzel *et al* have noted that the increased stress on the desirability of a one-party state was related to the formation of UPP. See C. Gertzel *et al,* 'Zambian's Final Experience of Inter-Party Elections: the Bye Elections of December, 1971', *Kroniek van Africa,* 2 (June, 1972), p.70.
11. *Zambia Daily Mail,* 26 September 1973.
12. For a discussion of Ghanaian politics, see D. Austin, *Politics in Ghana, 1946-1960* (Oxford, 1964); also see his latest book, *Ghana Observed.* Similarly, Kilson has noted that regulating competition and tension looms large in the concerns of African Single-Party systems — see 'Cleavage Management in African Politics: The Ghana Case', in M. Kilson (ed.), *New States in the Modern World,* (Cambridge, Mass., 1975) p.87.
13. The UNIP Manual of Rules and Regulations Governing the 1973 General Elections, *Background* No. 118/73 (Lusaka, Z.I.S., 8 October 1973).
14. The UNIP Manual of Rules, *op. cit.; The Constitution of Zambia Act 1973,* Art. 75(3)(a)(b)(c).
15. See R.V. Molteno and I. Scott, 'The 1968 General Elections and the Political System,' in W. Tordoff (ed.), *Politics in Zambia,* (Manchester, 1974), p.168.
16. E.E. Schattschneider, *Party Government,* (New York, 1942), p.64.
17. *Times of Zambia,* 19 October 1978.
18. *Zambia Daily Mail,* 30 October 1978.
19. *The UNIP Manual of Rules, op. cit.,* (emphasis added).
20. *Times of Zambia,* 24 July 1978.
21. R. Rose, *Influencing Voters: A Study of Campaign Rationality,* (London, 1967), p.13.
22. *Times of Zambia,* 5 December 1973; *Zambia Daily Mail,* 15 October 1973.
23. *Africa Confidential,* 14 (14 December 1973); see also J. Pettman, 'Zambia's Second Republic — the Establishment of a One-Party State', *The Journal of Modern African Studies,* 12 (1974), p.243.
24. See Table 1.
25. F. Fanon, *The Wretched of the Earth,* (New York, 1963), p.138; I. Wallerstein, 'The Decline of the Party in Single-Party African States,'

in J. La Palombara and M. Weiner (eds.), *Political Parties and Political Development,* (Princeton, 1966), p.208.

26.   F. Fanon, *op. cit.,* p.138.

27.   See, e.g., M.F. Lofchie, 'Representative Government, Bureaucracy and Political Development: The African Case', *The Journal of Developing Areas,* 2 (October, 1967), p.45.

28.   See I. Scott, 'The Organization of UNIP and Recruitment to Central Political Positions,' (mimeo., University of Zambia).

29.   R.V. Molteno and I. Scott, 'The 1968 General Elections and the Political System,' *op. cit.,* p.170.

30.   See for instance, I. Scott, 'Party Functions and Capabilities: The Local-level UNIP Organization During the First Zambian Republic 1964-1973, *Africa Social Research* No.22, (December, 1976), p.199; R.H. Bates, 'Rural Development in Kasumpa Village, Zambia,' *Journal of African Studies,* 2, (Fall, 1975), pp.341-42.

31.   *Sunday Times of Zambia,* 18 November 1973.

32.   I.U. Masumba, 'Ethnic Conflicts and Political Participation among the Lunda and Luvale of Zambezi District: A Case Study of Zambezi North Constituency in the 1973 Zambian General Elections,' (mimeo, University of Zambia, 1974).

33.   *Zambia Daily Mail,* 27 September 1978.

34.   *Ibid.*

35.   See M. Szeftel, 'The 1973 General Election on the Copperbelt,' (mimeo, University of Zambia, 1974).

36.   C. Gertzel, 'Tradition, Economic Deprivation, and Political Alienation in Rural Zambia: The 1973 General Election in Western Province,' (mimeo, University of Zambia, 1974).

37.   The Government engaged the services of a British political consultant, David Kingsley, as campaign adviser.

38.   See *Sunday Times of Zambia,* 23 April 1978; *Zambia Daily Mail,* 29 April 1978; *Zambia Daily Mail,* 18 September 1978.

39.   *Sunday Times of Zambia,* 16 July 1978; *Times of Zambia,* 19 July 1978.

Study Questions

1.   What do you understand by the term 'one-party participatory democracy.' ?

2.   Examine the major advantages which are expected to accrue from the establishment of a one-party participatory democracy.

3.   What is the major function of elections in a one-party participatory democracy?

4.   Since any member of the Party is free to contest elections, how does the Party exercise control?

5.   What was the major factor leading to the establishment of a one-party system by legislation in Zambia?

14. Robin Fincham and Grace Zulu

Labour and Participation in Zambia

The labour movement in Zambia grew in part at least from the demands of workers for a measure of autonomy in their places of work. From the early struggles against a harsh colonial and company regime, through to established trade unionism in the late 1940s, workers' autonomy emerged as an integral part of the country's industrial relations.[1]

At an early stage there was a demand by workers to be recognised as employees with the right to discuss their grievances with the employer and to expect satisfaction from him. The mine workers and the railway workers exerted considerable pressure to establish this right, The pattern of collective bargaining that eventually emerged in Northern Rhodesia was a response to this demand. It was based on a British industrial relations system known as 'voluntarism'. This system enshrines the right of a trade union to bargain with an employer and to be consulted on matters of welfare, albeit constrained within certain legislative limits. It fitted the needs of a colonial power which was familiar with such a pattern of industrial relations at home and agreed with a general policy of minimal intervention in the colony.

With the emergence of nationalist political parties and the growing struggle for independence, the relationship between party and union became important. Although the model of a 'class alliance against colonialism' fits certain independence struggles, it did not apply in Zambia. Indeed, there were conflicts between the largely petty bourgeois nationalist parties and the trade unions. No use was made of the strike weapon during the independence struggle nor were nationalist parties given access to trade union funds. The leadership of Lawrence Katilungu, who dominated the trade union movement throughout the 1950s, reflected the grass roots desire of the miners, for example, to retain their freedom of action in the industrial sphere.

State and Labour since Independence

With the takeover of state power at Independence the relationship between party and union changed. The insistence on trade union autonomy was resisted by the new Zambian state which was attempting to persuade workers to align themselves with the state's design for national development.[2] The immediate post-Independence period was characterised by frequent unofficial strikes and some major national strikes.[3] Independence had created high

214

expectations. The workers in particular anticipated, and had indeed been promised, improved wages and conditions. They also wanted to see an end to the huge gap between African and European wages.

The state's response was to initiate a number of public discussions and seminars on questions of a labour code and an incomes policy. These included the Livingstone Labour Conference in 1967, two national conventions in 1967 and 1969, and the Turner Report in 1969.[4] The Turner Report was directly critical of the pay rises won by workers shortly after Independence. Turner was concerned with an alleged fall in labour efficiency, regarding this as 'perhaps the most serious feature of wage inflation in Zambia'. The basic reason for this, he concluded, was that 'the colonial system of labour discipline has broken down and nothing has yet developed to take its place'. These discussions were a sign of an increased resolve on the part of the state to curb strike activity. The state began to employ additional strategies to cope with labour, including the centralisation of trade union power under a newly-constituted congress of trade unions; the informal incorporation of trade union leadership into a national development policy; and more comprehensive trade union legislation.

The Zambia Congress of Trade Unions
Already in 1965 the new UNIP government had moved to centralise the labour movement by creating a new congress, the Zambia Congress of Trade Unions (ZCTU). Prior to this, congresses had been troubled by splits and financial problems. The new Congress was to be a powerful agency for the regulation of trade union affairs. Member unions could not go on strike without its agreement, unions were compelled to affiliate or lose the protection of trade union law, and member unions had to pay 20% of subscriptions received to the Congress.

In 1972 a working party was set up under the auspices of the ZCTU's General Council to look into the matter of further increasing its powers. The committee came up with recommendations to give the Congress total power over member unions' finances and decision-making. These recommendations were rejected by all member unions, but subsequently the Minister of Labour managed to impose some of the committee's recommendations. Thus, subscriptions to the Congress were raised from 20 to 30% of member unions' receipts, the General Council of the Congress was given powers to reverse policy decisions reached by annual congresses of member unions, and the General Council was given the right to appoint an observer to wage negotiations by member unions. This represented a considerable increase in the centralisation of the trade union movement.[5]

The ZCTU is also one of the main structures for the communication of government policy to the unions. The Congress organises several meetings each year at which top government officials are given the chance to address labour leaders on labour policies. The government encourages the ZCTU to take part in conventions and seminars to gain support for national development plans. The theme in most of these seminars is labour's role in national development, and it is understood that the main task of the trade unions in this regard is to promote industrial peace and to support the government's policy of wage restraint. The ZCTU generally follows government policy though it does not always welcome government intervention in union affairs.

Incorporation of Trade Union Leaders

As early as 1963, when UNIP was part of a coalition government with the ANC, trade union leaders were brought into the government. In part this was simply a case of using the country's most able leaders at a time when organisational experience was in short supply. Later, however, the practice of giving lucrative but powerless posts to militants developed, as did the practice of extending incorporation to lower level union leaders.[6] Incorporation was becoming institutionalised to the extent that some trade union leaders began to regard a job in government as a part of their career development.

This overt form of incorporation is perhaps less important than the informal ties of friendship and cooperation that are fostered between government and workers' leaders — on delegations and at seminars, in courtesy calls and on local government committees. However, we should be wary of exaggerating the extent to which trade union leaders can be incorporated. While the pressures for it are considerable, there are countervailing pressures from membership who may reject leaders who have become too isolated from the shop floor.

Trade Union Legislation

The third aspect of incorporation is the legal one. The Industrial Relations Act of 1971 consolidated previous laws relating to employment and trade unions, principally the Trade Unions and Trades Disputes Ordinance and the Industrial Conciliation Ordinance. The Trade Unions and Trade Disputes Ordinance provided the basic legal framework for the protection and regulation of trade unions, and its provisions were incorporated virtually unchanged in the new Act. It provided protection against legal proceedings for damages caused to trade in the course of a dispute, and against victimisation for belonging to a trade union. It defined the relationship between the ZCTU and member unions, it enshrined the principle of 'one industry, one union', and it provided for the registration of trade unions.

The Industrial Conciliation Ordinance provided the arbitration procedure for resolving collective disputes. Under this Act the Labour Commissioner was given powers to bring together the parties in a dispute and to act as mediator in the first instance. In the event of a failure to agree the Minister of Labour could then appoint a conciliator to hold a more formal hearing. But at both of these levels arbitration was voluntary; the parties were not bound by the conciliator's decision. Under the Industrial Relations Act, however, a third tier was added, namely compulsory arbitration in the form of the Industrial Relations Court.

The Court is an important innovation. It has powers to resolve collective disputes and, unlike the previous conciliation bodies, its decision is final and binding. The Court is also the new registrar of collective agreements, and no collective agreement may be acted upon until it has been approved by the Court and gazetted. This gives the Court considerable powers, for example over wages. It may restrain wages by simply declaring that a particular agreement is not in the national interest, and ordering that the previous wage levels remain in force. The arbitration procedure also effectively makes strikes illegal as workers may not go on strike until they have exhausted this lengthy procedure. This body of labour law provides for complete intervention by the state in industrial relations. The principle of voluntarism, the traditional basis of Zambian industrial relations, still exists, and where a union is strong enough it can still bargain over conditions of employment. But this now falls under the close scrutiny of both the Labour Commissioner and the Industrial Relations Court and is bound by the limits set by wage restraints, the illegality of strikes and the registration of collective agreements.

Works Councils and Industrial Democracy [7]
At this point we shall break off the general discussion on incorporation of labour and turn to an account of one of its aspects – industrial democracy. The use of industrial democracy as a means of dealing with the demands of labour is now widespread in countries such as India, Tanzania, Yugoslavia, West Germany and Britain. Zambia too has recently followed this trend. Here the chief vehicle for 'industrial participatory democracy' – or IPD – as it is called, is the Works Council as provided for under the Industrial Relations Act. The particular section of the Act relating to councils did not come into force until May 1976, and there followed an introductory phase lasting until November 1977 during which workers were supposed to be educated in their new rights prior to the formation of councils. In July 1978 there were 113 works councils in existence, though in some private firms these existed only on paper.

Democracy in industry usually means participation by workers as a distinct aspect of worker-management relations. The term participation has come to mean something quite different from collective bargaining and relates to management decision-making. It refers to workers taking a part in decisions about production, investment and economic planning – areas previously decided by management alone. Proponents of participation believe that workers' horizons have hitherto been limited to issues of immediate interest to them, like pay, and that they should aspire to playing a much fuller part in the running of the organisations to which they devote so much of their lives. On the other hand, critics of participation have suggested that in the particular situations in which participation has been introduced – invariably at state or management initiative – it has been used to head off a radical upsurge in workers' demands.

Legal Provision for IPD: The notion of workers' participation in management arose from a Presidential initiative in 1969. Although a number of seminars were sponsored by ZCTU between 1969 and 1971 for the purpose of consulting trade unionists, the basic provisions were worked out by Presidential advisors and lawyers, and later amended by Parliament. President Kaunda called for worker participation in management through works councils and representation on the boards of directors of joint stock companies. Although little has subsequently been heard of the latter idea, the works councils appeared in much the same form as they were originally envisaged. 'The purpose of the works councils will be to provide machinery within the undertaking for the participation of the workers in management decisions. In clearly defined areas, which have been traditionally regarded as so-called "management prerogatives" decisions will only be taken with the participation of the works councils.'[8]

An excellent though unfortunately not widely available account of the passage of the relevant sections of the Act through Parliament, and of the way various business interests watered down the provisions, is given by Quemby.[9] She points out that the original intention had been to adopt the Yugoslav system of workers' councils, which have wide powers over the running of firms. However, in the final drafts of the Bill the Zambian government drew back from this potentially radical structure and instead adopted a model from West Germany, a capitalist country. Under the West German system of 'co-determination' the Yugoslav-type *workers'* councils are replaced by *works* councils, which include a sizeable management contingent. In West Germany the councils are usually dominated by management and have very little real power to intervene in the running of a firm.

In the Zambian legislation, workers in government and the civil service are excluded, as are domestic servants. During the passage of the Bill the commercial farmers' lobby was particularly active in restricting its scope still further. An early draft of the Act suggested that the legislation apply to undertakings employing 25 workers or more. However, last-minute amendments in Parliament raised this lower limit to 100 workers. In addition, a new category of worker, the 'eligible employee' was introduced. This category excluded workers hired to do part-time, seasonal or casual work. Much of farm work is of this nature. Taken together these changes meant that virtually the entire commercial farming sector did not have to form works councils.

Works councils have between three and fifteen members, two-thirds of them workers and one-third management. Most councils, since they have been formed in larger firms, have between twelve and fifteen members. The worker councillors are elected by secret ballot of the eligible work force, and management councillors are appointed by the chief executive. Councils are supposed to meet regularly, but not more frequently than monthly.

The powers granted to councils by the Act are defined at three distinct levels, for each of which there are specified powers: (a) Councils have a veto power in the field of personnel and industrial relations. Matters such as recruitment and remuneration of hourly-paid employees, discipline and redundancy require the approval of a majority of the council before they can be implemented; (b) Councils have consultative rights over matters of employees' health and welfare. In theory this confines them to the role of making suggestions. Management is required to bring a proposed decision before the council and to listen to workers' suggestions but not necessarily accept them. However, in practice, consultation and negotiation overlap and negotiation takes place on matters such as factory amenities, medical benefits, pensions and housing; (c) As regards investment policy, financial control and economic planning, the most important spheres of management, a council need only be informed after a decision has been taken. Here management's powers to run an enterprise alone remain unchanged.

A final provision that should be mentioned relates to the secrecy of a council's deliberations. The Act requires that any information concerning the 'financial affairs of any undertaking or any manufacturing or commercial secrets or working processes thereof' acquired by councillors must not be divulged to anyone outside the council. The breadth of this definition means that almost everything discussed by councils must be kept secret from the shop floor.

Attitudes towards IPD: In December 1977 a questionnaire on the usefulness of works councils was sent to all firms that had then formed councils; 121 questionnaires were returned — 81 from worker councillors and 40 from management councillors in 32 enterprises. The responses to some of the more interesting questions will now be discussed.

A large majority of both management and workers' representatives — about 70% — agreed that the councils were working well.

Table 1
'The system is working well considering its short period of operation'

	Management Representatives Agreeing		Worker Representatives Agreeing	
Private	7	(54%)	18	(82%)
Parastatal	21	(78%)	39	(66%)
Total	29	(72%)	57	(70%)

Table 1, however, shows that there were differences between respondents from the parastatal and private sectors. Management representatives from private firms were least enthusiastic about the councils, and workers in private forms were most enthusiastic. In the parastatals management representatives were a little more enthusiastic than workers. This probably reflects the fact that councils in parastatals have generally been established by initiative from the top, and that workers are for the most part relatively well represented by other mechanisms, such as Party committees and trade unions.

The councils appear to experience a fair amount of conflict in their deliberations. More than half the respondents said that agreement was reached with difficulty or rarely.

Table 2
'Agreement is usually reached . . . .'

	Easily		With Difficulty		Rarely	
	MRs	WRs	MRs	WRs	MRs	WRs
Private	5 (38%)	2 (9%)	7 (54%)	14 (64%)	1 (8%)	6 (27%)
Parastatal	14 (54%)	17 (31%)	9 (35%)	30 (55%)	3 (12%)	8 (15%)
Total	19 (49%)	19 (25%)	16 (41%)	44 (57%)	4 (8%)	14 (18%)

Management representatives were markedly less critical of cooperation at meetings than were workers; management representatives in private undertakings were rather more critical than those in parastatals. A similar pattern applied to workers. Thus it seems that councils in private undertakings experience the most conflict in decision-making.

A question testing the effectiveness of councils in terms of the frequency with which their decisions were implemented found management and worker representatives split in their judgement. Whereas 70% of management felt that 'agreed actions' were 'always' implemented, 73% of workers felt that they were only implemented 'sometimes' or 'seldom'.

Table 3
'Agreed actions are implemented . . . .'

	Always		Sometimes		Seldom	
	MRs	WRs	MRs	WRs	MRs	WRs
Private	13 (100%)	4 (18%)	0 (0%)	4 (18%)	0 (0%)	14 (64%)
Parastatal	15 (56%)	8 (25%)	3 (11%)	15 (47%)	9 (33%)	9 (28%)
Total	28 (70%)	12 (27%)	3 (8%)	19 (43%)	9 (22%)	23 (30%)

Management representatives in private undertakings were much more assertive, all of them maintaining that decisions were always implemented. This represents the clearest split between management and worker perceptions of councils, since only 18% of worker representatives in private firms agreed with this. Workers in private firms were also more critical than workers in parastatals — 64% of worker representatives in private undertakings feeling that agreements were 'seldom' implemented, whereas 47% of worker representatives in parastatals felt that they were 'sometimes' implemented.

Finally, a question was asked to try to establish the extent to which councillors felt able to participate freely in works council meetings. Respondents were asked if they felt their employment to be secure or insecure as a result of their participation.

Table 4
'When I speak on any item I feel my employment is . . . .'

	Secure		Not secure	
	MRs	WRs	MRs	WRs
Private	12 (92%)	10 (45%)	1 (8%)	12 (55%)
Parastatal	19 (83%)	29 (58%)	4 (17%)	21 (42%)
Total	31 (86%)	39 (54%)	5 (14%)	33 (46%)

We can see from the table that a substantial number of worker representatives (46%) felt insecure, a rather poor reflection on legal protection against discrimination afforded under the Act (Section 66 provides that 'no employee shall be discriminated against or made to suffer any penalty or disadvantage by reason of his membership of a council'). Worker representatives in private firms felt somewhat more insecure than those in parastatals. This can probably be attributed to the lower level of trade union organization in the private sector, and to the stronger tendency of management in private firms to be autocratic and suspicious of workers who emerge as leaders. There is, however, no firm evidence of this.

To summarize this attitudinal data, councillors thought of councils as useful though not consensual bodies. Manager councillors were less critical than worker councillors on a number of issues: the effectiveness of councils and their potential for cooperative action, and the extent of protection against victimisation. Councils in private firms were judged, on the whole, less favourably on these issues. Finally, there was a markedly higher level of conflict between manager and worker councillors in private firms.

The Rank and File: Apart from the questionnaire for councillors, a number of firms with works councils were visited and groups of workers were interviewed informally to try to find out the extent to which they were able to participate in councils. Virtually all the workers spoken to saw works councils as a means of improving communication between management and workers. However, their most common complaint was that their representatives never discussed agendas with them. In the words of one miner: 'How are we going to participate if we do not even know what goes on in the works council meetings?' Many workers were emphatic about wanting to know the agenda *before* meetings — aware that discussion with their representatives before decisions were taken was important. It seems that the great emphasis on secrecy in the Industrial Relations Act is having the effect of isolating councils from workers.

Some miners interviewed felt that their trade union was more representative than the works council. They gave examples of how their trade union leaders obtained views from workers and how they kept workers informed. These miners in particular regarded the council as a management platform, its meetings did not compare well with the union's which were well-publicised and open to all.

In two private firms visited, councils had not held any meetings. In one of the firms, which manufactured plastic and steel articles, management had disbanded the council. This was an interesting case as it showed how a crafty management can evade the law. The firm occupied one site under a single general management, but the premises comprised three separate buildings, each employing between 70 and 90 workers. Management had originally conceded that the whole firm could form a council, but then changed its mind, saying that each plant must be taken separately. Each was therefore below the minimum size required to form a council.

In another private firm, a clothing manufacturer, all the representative institutions — the Party committee, works council and trade union branch — were regarded by workers as being weak and under management control: 'You rarely hear of them', said one worker. Workers agreed that 'militancy among workers is not tolerated by management', and gave the example of a recent strike in which the leaders had been instantly sacked.

In summary, the usefulness of councils was doubted by workers, though they were in general well-disposed towards any chance to sit down with management.

The Business Establishment: We have so far looked at IPD mainly as a state initiative. We shall now look at businessmen's views on participation as expressed at a Presidential commission of inquiry set up in June 1977 — the Special Commission on Equity Participation. Its terms of reference were workers' participation in equity and the future of workers' participation in management.[10] Evidence was collected from a variety of sources, mainly from local and foreign businessmen. Evidence from special interest groups — for example, a judge and a church representative — were largely in agreement with the businessmen. The Commission report has not yet been published; the following data is taken from a file of evidence.

The Commission was told that management would accept worker participation if it did not interfere with traditional management decision-making. Most submissions showed a preference for participation through the present works councils. In particular they stressed that councils must be made to succeed before any further participation could be envisaged: 'The present objective should be to enhance the effectiveness of works councils. It is too early to evaluate the effectiveness of works councils because they have not worked for a long time' (Indeco) ; '. . . sufficient time should be allowed to implement this training (i.e. for further participation) before any further degree of participation is allowed and in this regard we consider that a period of 5—10 years should be considered.'(Zambia Sugar) ; 'Workers' participation is a good idea but needs to take a long process for an evaluation to succeed . . . Works councils are the best form of participation at the moment.' (Cleopatra Fashions) .

The commercial farmers, who were originally responsible for limiting councils to firms of more than 100 eligible employees, were least interested in participation. They stated that: 'The majority of workers in the agricultural industry are not disciplined. The industry should be allowed to organise itself better, raise productivity to feed the nation and produce surplus for export before it can afford to raise wages and introduce bonuses and lastly participation.' (Farmers Employers' Association).

One of the most common themes in the evidence was the threat to investment, particularly foreign investment, that might result from workers being given too much voice. That Zambia needs to 'attract' foreign capital was not questioned, and much of the commissioners' time was taken up considering whether particular forms of participation might make Zambia less attractive to potential investors. It was argued that: '. . . private enterprise can only be attracted when it is allowed to be directly responsible for managing and controlling its own business. If it were required to operate under a cooperative basis, special arrangements would have to be carefully worked out. We should appreciate the fact that for a long time to come, the country will continue to look to the private sector for new investment' (ZamAnglo). A legal adviser giving evidence: 'told the Commissioners that an investor who brings capital into the country from outside asks two basic questions: (a) is his capital safe? and (b) can he make a profit? If both questions are satisfactorily answered, he will be perfectly happy to take risks.'

And in his first summing up, the Commission's chairman stressed that participation might frighten off foreign investors. 'Commissioners were concerned to "work out how we are to attract foreign capital within the constraint of workers' participation". Zambia cannot do everything alone. She will need outside foreign assistance. We do not want a nation of beggars, it is undignifying. We want security which has its strength in economic power . . . Business is about management and money. Let us be consistent and define participation effectively to help prosperity.'

Many of the businessmen were aware of the West German system of codetermination. Bigger employers, such as Anglo-American, were particularly well-informed. All were clear that if participation had to evolve in Zambia these were the lines along which it should do so. 'The West German system of workers' participation seems to be more impressive and one needs to examine it more seriously. . . ZamAnglo would fly into Zambia an expert on the West German system of works councils at their expense if the Commission needed him' (ZamAnglo). One management, Zambia Sugar, saw workers' participation evolving as a junior partnership within management. This again is a variation on the West German model. 'Following the effective development of works councils we see the next stage as being the appointment of works council members to observer representatives at Board meetings and being selected for their contributions and training for sub-committees which may be set up by the Board to look into specific problem areas.'

From the above brief account it can be seen that business interests had a very clear idea of the kind of workers' participation they found acceptable, namely the works council. They were cautious about any changes.

Conclusion

Whether rank and file workers in Zambia still constitute the autonomous force
they were up to the mid-1960s is a difficult question. Certainly there are now
many forces ranged against the militant expression of workers' demands.
Since Independence the state has been increasingly adamant in its resistance to
wage demands, and the labour market has become less favourable from the
workers' point of view. Yet the incorporation of workers remains
problematic.

The small space left for manoeuvre by the wage freeze and the illegality of
strikes means workers have to find other means of furthering their interests —
for example, in winning recognition from management. This was illustrated in
our case study of works councils. The councils did not seem to be effective in
terms of the objectives for which they were set up, namely granting workers
'meaningful participation'. The value of councils as propaganda instruments,
considering the secrecy of their proceedings, must be virtually nil; and as a
channel of communication and influence over workers the councils have little
potency. Yet they appear to be at least as lively as some of the other
institutions for worker representation.   By no means all managers evaded
fulfilling their part in council meetings, and some parastatal managers expressed
positive attitudes towards councils. Furthermore there was a great desire by
workers for an additional channel of communication with management, at
whatever level. Workers were often optimistic about the councils, while at the
same time recognising their shortcomings.

Perhaps the central issue in industrial relations is whether the working class
has the strength to represent and further its interests. Indeed, for an industrial
relations system to exist at all workers must have some kind of strength —
otherwise there are no 'relations', only administration by state and employer.
Zambia's pattern of industrial relations lacks much of the structure existing
in advanced capitalist countries. Direct state intervention in disputes, poor
job security, and the absence in many places of shop stewards contribute to
an industrial relations system which is apparently haphazard. Whether or not
workers are represented at a particular place of work frequently depends on
the presence or absence of a strong personality willing to stand up to management. Workers are often driven to spontaneous action by the combination of
a docile (or absent) trade union leadership and an arrogant employer. For these
reasons the incorporation of labour is of less importance in a country like
Zambia than it would be in a country with a large and organised working class.
Of course, in relation to many African countries, Zambia's working class is
large and organised, and so we do see the subtle tactics of incorporation at
work. But even here incorporation is not the main tactic in the state's
armoury, it is one among others. In Zambia employers can rely on an inter-
ventionist state and a highly favourable labour market.

References

1. The theme of worker autonomy has been a fairly common one in interpreting Zambian industrial relations. See, for example, I. Henderson, *'Labour and Politics in Northern Rhodesia, 1900-1953: A Study in the Limits of Colonial Power'* (University of Edinburgh, Ph.D. thesis, 1972).

2. I am grateful to Ben Turok for this interpretation of the concept of incorporation. The particular phenomenon of the uncertainty of incorporation is nowhere more evident than on the Zambian copper mines. See R.H. Bates, *Unions, Parties and Political Development* (Yale University Press, 1972).

3. The frequency of strikes reported in the Monthly Digest of Statistics for 1965, 1966, 1967 and 1968 were respectively 114, 241, 222 and 206. These compare with frequencies in 1974, 1975 and 1976 of 55, 78 and 59 respectively. In addition, in 1965 and 1968 there were national strikes by railway workers, 1966 saw the last national miners' strike, and in 1970 the nation's last national strike occurred when the teachers came out.

4. *The Livingstone Labour Conference* (Lusaka, 1967); *National Convention on the Four-year Development Plan: Kitwe 1967,* (Lusaka, 1967); *Report of the Second National Convention on Rural Development, Incomes, Wages and Prices in Zambia: Kitwe 1969* (Lusaka, 1969); H.A. Turner, *Report to the Government of Zambia on Incomes, Wages and Prices in Zambia* (Lusaka, 1969).

5. See the *Annual Report of the Department of Labour, 1973*, p.19.

6. An interesting example of this is given by M. Burowoy, *The Colour of Class on the Copper Mines,* (Lusaka, 1972), p.83.

7. This section has been abbreviated from a forthcoming article: R. Fincham and G. Zulu, 'Works Councils in Zambia: The Implementation of Industrial Participatory Democracy'.

8. The Presidential Address in the *Report of the Second National Convention,* p.22.

9. Angela Quemby, 'Works Councils and Industrial Relations in Zambia', in E. Kalula (ed.), *Some Aspects of Zambian Labour Relations* (Lusaka: 1975), pp.85-104.

10. The meaning of 'equity participation' had not been defined by the Commission at the time of this research. Usually it refers to profit sharing in the form of a bonus paid out of dividends on shares held in trust for workers. At the time of writing interest in equity participation had died.

Study Questions

1. Explain the meaning of the concept, *'incorporation* of labour'; and answer the following questions about it. Why is incorporation an uncertain tactic? What are the range of tactics of incorporation open to the state? Why should the state wish to incorporate workers rather than employ some other tactic to deal with their demands? Why is it suggested that in a country like Zambia incorporation is not such an important tactic for the state?
2. In what ways has the state rationalised its labour policy in the 1970s?
3. What is understood by the term 'workers' participation in management'? What are the arguments for and against this form of industrial democracy?
4. What are the powers, composition and coverage of the work councils in Zambian industry? What is their role supposed to be in relation to the other institutions of workers' representation — i.e. the trade unions, Party committees and works committees?
5. Outline the attitudes towards works councils of the main groups that are concerned with them: rank and file workers, worker councillors, trade union leaders, management (private local, private foreign, parastatal) and commercial farmers.

15. Robert Serpell

Aspects of Intelligence in a Developing Country

When a psychologist discusses intelligence he generally uses a rather different approach from that adopted in everyday discourse. Because of his emphasis on technical aspects of measurement he tends to become unintelligible to those outside his specialised field of knowledge. There are two common reactions to this unintelligibility, opposite in their value judgements but both equally damaging to productive communication.

The sceptical reaction is to conclude that the psychometric approach to intelligence is irrelevant to the real issues of significance. It also implies that the discipline of psychological testing survives solely on the strength of a professional mystique, protected from public debunking by its facade of technical jargon and bewildering statistics. The opposite extreme is the reverential awe with which some politicians and administrators receive the pronouncements of psychologists as experts. Acknowledging the complexity of the statistical procedures involved as a technical necessity, the adherents of this position plead only for a simplified statement of the expert's findings and a practical indication of their implications.

I shall not in this article attempt directly to demystify the statistical aspects of psychometrics. My interest is in the underlying assumptions made by psychological tests of intelligence and the question of their validity across various cultures. Many of these assumptions are implicit and therefore as yet not fully absorbed into the technical terminology of the discipline. This makes them both easier to talk about in ordinary language, and more likely to be sources of weakness in the discipline as it enters new fields.

One aspect of the world 'intelligent' which is almost deliberately ignored by much of the psychological literature is that it has what the philosopher Hare has called a 'secondarily prescriptive' meaning.[1] This is to say that when you apply it to a person you are not only *describing* him but you are also *prescribing*, or advocating, a certain moral attitude towards him. Under certain circumstances, for instance, you are recommending that the intelligent man's judgement be relied on in preference to that of other, less intelligent men. This secondary moral content of the word has important implications for its use in a cross-cultural perspective. For in the modern world it is widely accepted that no single ethical yardstick can be applied universally to men of all cultures. Moral values are nowadays likened to aesthetic styles: the acceptance of polygamy by one society and of Old People's Homes by another is taken for granted in much the same way as the difference between European and Chinese music. Of course, some ideologies, like Christianity and Marxism, still maintain that in the moral sphere there exist certain absolute values to which various societies aspire and approximate in differing degrees. But it is common enough (especially in historical discussions) to find adherents even of these creeds making concessions towards cultural relativism by describing some eminent figure outside the fold as living 'unknowingly' or 'in his own way' in accordance with 'true' Marxist or Christian ideals. Whether we use this kind of formula, or whether we call him 'a good man by the lights of his culture', we are making a complex subjective evaluation, relating the criteria of another society in a very abstract way to those of our own.

Objective physical criteria, on the other hand, are generally accepted for assessing physical prowess. Either you can run a mile in four minutes or you can't. Testing conditions have to be equated, and the specialist will take into account not only the condition of the track and the force of the wind, but even the athlete's experience of that altitude and perhaps the intangible effects on morale of a 'home ground'. But these are technical details for adjustment so as to allow full scope to the only 'true' arbiter, the stop-watch. Curiously, intelligence testing is modelled more closely on athletics than on ethics. Yet intelligence, according to one authority, is the 'global capacity of the individual to act purposefully, to think rationally, and to deal effectively with his environment'.[2]

The claim that it is possible to measure objectively such a very abstract and very desirable attribute only became plausible in the West by a process of gradual evolution. The first step, and perhaps the most crucial, was to choose by intuition a set of appropriate tasks — to create a miniature environment within which the mind could demonstrate its purposeful, rational effectiveness. Little attention is given to the details of these tasks in much of the literature concerned with mental testing. Validation is principally based on correlations with other measures, like teacher ratings, university entrance and occupational success. These criteria bring out very clearly how much the values of the particular society have to do with the definition of intelligence. They also provide the main *raison d'etre* for IQ tests. Because the tests are more objective and more reliable than less formal methods of assessment, they are widely used in the West for selection. There is thus a self-confirming cycle: the tests were deemed valid because they agreed with society's criteria, and because they agree they are increasingly used by society as criteria themselves.

The tests are, of course, more than what they correlate with, and a massive literature has grown up around the question of exactly what they measure in psychological terms. But it is a significant fact that this literature (sometimes called psychometrics) makes only marginal contact with the mainstream of basic psychology. For instance, a very large part of the literature in experimental psychology concerns the nature of the process called learning. Yet the relation between measured intelligence and efficiency in learning remains very obscure. Likewise, the task of fitting in theoretical principles of perception and of language with the concepts evolved as 'factors' of intelligence has only just begun. In recent years the theoretical insights of Piaget concerning the nature of cognition and of Chomsky concerning the nature of language have been widely invoked in experimental psychology to throw light on changes observed in children's behaviour as they grow up. Yet neither of those theories features at all in the structure of currently prominent IQ tests. For the psychometrician, or test psychologist, predictive validity in application weighs more heavily than explanatory value of the test in its own right.

The difference of orientation between intelligence testing and experiments on the nature of intelligence leads to different conceptions of cross-cultural research. Thus in Eysenck's recent book *Race, Intelligence and Education,*[3] an environmentalist view of the determination of intelligence is evaluated on the basis of studies which attempt to 'equate' racially different samples for socio-economic and educational status. The rationale for this approach is drawn from studies confined to 'white', Western children showing that those living in poor housing conditions and attending overcrowded schools score, on average, lower on IQ tests than children of higher status. The idea of controlling these status factors in a cross-cultural study appeals to the test psychologist partly because it leaves untouched the assumptions about what his tests measure. The strategy is analogous to noticing that the average height of a defeated national team of runners was lower than that of the winning team, and asking for a repeat competition with runners from the two countries equated for height. The weakness of this approach is that in the case of IQ tests we have only a very tenuous theory of how environment affects test performance. It may or may not be right to assume that long legs make for fast running, but at least the structure of such a causal relationship is plausible and obvious. How exactly would poor housing affect a child's performance on an IQ test?

Vernon, the eminent test psychologist, recently published an ambitious study of the relation between intelligence and cultural environment, comparing eleven-year-old schoolboys from five countries.[4] In his conclusions he lists eighteen different explanations for the poor performance on IQ tests of what he calls the 'seriously handicapped groups' (Jamaican, Ugandan, Canadian Indian and Eskimo). Apart from genetic and constitutional factors which might be related to living in an impoverished environment, he distinguishes eleven environmental factors which are theoretically related to the development of intellectual potential. These range from the presence of books and TV in the home to a 'demanding' but 'democratic' family climate, emphasising internal controls, responsibility and interest in education'. Unfortunately, very little of the research backing up these theoretical ideas has actually manipulated on its own the variable which is supposed to be critical. Studies are more often designed along the lines of a survey comparing groups who have and have not bought themselves a TV set than of an experiment placing TV sets at random in half the houses of a relatively untouched community. In survey studies it is always a problem to control or to evaluate the hidden factors which may have caused the observed differences between the groups compared.

Another category of Vernon's explanations is labelled, significantly, 'extrinsic factors'. These are the variables which according to the general theory of testing shouldn't be there. They include anxiety, unfamiliarity with tests in general and with the particular testing conditions, linguistic difficulties in understanding instructions, and 'difficulties due to particular forms of items or materials'. In the manual for an IQ test, there is always a paragraph about the need to put the child at ease, to speak clearly, and so on, and there can be no doubt that when the tasks were first conceived a lot of imaginative intuition was brought to bear on how to make them attractive to children and easy to understand. But there is also little doubt that the intuition was derived from experience of children within a particular culture.

Evidently, a child must know the language of a verbal test if he is to score, and much research remains to be done on the difficulties caused by taking tests in a 'second language', the prevailing condition in most under-developed countries. Interest has focused recently on the possibility of analogous difficulties when the home dialect differs from that of the school, as happens for most 'black' Americans and West Indians in Britain. But what about non-verbal tests? The evidence points from many sources to the conclusion that here the differences between cultural groups are greater than on verbal tests. These tests rely mainly on visual perception to interpret the task directly without the assistance of words. Hence the relevance of experimental research into the influence of culture on visual perception. This field comprises, as yet, only a small number of studies. Within them we can distinguish three major strands of theory: linguistic relativity, cognitive style and perceptual learning. We will look at each in turn.

The linguistic relativity theory in its strongest form was proposed by Whorf, anthropologist and linguist.[5] It states that what man perceives is categorised and restricted by the language in which he thinks. The many fine distinctions among different kinds of snow made by Eskimos are underwritten by the complex snow vocabulary of their language; and the urban American child's capacity to pick out different kinds of automobile is based on his large vocabulary of brand-names. Conversely, if a language lacks the words to express a particular distinction its speakers will generally fail to perceive that distinction in the real world. Because in any language there are so many ways of expressing a single idea, this theory is difficult to put to a crucial test. But on one topic it has certainly fared rather badly: selective attention to colour and form.

Ask a child to match a red triangle with one of two other figures, a red square or a blue triangle and, strangely enough, he will usually make a quick and confident choice. The clue he chooses to use (colour or form), however, will vary according to several factors. In Europe and America several studies have shown that as children grow older they tend more and more to attend to shape in preference to colour in this kind of ambiguous task. It has also been shown that meaningful shapes, like a fish and a boot, make for more shape responses by young children than abstract shapes like squares and triangles.

In the last few years studies of this kind have been conducted in Liberia, Nigeria, Senegal, Uganda and Zambia.[6] In each case African children responded with a much greater preference for colour than European children of similar age.

Now in two of these studies the language situation was assessed. Wolof, the language spoken by the Senegalese children, has a rather meagre vocabulary for colours, and urban children tend to use French words instead. In Zambia the Bantu languages tend to have words for light and dark and for red, but abstract words for blue, green and yellow are seldom used, especially in the towns, where English colour terms prevail. From the colour vocabulary, then, the Whorfian hypothesis should predict, in both countries, not more but less attention to colour by African children than by European children. In the Zambian study we had used triangles and squares for the shapes, and for these concepts too the Bantu languages seemed to lack an abstract vocabulary. To see if this could explain the results, we compared two groups of children for whom, in a direct test, words came to mind equally for triangles and squares. The English-speaking children were about six years younger than the Zambian group, had spent rather less time in school, but came from much more privileged homes in terms of socio-economic class. Equal in shape vocabulary and better equipped with colour vocabulary, the English group still attended far more to shape than the Zambian group. In fact, they matched by shape as often as another comparable Zambian group had done with fish and boot in place of square and triangle. Probably familiarity with abstract geometrical shapes has a lot to do with this cross-cultural difference, but in young children at least it is not just a question of how easily the shapes are named.

Another major approach to cross-cultural studies of perception derives from the field-dependency theory of Witkin.[7] This describes a link between the individual's personality and his mode of perception, in the form of a general cognitive style. At one extreme is the field-dependent type, who relies heavily on his social environment for emotional security and displays a global approach to perceptual tasks. The opposite is the field-independent type, who is socially independent and more analytic in perception. Research supporting the theory has generally found that girls tend to be more field-dependent than boys. This is attributed to differences in upbringing. Cognitive differentiation, or field-independence, is said to be fostered best when parents emphasise self-control rather than conformity enforced by punishment. The idea that parental attitudes to boys and girls impart to them different styles of perception has been taken up and extended to cultural differences in traditions of child rearing.

Witkin's research introduced two rather unusual perceptual tasks, and related performance on them not only to personality variables but also to performance on other better-known tests. The idea of the original tasks is to place in conflict the directional pull of gravity as sensed by the body and the visual clues to true vertical. In one task he put children in a tilted chair and then tilted the whole room in which the chair was situated, asking them finally to adjust their chair until they were sitting upright. A less elaborate

231

task requiring a similar kind of judgement is used in the rod-and-frame test. Here the child sits in a pitch-dark room and adjusts until he thinks it is vertical a luminous rod which rotates independently in the middle of a luminous square frame. Because the walls of the room are invisible, field-dependent children can rely only on the luminous frame for a visual clue to the vertical, and by tilting the frame the experimenter puts the visual clues in opposition to the body clues from gravity. Children in Witkin's studies who succeeded in setting the rod at true vertical tended also to be good at finding embedded figures, a task in which again 'dependence' on the surrounding 'field' is a hindrance, as was shown many years earlier by the *Gestalt* school of psychology.

In one of the few experimental studies conducted by an African psychologist in his own country, Okonji gave the rod-and-frame test to undergraduates at Nsukka University.[8] He found that students raised as children in poor rural homes gave more field-dependent responses than those raised by middle-class parents in the city. The cognitive style explanation of this result is based on the differing patterns of family discipline in the two communities. But the perceptual skills of the urban group might also have been directly promoted by their educated parents and well equipped schools. A number of other cross-cultural studies have appealed to Witkin's analysis, but they often rely on paper-and-pencil tasks like the embedded figures test to measure field dependency. This raises further problems of interpretation, since in both Okonji's study and an earlier Nigerian study by Wober[9] much lower correlations were found between performance on embedded figures and the rod-and-frame test than are usual in Western populations. If the tests do not correlate, it is safest to assume they are not measuring the same thing.

Wober has an interesting solution to this dilemma: field dependency is still a valid concept, he argues, but it needs to be measured differently in Africa and the West.[10] In Africa cognitive style becomes elaborated mainly in the perceptual domains which are emphasised by African culture. Following the philosophy of McLuhan, he suggests that vision has become dominant in Western culture because it is the medium of mass communication in the printed word, advertisements and television.[11] In Africa, however, other kinds of perception are fostered by the emphasis on music, dancing and sculpture. The rod-and-frame test is therefore more appropriate as a measure of field dependency in Africans than the entirely visual embedded figures test. Moreover in two studies where their body was tilted West Africans made adjustments of the rod-and-frame type rather better than Europeans and Americans, whereas in other studies with the body erect Western groups performed better. The details of this experimental evidence are not entirely satisfactory and more research is required. But the theory presents a clear alternative to field dependency as the factor responsible for cross-cultural differences.

The idea that African culture promotes a different 'sensotype' from Western culture, with less emphasis on vision, more on hearing and the body senses, is one of several cross-cultural hypotheses which rely on the concept of perceptual learning. The common theme among these hypotheses is the suggestion that every culture actively promotes the learning of certain perceptual skills relevant to the performance of tasks which are considered important. In cultures where literacy and technology have become of paramount importance in education a lot of skills concerned with deciphering symbols on bits of paper have come to be regarded as essential and are taught to almost all children at a very early age. In many of the rural communities in Africa, Asia and South America, on the other hand, such skills are largely irrelevant to the valued activities of the local culture and are therefore not taught unless children enter the exceptional environment of a school, and even then they receive far less emphasis than in the technologically more developed countries. In particular the conventions of representing distance in pictures are much less well understood outside industrialised countries than is commonly assumed by the artists who illustrate school books.[12]

Other types of perceptual learning are less consciously promoted. One elaborate study has attempted with considerable success to show a link between the type of terrain in which a community lives and the extent to which its members are susceptible to certain visual illusions. Such illusions have long been a topic of interest to psychologists; some are also known as party games. Among the many different explanations proposed for the Muller-Lyer illusion, one is based on the idea that the oblique lines suggest a three-dimensional appearance: when they reach outwards, the centre is like the corner of a room indoors; when they reach inwards, it is like the corner of a building seen from outside. Now if the effect of the 3-D appearance is to trick the eye into thinking one centre line is farther away than the other, compensation for distance will make the far-away line (with obliques reaching out) be judged longer than the other. If this account is right, the illusion represents a case of perceptual learning misapplied. The eye has learned to make this judgement automatically because it is so often exposed to straight edges of this kind in the real world. Consistent with this view is the general finding that people from environments less 'carpentered' than those produced by Western culture are less susceptible to the illusion.

It might seem rather extravagant to postulate such an intricate explanation for a cross-cultural difference which could be accounted for under the general heading of differences in familiarity with drawings. But there is also striking support for the 'carpentered world' hypothesis in a study by Allport and Pettigrew.[13] A very compelling illusion for Westerners designed by Ames, artist turned psychologist, was presented to two groups of Zulu children, one living in remote villages composed of exclusively dome-shaped, thatched houses, the other in the city of Johannesburg. The illusion consists of a trapezoidal window frame which, when rotated at a certain speed presents the appearance of a normal, rectangular window oscillating to and fro. As predicted, the rural children were much less susceptible to the illusion than those in the city. Not having seen many right-angled windows before, the rural children had not acquired the perceptual bias which causes the illusion.

The horizontal- vertical illusion also has a 3-D explanation. The vertical line could represent a line extending away from the perceiver's eye, foreshortened

by perspective: compensation leads to the judgement that it is longer than
the horizontal line, which is all in one plane. Segall, Campbell and Herskovits
set out to test the idea that susceptibility to this illusion would also depend
on how frequently the perceiver had been exposed to similar arrangements in
his natural habitat.[14] In this case Western cities are not at the end of the relevant range of environments. People living in deserts or open plains would
probably see more foreshortened lines along the ground than city dwellers,
while those living in jungles or dense forests would presumably see fewer. By
enlisting the co-operation of anthropologists working in many parts of the
world they collected a mass of results which tend to support their analysis.
An important feature of this study is that the groups most susceptible to the
horizontal-vertical illusion turn out to be different from those most susceptible to the Muller-Lyer illusion. In order to explain such a result it is necessary
to go beyond the general argument on grounds of familiarity with pictorial
material to look at the relevant details of perceptual learning. Further research
is continuing on these lines, with various different types of visual illusion.

The link between perceptual learning and cross-cultural differences in performance on non-verbal tests of intelligence is an obvious one. But the details
of this relationship are likely to prove complex. A number of experimentalists
have adapted Piaget's intellectual tasks by using local materials in remote rural
communities. In some cases the conceptual development of children in a wide
variety of cultures appears to follow a remarkably similar time schedule to
that of children in the city culture of Geneva. But with other tasks the pattern
seems to be quite different.[15] Greenfield in Senegal explored children's
growing understanding of the fact that when water is poured from one vessel
into another of a different shape it does not change in amount.[16] Young
children tend to confuse the judgement of quantity with that of the dimensions
of the vessel or with the level to which the water rises.

For American children in Massachusetts an effective way of overcoming
their confusion and uncertainty was to screen the water levels until the child
had made a judgement of whether the quantity had changed. But for children
in remote Wolof villages who had never been to school the screening procedure didn't help at all. They did much better, however, if they were allowed
to pour the water themselves instead of watching the research worker do it.
Greenfield suggests that the critical factor in this was that it ruled out for the
children the possibility of some kind of 'action magic' inherent in the stranger's
way of pouring. Another explanation might be that, for children of an African
'sensotype', handling is in general more important than watching. Or, still
more simply, we might suggest that the formal demonstration which was
effective for schoolchildren requires an element of perceptual learning to be
understood at all, learning which is imparted in the preliminary stages of
Western education.

A remarkable study informed by this kind of perceptual learning approach
was conducted in Mexico by Price-Williams, Gordon and Ramirez.[17] Their
interest was in the impact on performance of Piaget's intellectual tasks of
perceptual skills acquired in the home environment. They chose for comparison

two groups of children in each of two Mexican villages: one group from families who were traditional potters, the other group from families with other occupations. The first group are introduced at an early age to the family craft and are soon fully involved in production. In the course of this professional training they learn, of course, that the same piece of clay can assume many shapes. As it happens, Piaget used exactly this phenomenon as a parallel to the water task described above. But his theory interprets the ability to judge the constant amount of clay or water under various transformations as evidence of a profound intellectual growth. The Mexican study found that at the same biological age children without the special experience of making pottery were far behind the other children on this task. In one village this difference between the groups extended to a great variety of such tasks, using not only clay but also materials quite unrelated to the pottery skills. In the other village the difference was confined to the clay task.

One of the confusing aspects of so much cross-cultural research is that we always seem to be testing how good non-Western people are at doing Western tests. Whenever they do poorly the question can be raised: is this because they have not learned the perceptual habits necessary for interpreting the test, or does it reflect a deeper, conceptual deficit or an intellectual handicap? We have seen that in the case of visual illusion non-Western people often fail to make the mistakes characteristic of a Western population. But, of course, Western tests of intellectual potential rightly avoid the use of items like these which are known to cause confusion in Western populations. A fairer test of the notion that non-verbal Western tests include a hidden perceptual bias would be to go back to the first intuitive stage of test construction and devise a test appropriate to a different cultural group. If this could be done in all innocence, the prediction would be made that Westerners should experience a perceptual learning handicap and score lower on the test than the 'normal' population on which it was standardised. Speaking of just this possibility, Eysenck writes, 'it may confidently be predicted that any attempts to find such tests will end in failure.'[18]

The first problem in this undertaking is one of innocence. The kind of research worker likely to attempt such a task is bound to know a certain amount about the perceptual and intellectual skills of Western children. A second and more serious problem is the scope of intuition. What is required is an appraisal of what constitute within the culture in question the most highly valued instances of purposeful action, rational thought and effective dealing with the environment. How many people can credibly claim to have made such an appraisal of any culture other than the one in which they were reared? And for the growing number of non-Western psychologists there is the additional problem that their very conception of these aspects of thinking and behaviour has been developed in the context of a largely Western education. We have recently begun a programme of research in Zambia which is aimed at tapping some of the latent wisdom of rural parents about what aspects of children's intellect are cherished and promoted in their village communities. After identifying a group of children of roughly the same age, we ask an adult familiar with them to indicate which child he or she would select for each of a variety of hypothetical everyday tasks. This is followed up with questions designed to clarify the criteria which an informant has applied in making each choice. It is too early to tell whether this indirect approach will yield any valuable insights: it would be surprising if there were no areas of overlap with concepts of intelligence in the West. But perhaps there will be differences of emphasis. Wober, for instance, has shown that a Luganda word which translates most readily as 'intelligent' is perceived by rural Ugandans as having much less to do with speed than is the case for the English word as judged by American students.[19]

A less daunting project which goes some of the way towards testing the hypothesis which Eysenck rejects starts by accepting the Western definition of a particular intellectual skill. The definition is accepted in very abstract terms, however, and intuition is applied within another cultural setting to devising an appropriate task. As with Price Williams's Mexican study described above, the emphasis here is on the form of certain tests as distinct from their intellectual content. The guiding assumption is that a major contribution to an individual's score is the extent of his perceptual skill in the medium, as distinct from his underlying abstract intelligence. An attempt to test this idea for the skill of copying was made recently for urban Zambian boys.[20] Several Western IQ tests require the copying of shapes or designs, and Africans generally score rather low on these tasks. A series of studies in Zambia led to an increasing emphasis on the difficulty inherent in the copying process itself as distinct from the mere perception of shapes.[21] Drawing with a pencil, and arranging patterned blocks like a jigsaw, the usual modes of copying required, are both skills which Western children pick up at home and in school very early in life. What kinds of skill does a child growing up in a Zambian city slum pick up which could be tapped in a copying task? Pencils and paper are scarce, jigsaws and building blocks unknown.

One kind of copying requires no tools at all, and this is mimicry. So we devised a mimicry task of copying hand positions, starting with very simple items like the hands clasped in prayer, and ending with complex arrangements of intertwined fingers. Another likely candidate was the skill of bending wire. A very popular hobby among boys in Lusaka is to build skeleton cars out of old bits of wire. The models can be quite intricate, with suspension and steering, and the bodywork is carefully styled for various makes. The game is played almost exclusively by boys, and it has no obvious counterpart in Britain. Our test of ability based on this used a series of wire shapes, starting with a plain circle and ending with a stick figure of a man. The child has to copy each model with a length of pliable wire.

A number of children were tested on these tasks, as well as on closely parallel tasks with paper and pencil and with plasticine. The following results were obtained for eight-year-old boys and girls from poor homes in Lusaka and eight-year-old boys and girls from a slum district of Manchester. These children had all attended school for about two years; their parents were in both cases people of little education, but belonging to quite different cultures. The skill of copying hand positions was equally developed in both communities. Older Zambian children, in their sixth year at school, scored much higher on this test, and mentally handicapped eight-year-olds in Manchester scored much lower, but the two groups of 'normal' eight-year-olds did equally well. The wire-modelling task gave quite different results. Zambian eight-year-old boys scored much higher than their English peers. Girls in each group did less well than boys, but even Zambian girls scored higher than English boys. Yet when almost the same shapes were copied in the pencil and paper medium, English children scored much higher than their Zambian peers. Not only do English schools lay much greater emphasis on drawing than Zambian schools, but the English children were more likely to practise this skill at home. The results for plasticine were less clear-cut, with neither cultural group excelling over the other: probably the English children's greater experience with this medium in school is offset by the extensive practice of Zambian children at modelling in the similar medium of earth and water.

These results clearly follow the general pattern predicted from the children's opportunities for particular kinds of perceptual learning. It is hard to see why the medium in which a child is asked to copy (be it bending wire, moulding plasticine or drawing with a pencil) should affect the amount of general ability to think rationally which he displays. Children learn to deal effectively with the environment in which they live: this means acquiring quite specific perceptual skills. We looked, incidentally, in this study at the broader concept of 'sensotypes' proposed by Wober.[22] Half the children in each group did the modelling tasks with their eyes blindfold. The effect of losing vision was disastrous in either culture. No doubt in some cultures the skills of carrying water on the head or of making pottery are learned more generally than in the West. But to tap children's ability we must use tasks in which they can perceive how to apply the skills they have learned. Zambian boys were better at bending wire than English children even blindfold, but their superiority was most marked when the task was presented in its familiar, visual form. Likewise, neither group copied hand positions better blindfold: this test too taps a mainly visual skill.

It may be instructive to contrast the design of this study with that of a study by Jensen, 'Comparison of "culture-loaded" and "culture-fair" tests'.[23] He compared performance on two tests by three groups of schoolchildren, lower-class Mexican Americans and U.S. Negroes, and middle-class U.S. whites. (Since I am quoting, I will beg the controversial question of how these groups should properly be named by using the author's terminology.) The reasoning which guided his choice of tests was as follows: a highly culture-loaded test was defined as one in which 'the more difficult items are those calling for information with lower probability of being acquired in the culture — for example, being able to identify a picture of an aardvark as compared with a picture of a dog'. As an extreme example by this criterion he chose the Peabody Picture Vocabulary Test, in which he showed that as the items get more difficult they also become rarer words in the English language. (In this test each item consists of four pictures, one of which represents a word which

the tester speaks, and the child is required to point out the correct picture.)
At the other extreme, as a 'culture-fair' test, he chose Raven's Coloured Progressive Matrices, a non-verbal test in which a logical sequence must be
detected within an array of abstract shapes. The more difficult items in this
test are no rarer in American culture than the easy ones, since all the shapes
are meaningless. The results of the study showed that, while middle-class
white children scored highest on both tests, on the Vocabulary test Negro
children scored higher than Mexicans and on matrices Mexicans scored higher
than Negroes.

At first sight this study appears similar in conception to the Zambian-
English experiment. But the difference in criteria for choosing the tests is
all-important. Jensen assumes that these tests, standardised on 'white'
American children, measure what they purport to measure, no matter to
whom they are given. Culture loading for him is defined by the content of the
test. Mexicans are at a disadvantage on the Picture Vocabulary test because
the vocabulary itself is not provided in their homes. The possibility raised by
cross-cultural studies of perception is that the pictures, technically the form
of the test, could be an additional source of bias, as distinct from the words,
which are the content. Not only Africans but also 'lower-class U.S. Negroes'
have been shown to experience more difficulty in classification and abstraction
when the items used are pictures instead of familiar objects, although these
two forms of test are quite equivalent for middle-class 'white' American
children.[24] US 'whites', for whom both Jensen's tests were originally devised,
are closer in home language to US Negroes than to Mexican Americans, but in
use of pictorial materials they may be closer to the Mexicans. If so, the results
obtained can be explained in terms of perceptual learning. Experience in
problem solving with pictorial materials may be of great importance in determining scores on both these tests, especially Raven's Matrices. Both tests are
biased against the Negro groups in form, but in the Vocabulary test this factor
is outweighed by the verbal content. Because he considers only the content of
the tests, Jensen instead interprets the results as revealing less abstract ability in
the Negro than in the Mexican group.

Much has been said and written recently about the motives underlying
research on intelligence. It is probably not sufficient to rely on the traditional
academic argument that 'facts are one thing, attitudes are another'.[25] Desirable
as it may seem that science should concern itself only with facts, every human
research worker can trace part of his endeavours to his own attitudes. These
become especially significant when he is trying to spell out practical implications. Research seldom covers more than a few of the factors relevant to
practical policy, and there is great scope for subjective bias in deciding how
much emphasis to apply to the 'facts' one has discovered. On the other hand,
it is all too easy for those who have no respect for facts to undermine the
value of research by oversimplifying the motives which guide it. In our present
state of knowledge the theoretical assumptions made by 'test' psychologists
lead some of them to interpret their results in a way which coincides with
judgements made on quite different grounds by racialist politicians. But to

share certain opinions is not the same as sharing objectives.

The different theories discussed above should be confirmed or rejected only on grounds of factual evidence. But because there is so much scope for discretion in where to lay emphasis, and because it takes a long time to rule out any theory conclusively, it is worth looking in practical terms at their various implications. The linguistic relativity theory has a number of modern adherents in a slightly more up-to-date form. Instead of suggesting that language restricts perception, they argue instead that it moulds abstract concepts. For an independent nation, 'emerging from backwardness', on this view there are strong grounds for introducing education in the medium of one of the languages of industrialised nations. The thought processes of the next generation will thereby attain higher levels of abstraction. Field dependency theory sees as critical the style of parental discipline, so to raise the nation's capacity for analytic perception requires a campaign of parental enlightenment. Perceptual learning theory allows of two different approaches: to modify the tests or to modify the people.

Already some 'test' psychologists in underdeveloped countries favour the idea of practice runs on intelligence tests. Western tests, they argue, are the best we have got, and they do predict school achievement even in non-Western societies. If everyone is given some practice, they will quickly learn the knack. The idea is analogous to letting athletes from low-altitude countries do their training in Mexico for the 1968 Olympics. There is good evidence that practice does improve performance on IQ tests much more in underdeveloped countries than for the population on which they were standardised. But it is also very likely that early experience is more valuable than later in life. So, in parallel, this perceptual learning approach leads to advocating pre-school enrichment programmes, providing jig-saws and other constructional toys in day nurseries and the like. Like all the other policies listed so far, this is one of 'raising the level of ability' to that of Western man. They differ only in the methods they propose for achieving this end.

The great danger of such policies is that they are entirely Western-centred. Vernon justifies this on the grounds that underdeveloped nations have opted for a Western industrial economy. But underdeveloped nations tend to be eclectic about Western values: they aim for computers and motor cars but not for Old People's Homes. To what extent do we defeat this aim by insisting that to enter the space age they must develop their minds along Western lines? The predictive validity of Western tests in African education may simply reflect the fact that education in Africa is modelled on Western lines.

Some political observers might argue that in underdeveloped countries at present Westernisation is a better qualification than intelligence for success in industry or government administration. But if we hold on to the value judgements with which the concept of intelligence is so heavily loaded, what kind of society would we build based on selecting men for employment on these terms? We would be guiding into positions of authority and responsibility not those endowed with the greatest 'capacity to act purposefully and think rationally' but those who by accident or design have made the fullest adjustment to the culture of the West. The political objections to this aim are only too obvious in nations which have struggled so intensely to throw off the oppressive culture of colonial powers. Yet the possibility that this is the objective towards which we are working is obscured by formulations of policy aimed at 'raising the level of ability' of a whole nation. This is for me a most potent reason for exploring by experiment what exactly we are measuring with so-called tests of intelligence and how the various skills involved are related to different cultures.

References

This essay was first published in *Africa Social Research*, 17, (June, 1974).
1. R.M. Hare, *Freedom and Reason*, (Oxford, 1963).
2. D. Wechsler, *The Measurement of Adult Intelligence*, (Baltimore, 1944).
3. H.J. Eysenck, *Race, Intelligence and Education*, (London, 1971).
4. P.E. Vernon, *Intelligence and Cultural Environment*, (London, 1969).
5. B.L. Whorf, *Language, Thought and Reality: selected writings of Benjamin Lee Whorf*, (New York, 1956).
6. H.M. Irwin and D.H. McLaughlin, 'Ability and preference in category sorting by Mano schoolchildren and adults', *Journal of Social Psychology, [JSP]*, 82 (1970), pp.15-24; R. Suchman, 'Cultural differences in children's colour and form preferences', *JSP*, 70 (1966), pp.3-10; T.P. Kellaghan, 'Abstraction and categorisation in African children', *International Journal of Psychology [IJP]*, 3 (1968), pp.115-20; P.M. Greenfield, L.C. Reich, and R.R. Olver, 'On culture and equivalence: II', in *Studies in Cognitive Growth*, (New York, 1966), pp.270-318; J.L. Evans and M.H. Segall, 'Learning to classify by colour and by function: a study of concept-discovery by Ganda children' *JSP*, 77 (1969), pp.35-52; R. Serpell, 'Cultural differences in attentional preference for colour over form', *IJP*, 4 (1969), pp.1-8; R. Serpell, 'The influence of language, education and colour on attentional preference between colour and form', *IJP*, 4 (1969), pp.183-194.
7. H.A. Witkin, 'The perception of the upright', *Scientific American.* 200 (1959), pp.50-6.
8. M.O. Okonji, 'The differential effects of rural and urban upbringing on the development of cognitive styles', *IJP*, 4 (1969), pp.293-305.
9. M. Wober, 'Adapting Witkin's field independence theory to accomodate new information from Africa', *British Journal of Psychology*, 58 (1967), pp.29-38.
10. *Ibid.*, M. Wober, 'Sensotypes', *JSP*, 60 (1966), pp.181-9.
11. M. McLuhan, *The Gutenberg Galaxy*, (London, 1962).
12. W. Hudson, 'The study of pictorial perception among unacculturated groups', *IJP*, 2 (1967), pp.89-107; J.B. Deregowski, 'Pictorial perception and culture', *Scientific American*, 227, 5 (1972), pp.82-8.
13. G.W. Allport and T.F. Pettigrew, 'Cultural influence on the perception of movement: the trapezoidal illusion among Zulus', *Journal of Abnormal and Social Psychology*, 55 (1957), pp.104-13.

14. M. H. Segall, D.T. Campbell, and M.J. Herskovits, *The Influence of Culture on Visual Perception*, (New York, 1966).
15. J. Goodnow, 'Culture variations in cognitive skills', in *Cross-cultural Studies*, (Harmondsworth, 1969).
16. P.M. Greenfield, 'On culture and conversation', in *Studies in Cognitive Growth*, (New York, 1966), pp.225-56.
17. D.R. Price-Williams, W. Gordon and M. Ramirez, 'Skill and conservation', *Development Psychology*, 1 (1969), p.769.
18. Eysenck, *op. cit.*
19. M. Wober, 'Towards an understanding of the Kiganda concept of intelligence', in J.W. Berry and P.R. Dasen (eds.), *Culture and Cognition*, (London, 1973).
20. R. Serpell, in preparation.
21. R. Serpell, 'Cross-cultural differences in the difficulty of copying orientation: a response organization hypothesis', *Human Development Research Unit Reports*, No.12 (University of Zambia, 1969).
22. Wober, 'Sensotypes'.
23. A.R. Jensen, 'Comparison of 'culture-loaded' and 'culture-fair' tests', in 'An experimental analysis of learning abilities in culturally disadvantaged children', (Office of Economic Opportunity, Contract No. OEO 2404, 1970), pp.90-102.
24. I. Sigel, L.M. Anderson, and H. Shapiro, 'Categorization behaviour of lower and middle-class Negro pre-school children: differences in dealing with representation of familiar objects', *Journal of Negro Education*, 35 (1966), pp.218-19.
25. Eysenck, *op. cit.*, p.12.

Study Questions

1. Why are some factors influencing performance on intelligence tests regarded by certain psychologists as 'extrinsic'?
2. How does the linguistic relativity theory interpret the relation between language and perception? Describe an alternative possible view of this relationship.
3. On what grounds does field-dependency theory explain the observed tendency for African students raised in rural homes to perform less well on the Embedded Figures test than those raised in towns? Describe one or more alternative explanations for this observation.
4. What evidence is there that prolonged experience with a certain kind of environment leads to a bias in perception? What are the implications of this phenomenon for the interpretation of performance on intelligence tests?
5. Discuss the concept of a 'culture-fair' test of intelligence.
6. How does the use of 'intelligence tests' affect manpower policy in a Third World country?

16. Muyunda Mwanalushi

Dimensions of Stress Among Zambian Youth

Adolescence is the period of transition from childhood to adulthood. It begins with puberty (about 11 to 13 years), culminating in the assumption of full adult responsibilities, such as marriage, parenthood, independent living, etc. The concept of 'adolescence' is unrecognised in many socities, but youths everywhere must at some point pass from sub-adulthood to full adult status. It is this transition which is called adolescence.

As a transitional period, adolescence has often been viewed as a period of considerable emotional stress. Adolescent stress refers to any signs of internal turmoil, emotional crisis, distress or upset, personal conflict, unhappiness, tension or maladjustment during the period of adolescence. The belief that adolescence is inevitably a period of stress is so widespread and so generally accepted that some behavioural scientists regard the belief as a truism. For instance, Gustin states, in no uncertain terms, that: 'The inescapable fact is that this is everyone's dilemma at adolescence. No one is exempt — no matter how warm and understanding the family background ... For this conflict follows the law of nature. It is the self-actualizing principle that provides the impetus toward growth.'[1] And Ames warns parents to 'prepare themselves for the adolescent rebellion ... It's an almost inevitable stage in the emotional development of a healthy child.'[2] Greenacre also maintains that adolescence is a 'time of painful emotional evolution with a great variety of external manifestations as well as inner stress.'[3] And Spiegel goes so far as to draw a parallel between adolescence and adult psychotic states.[4] But Erikson is quick to point out that '. . . in spite of the similarity of adolescent "symptoms" and episodes to neurotic and psychotic symptoms and episodes, adolescence is not an affliction, but a *normative crisis,* i.e. a normal phase of increased conflict characterized by a seeming fluctuation in ego strength. . .'[5] To Erikson, adolescence represents a time of identity crisis for the growing person; it is a period during which he is constantly asking himself 'Who am I?' and trying to establish a satisfactory identity for himself — a process supposedly fraught with considerable stress and disorganisation.

This view has not gone unchallenged. For instance, Bandura is of the opinion that the 'storm and stress' view has been exaggerated due to an over-emphasis on the biological determinants of heterosexual behaviour, mass media 'sensationalism', overgeneralization from samples of deviant

242

adolescents, the self-fulfilling prophecy (when society labels adolescents and expects them to be wild and rebellious, so wild and rebellious they will be!), etc.[6] And Douvan insists: 'For the most part, the evidence bespeaks a modal pattern considerably more peaceful than much theory and social comment would lead us to expect. "Rebellious youth" and "the conflict between generations" are phrases that ring, but, so far as we can tell, it is not the ring of truth they carry so much as the beguiling but misleading tone of drama.'[7] The controversy rages on! However, if youth protest, rebellion, delinquency, drug abuse, etc. are considered as manifestations of stress among the youth, then there is no shortage of 'symptoms'. Recently, Rutter and his colleagues wondered whether adolescent turmoil was 'fact or fiction'. They subjected a total of 504 adolescents in the Isle of Wight (UK) to intensive psychiatric interviews and psychological diagnostic tests. On the basis of their findings they declared: '. . . "Inner turmoil" as represented by feelings of misery, self-depreciation and ideas of reference are quite common . . . These feelings cause appreciable personal suffering but often they are unnoticed by adults.'[8] Apparently, adolescent turmoil is a fact!

However, this conception of the adolescent's emotional state implies some form of constant emotional crisis – probably an overstatement. Furthermore, the sceptic is justified in questioning the generality of this phenomenon. Surely it seems reasonable to expect some cultural differences. The theoretical basis for expecting a substantial relationship between culture and the psychology of adolescence is that different cultural groups afford different opportunities for social learning and have different ways of handling problems. Clearly, this argues for the serious empirical cross-cultural study of adolescence. However, cross-cultural studies of adolescent 'storm and stress' are conspicuous by their absence. The early anthropological reports about so-called 'simpler' societies are no longer appropriate. The present study is part of a long-term research project on problems of growing up in contemporary Zambia.

Method

Subjects: Two samples have been used in the present study. The first comprised 38 University students. The sample was composed of 26 male and 12 female students, with the median age of 20.5 years and the mode at 19 years. The other sample was drawn from a rural secondary school in the eastern part of Zambia. This comprised 45 male and 31 female (N = 76) pupils, with the median age of 17 years and the mode at 18 years.

Materials and Procedure: The subjects completed questionnaires on adolescent stress and related problems. The questionnaire consisted of:
i. Direct questions concerning specific aspects of adolescent experience; such as whether or not they are experiencing their adolescence as stressful, whether or not there are 'growing up' problems confined to adolescence, what the causes of adolescent problems could be, etc.
ii. A ranking procedure, in which respondents are required to rank specific 'areas of concern in life' in the degree to which they are experienced as personal

problems. This procedure was devised by Symonds and the Symonds checklist, consisting of 15 areas of concern, was used.[9] The items on the checklist include: health, sex adjustments, money, home and family relationships, personal attractiveness, getting along with other people, etc. (each followed by a few words of explanation as given in the original checklist).

Results

For the University sample, 73.7% felt that there are problems related to growing up confined to the period of adolescence and 52% reported experiencing their adolescence as a stressful period. The figures were 81.1% and 50.7% respectively for the secondary school sample. Problems considered characteristic of this period by the University sample are shown in Table 1.

Table 1
Problems Characteristic of Adolescence in Zambia

Categories	Percentage of total
Confusion: 'trying to adjust to a changing world' and 'not knowing what to do due to adult demands'	12.72%
Unemployment	19.08%
Lack of education in heterosexual relations	16.96%
Misunderstood by elders	10.60%
Uncertainty of future	10.60%
Lack of sense of direction	8.48%
Others: 'no recognition from elders of youths as responsible persons' and 'having little say in one's affairs'	8.48%

Evidently, there is not shortage of problems during this stage. These results suggest that a substantial proportion of our youth does experience adolescence as a stressful period. There is a sense in which these problems can be said to be interrelated. For example, ambiguity of the stage means that the adolescent does not know what to do or what is expected of him due to conflicting cues from a 'changing world' and 'adult demands'. This gives rise to a feeling of 'lack of sense of direction' which in turn generates insecurity and anxiety born of uncertainty. This is probably what the psychiatrist Lowrey meant when he referred to adolescence as a *'not quite'* stage: the adolescent is *not quite* a child, *not quite* an adult and *not quite* sure of himself.[10] This state of affairs is confusing to the growing person. This is probably accentuated by lack of adult understanding and guidance. Some parents, for instance, do not revise their treatment of the growing person in the light of his changed status − they continue treating him as a child; other parents are guilty of applying double-standards. Similarly, unemployment and the consequent financial dependency on parents are obstacles that prevent the adolescent from doing what he wants to do. Lack of money, for instance, makes it difficult for him to have the clothes, recreational facilities, etc. that he desires.

The secondary school sample was further examined in terms of the two variables of sex and initiation. When the sample was divided according to sex, it was found that 61.8% of the girls reported experiencing stress as against 40.5% of the boys. This difference is, however, not reliable ($X^2 = 2.4$; df = 1; p $>$ .05).

We now sought to determine the effect of initiation (puberty rites) on adolescent stress. The sample was thus divided according to whether or not the subjects had undergone initiation at puberty. For girls the differences were substantial (as Table 2 indicates), but again, failed to attain statistical significance ($X^2 = 3.37$; df = 1; p $>$ .05).

Table 2
Reported Stress, by Sex and Initiation

Categories		Stress	No Stress
Boys*	Initiated	18.9%	13.5%
	Not Initiated	21.6%	45.9%
Girls	Initiated	47.1%	14.7%
	Not Initiated	14.7%	23.5%

* $X^2 = 1.37$; df = 1; N.S.

Although the effect of initiation is not significant, the trend is interesting and calls for comment. It seems that initiation creates a conflict for the adolescent. Puberty rites are supposed to usher the adolescent into adulthood. For instance, the young person who has undergone initiation has been prepared, and is ready (it is believed) for marriage. But in present-day Zambia the sexual behaviour of the adolescent in school or in a higher institution of learning is subject to strict surveillance (parental or otherwise) due to the prolonged period of formal education and the consequent delayed assumption of adult roles. The conflict which ensues gives rise to some emotional stress.

For the Symonds checklist items the Spearman rank correlation coefficients were computed and the results are shown in Table 3.

The results indicate that our youth experience similar problems to a comparable degree. For the females there is lack of agreement on 'personal attractiveness'. Whereas this represented a pressing problem for the university female students (ranked no.2), it was not experienced as such by the secondary school girls (ranked no.11). 'Home and family relationships' was ranked highest (No.1) by 75% of the subject population. Table 1 shows that the problem relating to relationships with adults ranks highest (confusion/misunderstood by elders/lack of parental guidance/others: 44.52%). A tentative explanation of this finding will be given in the following section.

Table 3
Spearman Correlation Coefficients

Comparison	*Spearman's Rho*
University vs. Secondary School	.46*
University: females vs. males	.603**
Secondary School:	
females vs. males	.82***
University males vs. Secondary School males	.45*
University females vs. Secondary School females	.43+

* p<.05   **p <.01   ***<.001   +m.s.

Discussion

This essay is based on data obtained from a small number of adolescents. As a statistical sample, it leaves much to be desired, and the conclusions drawn should be generalized with the greatest caution. This initial inquiry does not purport to do more than present a picture (as it is beginning to emerge) of the emotional problems of growing up in contemporary Zambia.

It is quite clear that the youth in Zambia are faced with a conflict. This conflict apparently emanates from two sources: social adjustment and relationships with parents. It seems to me that the explanation for these problems should be sought in the nature of the Zambian society of today. In discussing adolescent alienation in technological societies, Goettlieb and Ramsey identified four contributory factors: a highly industrialized society with a complete division of labour, an open-class system offering individual occupational mobility, a system of public education requiring school attendance to a given age, and a labour force whose members choose their occupations with little attention to society's immediate needs. The second and third factors and, in a modified form, the first factor apply to the Zambian situation. (The proposed education reforms are aimed at, among other things, combatting the fourth factor.) Over the last fourteen years (since independence) Zambian society has become relatively more complex as a result of a high rate of industrialization which has brought with it a complex division of labour and the consequent prolonged period of preparation for the attainment of skills necessary to fit one in society. The knowledge and skills necessary to be an adequate and effective parent, employee and citizen are becoming more and more complex with the result that the youth cannot simply look to their parents for guidance.

Moreover, society presents the Zambian youth with a confusing and incoherent array of values and expectations. This is because our adolescents are making their transition from childhood to adulthood in a society undergoing rapid social change, thereby being exposed to an enculturative dilemma. Enculturation is the process by which individuals learn the culturally prescribed and valued behaviours of their society. The goal of the process is to develop responsible adults who perform adequately in terms of culturally accepted norms. The situation regarding culturally accepted norms in present-day Zambia is somewhat diffuse. New values, such as those fostered by western-type education, urbanization and industrialization, have emerged. These values, in most cases, are not consonant with traditional values. Most parents of the youth of today in Zambia are still traditionally-oriented. They are overwhelmed by the new system, confused about what standards of behaviour to expect and demand from their adolescent children, and therefore unsure about what values to inculcate in them. The adolescents, on the other hand, feel misunderstood and alienated. All these factors make socialization somewhat uncertain and therefore cause major difficulties for young persons to establish a bridge towards the assumption of adult roles.

Furthermore, adolescence is itself a period of change, and rapid change is not unusual: it is a time of physical maturation; it is marked by changes in values, attachments, behaviours, etc. and attended by many new experiences such as living away from home, starting to drink, experimenting with sex; it is a time of acquisition of educational, occupational and interpersonal skills which will be relied upon during adulthood. In short, this is a period of trans-formation for the growing person. These changes have far-reaching effects on the adolescents, on their self-perception and the way they are perceived by others. Thus Erikson states: 'The growing and developing youth, faced with this physiological revolution within them and with tangible adult tasks ahead of them, are now primarily concerned with what they appear to be in the eyes of others, as compared with what they feel they are, and with the question of how to connect the roles and skills cultivated earlier with the occupational prototype of the day . . .'[12] Thus adolescents have to adjust to a new mode of social functioning. In the process, they experience some strains and stresses accruing upon the discontinuity for, as Benedict observed, the change from one mode of interpersonal relationship to another creates discontinuity in the growth process.[13] The degree to which the change is experienced as continuous or discontinuous affects the smoothness with which the transition is accom-plished. By and large, when the change is attended by continuity in cultural conditioning (as was the case in traditional society) the transition is likely to be gradual and smooth; on the other hand, discontinuity in cultural condit-ioning gives rise to emotional strain.

It can be seen that adolescent stress is embedded in a multivariate, psycho-social network. The hypothesized relationships are actually complex and should be seen within the context of a broader theoretical framework. For this purpose the concept of the 'perceived environment' provides such a con-ceptual framework.[14] The perceived environment refers to the view that the environment of action is, in the final analysis, constituted by the actor. This derives from the sociological view that man lives in a symbolic environment which mediates the relation of the physical environment to him and therefore social interaction is an interpretative process. Within this frame of reference, variables which are directly implicative of a specific behaviour are character-ized as 'proximal', and those variables which are not immediately connected with the behaviour referred to as 'distal'. From this perspective, rapid social change and industrialization are here considered to be distal variables which give rise to an increased complexity of present-day Zambian society. In so-called 'simpler' societies of the past, where the son followed in his father's footsteps and might have served as an apprentice in early adolescence, the period of transition was shorter, simpler and less stressful. The situation is somewhat different for a large proportion of Zambian adolescents today. Nowadays, adolescents have often exceeded their parents' education, often plan to have different jobs from their parents, and are exposed to different (often conflicting) sets of values. This situation gives rise to, on the one hand, anxiety born of uncertainty and, on the other, the difficulties in relationships between adolescents and their parents, both of which are seen as contributing to adolescent stress. In addition, adolescence is a period of change in the individual's life which inevitably leads to some problems of adjustment.

References

The research reported here is part of a larger project on 'Adolescence in Zambia'; this paper derives from two previous papers presented at the Second Pan-African Conference on Psychology held at Nairobi University, Kenya, from 29 December 1975 to 2 January 1976, and the Third International Conference of the International Association for Cross-Cultural Psychology held at Tilburg University, The Netherlands, from 12 - 16 July, 1976. I am grateful to Dr. John Coleman of the London Hospital Medical College who read the manuscript and made helpful suggestions.

1. J.C. Gustin, 'The Revolt of Youth', *Psychoanalysis and the Psychoanalytic Review,* 98 (1961), pp.78-90.
2. L.B. Ames, 'Rebellion's as natural as losing baby teeth', *Hertford Times,* 13 October 1970.
3. P. Greenacre, 'Youth, Growth and Violence', *Psychoanalytic Study of the Child,* 25 (1970), p.340.
4. L.A. Spiegel, 'Disorder and consolidation in adolescence', *Psychoanalytic Study of the Child,* 6 (1951), pp.375-393.
5. Eric Erikson quoted in M. Rutter *et al,* 'Adolescent Turmoil: fact or fiction?', *Journal of Child Psychology and Psychiatry,* 17, (1976), p.36.
6. A. Bandura, 'The stormy decade: fact or fiction?' in D. Rogers (ed.) *Issues in Adolescent Psychology,* (New York, 1972).
7. E. Douvan and H. Gold, 'Modal patterns in American adolescence', in L.W. Hoffman and M.L. Hoffman (eds.), *Review of Child Development Research,* Vol.2, (New York, 1966).
8. Rutter *op. cit.,* p.54.
9. Symonds (1936).
10. L.G. Lowrey, 'Not-Quite Age', *Science Newsletter,* 62 (1952), p.356.
11. R. Gottlieb and C.E. Ramsey, *The American Adolescent,* (Chicago, 1964).

12.   E.H. Erikson, *Childhood and Society*, (New York, 1950).
13.   R. Benedict, 'Continuities and discontinuities in cultural conditioning', in W.E. Martin and C.B. Stendler (eds.), *Readings in Child Development*, (New York, 1954).
14.   R. Jessor and S.L. Jessor, 'The perceived environment in behavioural science: some conceptual issues and some illustrative data', *American Behavioural Scientist*, 16 (1973), pp.801-828.

Study Questions

1.   What is the significance of correlation in test results?
2.   What is an open-class system?
3.   How is 'social interaction' used in this essay?

Appendices (Prepared by Ilse Mwanza)

A. Chronology of Events in Zambia since Independence

1964 Zambian Independence — October 24
Economic survey mission on the economic development of Zambia.
Report of the UN/ECA/FAO Mission (Seers Report)

1965 Speech by President Kaunda at National Rally, Lusaka, April 11
U.D.I. November
Emergency (transitional) Development Plan

1966 First National Development Plan, July
Report on the Grading, Structure and Salaries Commission (Whelan Report)
Report of the Commission of Enquiry into the Mining Industry (Brown Report)

1968 'Zambia's Economic Revolution', Address by President Kaunda in Mulungushi, April
'Zambia's Guidelines for the Next Decade', Speech by President Kaunda, Lusaka
'Zambia towards Economic Independence' Speech by President Kaunda, Lusaka
'The Rich and Poor Nations', Address by President Kaunda to the World Council of Churches, July (all indicating economic reforms)

1969 'Towards Complete Independence', Address by President Kaunda at Matero Hall, Lusaka, August (51% take-over of mining shares announcement)
ILO Report to the Government of Zambia on incomes, wages and prices in Zambia: policy and machinery (Turner Report)

1970 'Now Zambia is Ours' Speech by President Kaunda on economic reforms, Lusaka
51% take-over of mining interests
Address by President Kaunda at the opening of workers' seminar, Mufulira March (on workers' participation)
Mufulira Mine disaster, September

1971 'A Path for the Future', Address by President Kaunda at the opening of UNIP General Conference, Mulungushi

Abolition of fees for hospitals and schools
1971 51% take-over of mining interests, final stage (total redemption of bonds)
Second National Development Plan, 1972-1976, December
1972 'A Nation of Equals', Speech by President Kaunda (the Kabwe
Declaration)
Report of the Commission on the Establishment of a One-Party
Participatory Democracy in Zambia, Lusaka
Ban of Kapwepwe's United Peoples Party (UPP)
Report of the working party appointed to review the system of decen-
tralised administration, May (Simmance Report)
1973 Census of Population and Housing, 1969. Final Report
'The Challenge of the Future', Speech by President Kaunda, Lusaka
Rhodesian border closure, January
UNIP Party Programme, 1974-1978, August
1975 Summary of the main recommendations of the 'Commission of Enquiry
into the Salaries, Salary Structures and Conditions of Service'
(Mwanakatwe Report)
Sample Census of Population, 1974, Preliminary Report
Address by President Kaunda to UNIP Council, Lusaka, June 30
(Watershed Speech)
Closure of Benguela Railway
Opening of TAZARA (Tanzania-Zambia Railway), October 24
1976 Recommendations on a national programme for action for human
settlements in Zambia
TAZARA in full operation, August
1978 IMF approved standby arrangement for SDR 250 million
Re-opening of Rhodesian border, November

3. Information on Zambia

Area

752,600 km^2 (on a plateau between 915- 1,500 m)

Population

4,067,000 (1969 Census)

5,472,000 (1978 estimate):   85,000 non-Zambian

39.3% in urban areas

Density: 7 per km^2

Growth: 3% per annum

Neighbours:

Zaire

Tanzania

Malawi

Mozambique

Zimbabwe

Botswana

Namibia

Angola

Member of:

Commonwealth of Nations

Organization of African Unity (OAU)

International Monetary Fund (IMF)

World Bank (IBRD)

African Development Bank

Copper-producing Countries (CIPEC)

9 Provinces:

Central

Copperbelt

Northern

North-Western

Western

Southern

Eastern

Luapula

Lusaka (divided into 51 districts)

Each province is represented in the Central Committee by 1 member and is headed by a Governor.

Political Institutions:

National Assembly – 125 members

Central Committee of UNIP (the supreme policy-making body), elected by General Council of UNIP – consists of 19 members.

Ministries (17 as of 2 January 1979):

National Guidance (A. Simuchimba)

Home Affairs (W. Phiri)

Foreign Affairs (W. Chakulya)

Legal Affairs (F. Chomba)

Education and Culture (L. Goma)
Health (R. Kunda)
Finance and Technical Cooperation (J. Lumina)
Commerce, Industry and Foreign Trade (R. Chisupa)
Mines (M. Mumbuna)
Power, Transport and Communications (K. Chinkuli)
Works and Supply (H. Mwale)
Labour and Social Services (D. Banda)
Tourism (R. Sakuhuka)
Information and Broadcasting Services (M. Tambatamba)
Youth and Sports (K. Musokotwane)
Agriculture and Water Development (A. Chikwanda)
Lands and Natural Resources (C. Mwananshiku)
Each minister is assisted by a minister of state and a permanent secretary.

Gross National Product:
1977 approx. K1921.3 million (or K351.1 per capita)

Income Distribution (1973 figures):
60% of population receiving 20% of national income
30% of population receiving 34% of national income
10% of population receiving 46% of national income

Employment: Formal Sector wage-employment: 384,000 (1973)

Gross Domestic Product (1978): K1001.1 million

Agriculture, Forestry, Fishing	K 142 m
Mining and Quarrying	K 245.6 m
Manufacturing	K 98.9 m
Electricity, Gas, Water	K 61 m
Construction	K 64 m

C. Bibliography

Bates, M.R. (1977) 'UNIP in Post-Independence Zambia. The Development of an Organizational Role', Ph.D. Harvard University.

Bates, R.H. (1971) *Unions, Parties and Political Development: A study of mineworkers in Zambia.* New Haven and London: Yale University Press.
(1976) *Rural Responses to Industrialisation: A study of village Zambia.* New Haven and London: Yale University Press.

Baylies, C. (1974) 'Class Formation and the Role of the State in the Zambian Economy'. Lusaka, UNZA, seminar paper.
(1978) 'Patterns of Interaction among Governmental Business and Labour Organization in an Export-based Economy.' Ph.D. University of Wisconsin, Madison.

Berger, E. (1974) *Labour, Race and Colonial Rule: The Copperbelt from 1942 to Independence.* London: Oxford University Press.

Beveridge, A.A. (1973) 'Varieties of African Businessmen in the Emerging Zambian Stratification System.' Syracuse: 16th African Studies Association Conference, paper.
(1973) 'Converts to Capitalism: The emergence of African entrepreneurs in Lusaka, Zambia.' Ph.D. Yale University.
(1974) 'Economic Independence, Indigenization, and the African Businessman: Some effects of Zambia's economic reforms.' *African Studies Review,* 17 (3): 477-492.

Bhagavan (1976) 'Zambia: State, Industry and Class Struggle.' Uppsala: Nordic Seminar on the State in the Third World, paper.

Bloom, L. (1972) 'Some values and attitudes of young Zambians: Studies of three spontaneous autobiographies.' *African Social Research,* 14:288-300.

Bratton, M. (1976) 'The Social Context of Political Penetration in Rural Zambia: Ward and village committees in Kasama District'. *African Social Research Communication,* 15 (in press).
(1977) 'Peasant and Party-State in Zambia: Political Organization and Resource Distribution in Kasama District.' Ph.D. Michigan State University.

Burawoy, M. (1971) 'Zambianisation: A study of the localisation of a labour force'. Unpublished manuscript.
(1972) 'Industrial Conflict: The relationship between effort, remuneration and output'. Lusaka, UNZA, paper.
(1972) 'The Colour of Class on the Copper Mines: From African advancement to Zambianisation'. Lusaka: IAS, *Zambian Papers,* 7 and Manchester U.P. for I.A.S. 1976.
(1972) 'Another Look at the Mineworker'. *African Social Research,* 14.
(1974) 'Constraint and Manipulation in Industrial Conflict: Comparison of strikes among Zambian workers in a clothing factory and the mining industry.' *IAS Communication,* 10.
(1976) 'Consciousness and Contradiction: A study of student protest in Zambia'. *British Journal of Sociology,* 27 (1): 78-98.

Burdette, M. (1976) 'AMAX and ANGLO: Corporate or National Interests? An analysis of mining company behaviour in Zambia. An Outline.'

Unpublished manuscript.

Chaput, M.J. (1976) 'Zambian State Enterprise: The politics and management of nationalized development'. Ph.D. Syracuse University.

Clarke, D.G. (1975) 'The Political Economy of Discrimination and Underdevelopment in Rhodesia, with special reference to African workers, 1940-1973.' Ph.D. St. Andrews University.

Collins, J. and I. Muller (1975) 'Economic Activity, the Informal Sector and Household Income: Some findings from a survey of Chawama, Lusaka'. Lusaka, UNZA, paper.

Cross, S. (1974) 'Politics and Criticism in Zambia'. *Journal of Southern African Studies,* 1 (1): 109-115.

Curry, R.L. Jr. (1976) 'Global Market Forces and the Nationalization of Foreign-based Export Companies'. *Journal of Modern African Studies,* 14 (1) : 137-143.

Damachi, U.G. (1976) 'Kenneth Kaunda: Humanism in Zambia'. In U.G. Damachi (ed.), *Leadership Ideology in Africa: Attitudes toward socioeconomic development.* New York.

Davidson, B. (1971) 'Pluralism in Colonial African Societies: Northern Rhodesia/Zambia'. In L. Kuper and M.G. Smith (eds.), *Pluralism in Africa,* London.

Dore, M.H.I. (1975) 'Planning Industrial Development in Zambia'. Ph.D. Oxford University.

Dresang, D.L. (1971) 'The Zambia Civil Service: A study in development administration.' Ph.D. U.C.L.A.

(1972) 'Entrepreneurialism and Development Administration in Zambia'. *African Review,* 1 (3).

(1974) 'Ethnic Politics, Representative Bureaucracy and Development Administration: The Zambian Case'. *American Political Science Review,* 68 (4).

(1975) 'The Political Economy of Zambia. In R. Harris (ed.), *The Political Economy of Africa'.* Cambridge, Mass.: Schenkmann.

(1975) *The Zambian Civil Service: Entrepreneuralism and Development Administration.* Nairobi: East African Publishing House.

Dumont, R. and M. Mazoyer (1973) *Socialism and Development: Kenneth Kaunda's Humanist Socialism in Zambia.*

Elliott, C. (ed.) (1971) *Constraints on the Economic Development of Zambia.* Nairobi: Oxford U.P.

(1972) 'Income distribution and social stratification: some notes on theory and practice.' In N. Baster (ed.), *Measuring Development. The role and adequacy of development indicators.* London.

Eriksen, K. (1978) 'Class Formation and Detente'. *Review of African Political Economy,* 9.

Fagan, B. (ed.) (1966) *A short history of Zambia from the earliest times to AD 1900.* Nairobi.

Fortman, B. de Gaay (ed.) (1969) *'After Mulungushi: The economics of Zambian Humanism'.* Nairobi.

Fry, J. (1970) 'The Turner Report: A Zambian View'. Lusaka: UNZA, Dept. of Economics discussion paper. And in *Times of Zambia,* 3 and 10 April 1970.

Fry, J. (1974) 'An Analysis of Employment and Income Distribution in Zambia'. Ph.D. Oxford University.

(1975) 'Rural-urban terms of trade, 1960-1973, Zambia: A note'. *African Social Research,* 19.

Gertzell, C. (1975) 'Labour and the State: The case of Zambia's Mineworkers' Union', *Journal of Commonwealth and Comparative Politics,* pp.290-304.

Gupta, D.B. (n.d.) 'Labour supplies and economic development in Rhodesia'. M.Sc. University of London.

Hall, R. (1973) *The High Price of Principles: Kaunda and the White South* Harmondsworth: Penguin (revised edition).

(1977) *Zambia 1890-1964.* London: Longman.

Hall, R. and J. Peyman (1976) *The Great Uhuru Railway: China's showpiece in Africa.* London.

Harries-Jones, P. (1969) ' "Home-boy" Ties and Political Organisation' in J.C. Mitchell (ed.), *Social Networks in Urban Situations.* Manchester U.P.

(1970) 'Tribe, Politics and Industry on the Zambian Copperbelt'. Ph.D. Oxford University.

Hatch, J. (1976) *Two African Statesmen: Kaunda of Zambia and Nyerere of Tanzania.* London: Secker and Warburg.

Harvey, C. (1973) 'The Control of Credit in Zambia'. *Journal of Modern African Studies,* 11 (3):383-392.

(1973) 'International Corporations and Economic Independence: A view from Zambia'. In D.P. Ghai (ed.), *Economic Independence in Africa.* Nairobi.

(1976) 'The Structure of Zambian Development'. In U.G. Damachi *et al* (eds.), *Development Paths in Africa and China.* London: Macmillan.

Harvey, C. and M. Bostock (eds.) (1972) *Economic Independence and Zambian Copper: A case study of foreign investment.* New York.

Heimstra, Y.C. (1976) 'The Financing of Small-Scale Farmers in Zambia'. M.Sc. University of Reading.

Heisler, H. (1971) 'The Creation of a Stabilised Urban Society: A turning point in the development of Northern Rhodesia/Zambia'. *African Affairs,* 70 (279):224-245.

(1974) *Urbanisation and the Government of Migration. The inter-relation of urban and rural life in Zambia.* London: C. Hurst

Henderson, I. (1970) 'The Origins of Nationalism in East and Central Africa: The Zambian Case'. *Journal of African History,* 11 (4):591-603.

(1972) 'Labour and Politics in Northern Rhodesia, 1900-1953: A study in the limits of colonial power'. Ph.D. University of Edinburgh.

(1973) 'Wage Earners and Political Protest in Colonial Africa'. *African Affairs,* 72:288-299.

(1974) 'The Limits of Colonial Power: Race and labour problems in colonial Zambia, 1900-1953'. *Journal of Imperial Commonwealth History,*

2 (3):297-307.

(1975) 'Early African Leadership: The Copperbelt disturbances of 1935 and 1940'. *Journal of Southern African Studies*, 2 (1):83-97.

I.L.O. (1977) *Narrowing the Gaps. Planning for basic needs and productive employment in Zambia.*

I.M.F. (1971) *Surveys of African Economies: Zambia.* Vol.4. Washington.

Indeco (1970) *A Survey of Zambian Industry.* Lusaka.

Jolly, R. (1969) 'How successful was the First National Development Plan?' In 'Six Years After', Supplement to *Zambia Daily Mail* (November).

(1971) 'The Seers Report in Retrospect'. *African Social Research*, 11.

Jolly, R. and M. Williams (n.d.) 'Macro Budget Policy in an Open Export Economy: Lessons from Zambian experience.' *Eastern African Economic Review.*

Jones, M. (1974) 'The Politics of White Agrarian Settlement in Northern Rhodesia, 1898-1928'. M.A. University of Sussex.

Kandeke, T. (1977) *A Systematic Introduction to Zambian Humanism.* Lusaka: NecZam.

Kapferer, B. (1972) *Strategy and Transaction in an African Factory: African workers and Indian management in a Zambian town – Kabwe.* Manchester U.P

(1976) 'Conflict and Process in a Zambian Mine Community: An appreciation of some of Max Gluckman's theories of conflict'. *Political Anthropology*, 1 (3/4).

Kaplinsky, R. (1975) 'Control and Transfer of Technology Agreements'. *IDS Bulletin*, 6 (4):53-64.

Kashoki, M. (ed.) (1978) *Language in Zambia.* Manchester U.P.

Kaulua, E. (1975) *Some Aspects of Zambian Labour Relations.* Vol. 1. Lusaka: UNZA.

Kaunda, K.D. (1962) *Zambia Shall be Free.* London.

(1967) *Humanism in Zambia* Part I.

(1974) *Humanism in Zambia.* Part II.

Kay, G. (1967) *A Social Geography of Zambia.* London.

Keller, B. (1978) 'Second-Hand Women. Elopement marriage in Southern Zambia'. Lusaka: UNZA, seminar paper. In *ASR*, 27 (in press).

(1979) 'Marriage and Medicine: Women's search for love and luck', *African Social Research*, 26.

Kessel, N. (1971) 'The Mineral Industry and its Contribution to Development of Zambian Economy'. Ph.D. University of Leeds.

(1971) 'Mining and the Factors constraining Economic Development', In C. Elliott (ed.), *Constraints on the Economic Development of Zambia.* Nairobi: Oxford U.P.

Kingsley, J. (1978) 'Pre-Colonial Trade among the Bisa of Chiundaponde (Mpika District)'. Lusaka: UNZA, seminar paper.

Koloko, M.E. (1974) 'Rural to Urban Migration in Zambia'. M.A. thesis University of Pittsburgh.

(1976) 'The Manpower Approach to Educational Planning. Theoretical issues and evidence from Zambia'. Ph.D. thesis University of Pittsburgh.